Inside My Outside

ALSO BY SARA PYSZKA

Dancing Daisies
Switch the Song

Inside My Outside

An Independent Mind in a Dependent Body

Sara Pyszka

Text by Sara Pyszka
Cover photograph by Matthew RC
Cover design by Kerri Frail
Edited by Nicole Frail

Print ISBN: 9798621505226
Also available as an ebook.

Printed in the United States of America

For anyone who has a great life but may be going through a rough patch. Be annoyed, get pissed, scream loud, cry hard. Afterward, take a deep breath, reflect, and smile. The experience will top any lesson learned in a classroom.

Dear Reader,

Thank you for taking the time to read my memoir. You are either familiar with my other two books, *Dancing Daisies* and *Switch the Song*, or you know me personally, or you've attended one of my presentations, or your teacher assigned you this book so you can get a better understanding of what it's like to have a disability.

If you don't know me and randomly came across this book, props to you for taking a chance on something new from someone you don't know!

Regardless of why you are reading this book, I thank you, and I'm so excited to share my experiences from living a pretty fricking unique life.

Ever since I was a teenager, people have suggested I write a memoir or an autobiography of some kind. Someone even wanted to write one with me. I think they even had connections to a publisher or something like that. But even as a teenager, that just didn't sit right with me. Somebody else writing about my life?

Thank you, but I think I'll pass.

At that young age, an "autobiography" to me was just facts, facts, and facts.

Oh, yeah, and more facts.

What teenager wants to write about facts?

Not me!

I wanted to make things up and create a character who was just like me and have her go on adventures I would never get to do. I wanted to write about camps and have this character fall in love, and . . . I just wanted to make things up.

I still want to make things up, damnit!

I swore I would never write a nonfiction book.

I was going to be a fiction author, because I believed people learn a lot from stories.

I was going to be the best damn fiction writer, and my books were going to be the next *Twilight*, and I was going to change the world with my writing.

That's really what I thought.

Seriously.

Also, don't judge me—*Twilight* was taking over the world at that time, and I just wanted my books to have that kind of success.

It wasn't until my late twenties that I entertained the idea of writing anything that wasn't "entertainment."

I finally realized nonfiction wasn't just facts, facts, and more facts.

Memoirs *are* stories.

Memoirs can actually be fun, interesting, engaging stories that also happen to be true.

Moron moment.

Right here.

Once I wrapped my head around that and accepted the idea of writing nonfiction, I still wanted to put my own unique twist on it. Because I can't really do much for myself, I have to have personal care assistants. These assistants are usually females in their twenties. After watching female after female after female make the same mistake, I had an idea.

Hey! I just got my heart ripped out by some guy after making the same mistake every other girl makes! I will help girls not get hurt like I just did! I will write an advice book for girls my age transitioning to adulthood!

Me being me, I polled my readers on Facebook. I asked them: "If you could ask me about anything, what would it be?"

Nobody wanted to know how to handle heartbreak.

Nobody wanted me to tell them how to be honest.

Nobody wanted to know about money management.

They wanted to know how I graduated college with a disability.

They wanted to know how I live on my own.

They wanted to know about *my* life.

Well. Crap.

There went my little unique twist on writing a memoir.

Back to writing my third Brynn book.

(If you're not familiar, that's the name of the main character in the Just Be series, which *Dancing Daisies* and *Switch the Song* belong to.)

A few weeks went by, and I had the brainstorm of all brainstorms.

I often feel like nobody understands me. There are very few people who try to understand me, and I appreciate them more than they will ever know.

But do I have one person who I can run to at any time of the day, vent about whatever I need to, and have them comfort me exactly how I needed to be comforted?

No.

So, I was sitting in my bedroom, trying to get some work done, feeling so alone I wanted to cry . . . and . . . bam!

There it was!

My brainstorm!

The twist I needed!

The project that was going to make everybody understand me better!

But I'm writing my third novel.

The brainstorm kept growing.

But you need to finish this novel!

No! You need to start this project, which will make everybody understand you better and maybe help people understand others like you!

Once I knew what I could do to make this book as unique as I am, I immediately felt better.

I didn't want to break down crying anymore.

I wanted to tell *my* story *my* way.

I didn't feel as alone anymore.

I wanted to make people understand exactly what I was going through.

I spent a week trying to force myself to work on my third novel.

It just wasn't working. I kept thinking about this idea.

And so, here I am. About to spill my guts on pages upon pages so I can feel better.

. . . And I guess so I can help spread awareness for people like me, too.

Let's not be too selfish here, Sara. Geez!

I was raised like I was anybody else. My parents taught me to think I could do anything I wanted to do and expected nothing less than awesome from me. Nobody acted like I had a disability. Everybody believed I would have a "normal" life and that I was just like everybody else.

However, I'm not like everybody else.

I'm *so* not like everybody else.

From the moment I get up in the morning until the moment I go to bed, my disability affects me in one way or another. The majority of people don't have to do what I have to do.

I am not like everybody else.

I will never lead a "normal" life, as some people like to call it. I don't include myself in that group.

Don't get me wrong. I'm not against people treating people with disabilities like everybody else. In fact, that is what I advocate for. However, growing up *with* everybody treating me like I was *just like everybody else* put certain expectations in my head, and those expectations were not necessarily a good thing.

I'm not writing this book to blame my family and friends who treated me this way. I'm not one of those people who like to whine: "My family raised me wrong. Boo hoo hoo. Now I'm so screwed up."

Please don't think this is anything like that.

I'm writing this book because I think I have a one-of-a-kind perspective with the same thoughts, feelings, dreams, goals, wants, and needs as anybody else, but with a body that says, "Nope. We are not going to do it like that. We are going to do it like this."

This book is called *Inside My Outside*. Everybody sees what I am doing on the outside, but they have no fricking idea what I am thinking—of what I am capable of—on the inside.

This book is going to have not one, but two really cool and unique formats.

First, I am going to introduce you to two versions of myself:

There's Sara without a disability. Let's call her . . . Inside Sara. She's representative of my mind. Really, she's the person who I think I would be if I didn't have a disability. She's going to pop up every once in a while to show what I'd do if I didn't have a disability.

Then, of course, there is me. The real me.

So, it's really kind of like Sara's mind versus Sara's reality. Pretty cool, huh?

The other spin I wanted to put on this is related to the time period in which the book takes place. Throughout these pages, you will live four typical days of my life with me, morning to night. Most memoirs comprise essays about significant events in somebody's life, sometimes not even chronologically. I tried that for about two months, and it just wasn't working for me. I discovered that the ten-second, everyday moments are, to me, just as important as my big life events, and I have to share those everyday moments with the people who choose to read this if I want them to understand me better.

So . . . just a few disclaimers before we start.

Even though I'm an adult, some people think that just because I have a severe disability, other people decide everything I do and how I do it. This was especially evident when I did a photoshoot for a magazine. I was wearing a spaghetti-strap tank top, because, ya know, I was twenty-one and that was the style at the time. Someone called the magazine and said, "Her mother should be ashamed of herself for dressing her that way."

Umm. Thanks for your concern, Person I Don't Know, but I picked out my outfit for that day.

Actually, my mom didn't even help me get dressed that morning.

You're going to read outrageous situations I've been in. Just know that I always have a choice of how I want to handle them. I'm not being forced into anything I don't want to do, and sometimes, I'm okay with the challenge of these outrageous situations. I also think it's important for you to see someone with a disability not being perfect and not always making the best decisions.

You are going to see me love.

You are going to see me hate.

You are going to see me conquer.

You are going to see me defeated.

You are going to see me hurt.

You are going to see me heal.

I think it's so important to see someone with a disability who's living a very real life.

It's also extremely important to know that I am just one person with a disability. This is *my* story. It doesn't represent everybody with a disability. I was actually hesitant to write a memoir like this, because I know some people will take it as a rule of thumb for all people with disabilities. However, even though a lot of people with disabilities feel and experience the same things that I do, if you and I understand that I am telling *my* story, and *my* story only, I think we'll be good to go.

Unfortunately, my life is flooded with people. I'm with someone as soon as I wake up, I'm with someone right when I go to bed, and I'm with people everywhere in between. Not writing about people is absolutely impossible because of this, so I have done my best to protect the innocent, or, rather, the not-so-innocent. I will not be using any names of real persons, places, or things.

To make sure nobody feels like I'm publishing their own business for my readers and, really, to prevent my ass from getting kicked all the way to another country, I've created four completely fictional personal care assistants. These assistants have never existed, but everything these characters do is something I have experienced with one assistant or another.

My goal is to roll the education in—not call the people out.

And if you think I'm talking about you . . . don't be so quick to judge!

One more thing: This is a work of my memory with an emphasis on how I felt during these events with reflections on how I would've handled it differently if I had the knowledge I have today. I don't know what anyone else was feeling at that time. These are just *my* feelings, *my* thoughts, and *my* reflections. If you remember something happening differently from what I'm describing . . . well . . . then . . . good for you!

Alright.

Here goes . . . everything!

Day One

7:32 a.m.

A S MY EYES DART OPEN, I hear the sound of my neighbor's motorcycle fade down my street. I slowly turn my head to the alarm clock. *Damn you, Grumpy Naked Man! I think I was actually going to sleep until my assistant came for once! Why'd ya have to go waking me up with your motorcycle?*

Okay, he's not always entirely naked. I've just seen him more times than I'd like to without a shirt, and trust me, it's not a pretty sight.

I look at my digital clock again.

7:33.

I close my eyes again just to make sure there's not a chance I can go back to sleep for a few. Not that I want to go back to sleep for a few—it actually makes me groggier than if I would've slept all the way through—but I have some time to kill.

My eyes pop back open within seconds.

Yep. Definitely awake now.

If I was able-bodied—if I was Inside Sara—I would get up right now. Maybe I would take a shower. Maybe not. Perhaps I would sip on a cup of coffee, cradling the mug with both of my hands, sitting curled up in my big comfy recliner. Maybe I would turn on the news for a little. Maybe I would scroll through social media until I get bored with it.

Instead, I have to wait for someone to come to my house to get me up.

I've been having my personal assistants come at eight o'clock, because I think about what's best for *other people* way too much—to the point that I moderately believe one day I will lose my crap, combust, and there will be little scraps of Sara throughout my house.

Working on prioritizing myself more.

I swear.

I originally chose eight o'clock because I believed it was not too early for somebody to come to "work" and also not too late for me to get up. With every day, though, I vow to have my next group of assistants come a lot earlier.

Not just because of Grumpy Naked Man.

Because I usually get up around 7:30 anyway, give or take a few minutes.

As I lay there waiting, I think about the day ahead.

Today, I'm happy I have Amber as my assistant.

Contrary to popular belief, I really don't like saying I have *the best* assistants, but I have *the best* assistants, and Amber is one of them.

Knowing I have Amber today, I immediately feel relaxed.

I know she will show up in just a few minutes, guaranteed.

I know there won't be any drama or attitude today.

I know I can do whatever I want to do and go wherever I want to go.

For a moment, I actually feel sad that I'm so glad I have Amber today. My entire mood for the day, everything I want to do for today, is decided when I realize which assistant is scheduled that day.

What the hell is my life becoming?

I shake away the thoughts.

Little things, dude. Little things.

So what if you're relieved Amber will be with you for the day?

Amber is coming.

You're happy about it.

That's all that matters.

I hear my front door open and shut, and I'm 100 percent at ease now.

She came.

It's all good.

I hear her put her food for the day in my refrigerator and walk back to my bedroom.

"Good morning." She pops her head in my door before heading to my bathroom. I hear her turn the water on, knowing she's getting three washcloths: one soapy, one with just water, and a dry one.

She enters my bedroom and puts the cloths on my nightstand. "How are you doing?"

I turn my head toward her, and I nod.

"That's good." She uncovers me and turns me on my back. "How did you sleep?"

I nod again.

"Me too. When my neighbors upstairs finally shut up!"

I frown to tell her I'm sorry.

"Eh, it is what it is. Are you ready?"

I give her the go ahead.

I sweat a lot in the night, and my G-tube, which is really a tiny button inserted into my stomach, leaks a lot, and (can't believe I'm actually going to write about this) I wear diapers during the night. One can only imagine how disgusting I feel in the morning.

Okay, it's not *that* disgusting. This is coming from a girl who gags at the mere mention at any bodily fluid, so I'm not just saying, "Hey, I have stuff coming out of me at multiple points, but I'm just going to downplay it for my book, because I really don't want people to think less of me!" It's just really not that gross, I swear! But I'm an uberly clean person.

My goal is to have the option of getting a shower every morning and every night, but that will require more than people could ever realize, so until then, the cloths will have to do.

Once I'm de-sweatified from the night, I start getting dressed for the day, starting with a pull-up.

Just a really quick side note about diapers (adult briefs, depends, pull-ups, protective underwear, whatever you prefer to call them). Again, I can't believe I'm writing about them, but they are very much a part of my story, and if I'm going to share any parts of my life, especially if it's an embarrassing part, I want to make sure you can understand every little detail about it.

I know adult diapers have a bad rep overall. They are gross. They are disgusting. People make jokes about them. I once heard a grown man actually telling his son that if he ever had to wear adult diapers, his son should just shoot him in the head. That completely and utterly blew my mind, but hey! He's human.

Humans are sometimes just too human-y.

I have full control of my bladder. Make no mistake about that. If I can manage it, I will always, always go in a toilet rather than a weird, sweaty, plastic-y-but-cotton-ball-y thing that's on me. However, a few years ago, I guess I was getting older or some crap like that, and I started needing to pee in the middle of the night.

Now, I cannot walk. I cannot use my hands. I cannot talk, although, for once, that doesn't have anything to do with the situation at hand here. At three, four, five o'clock in the morning, I would wake up needing to pee and couldn't go back to bed. Sometimes, it took everything I had to hold it. Needless to say, that was not good for my bladder, my body, or my stress level.

I needed to make a decision. Did I want to spend half my night awake and in distress, or did I want to take the plunge and give up my cute, colorful undies?

The decision was a no-brainer. I went online, did a lot of research about different brands . . . and yeah, I'm going to stop talking about what I wear at night, because you now have all the information you need to come to the same conclusion I did. Even though I just tackled it, this is not a topic I particularly enjoyed sharing. In a book. That is going to be linked to my name. Forever.

Flash forward a couple years to when I got my G-tube button. I started taking in a lot more liquid, which, naturally, made me have to pee more, which, of course, required me to get out of my wheelchair more, and that required me to need more help, and so, it resulted in me holding it to the very last possible minute and ended with a lot of unnecessary "rivers" in my chair.

I finally got over the fact that I needed to use the bathroom more, and now I have the mindset of: "If I have to go, I have to go, and people can just deal with it." Still, I choose to wear pull-ups during the day for the times I can't get to the toilet right away and have the occasional "river."

Okay. I'm done talking about pee.

Actually, wait.

Final thought. Not a day goes by where I miss my pink, lacey, flower undies or my black undies with multicolored polka dots. I would do anything, anything to be able to wear something cute again. If anybody invents something that collects more than a few drops of pee, isn't invasive, doesn't smell, isn't gross, and preferably has lace on it, sign me up!

Once I'm clean, Amber asks me if I want to wear jeans. About 98 percent of the time, that's what I want. When I'm training an assistant, I tell them to ask my voice-activated speaker to read me the weather before I decide on my clothes.

If I'm going somewhere special, or, hell, if I just want to be cute for myself that day, I choose leggings with regular socks. I actually like to wear leggings more than I do, but with my CP and uncontrollable movements, the more weight on my legs, the better, so that's why I almost always go with good, old-fashioned, flare, no-rips-in-them jeans.

Now, if I were Inside Sara? Leggings. Every day.

Leggings with any kind of a cute top.

Once my lower body is fully dressed, Amber turns my entire body sideways on the bed. This is one of the times my assistants have to be careful and aware of my flying arms, because if they don't know their pattern, I can accidentally hit somebody.

A lot of people actually have said to me, "That's so awesome! If you don't like somebody, you can give them a good whack and you have an excuse! You can say it was an accident!"

No, no, kids! I'm sorry to break it to you, but that is *so* not how that works! When you uncontrollably hit somebody within thirty minutes of starting your day, it doesn't make you feel awesome. You feel completely horrible. You feel like a crap of a person.

Even if you don't necessarily get along with somebody. Yeah, that's really not going to make you feel better. Chances are they will understand it was an accident (but maybe not), but they're probably not going to have that understanding, laugh-it-off reaction. It will make you feel like even more of a crap of a person.

Just sayin'.

When I'm half-dressed and sideways on the bed, Amber rolls my transfer device to my feet, stands it up, and props it up with a wooden block I had somebody duct tape together. The lift basically looks like a refrigerator dolly for human beings, and for those of you who read my other books, yes, I did make Brynn, my main character, use one. It works awesome, but unfortunately, manufacturers don't make it anymore.

Once my transfer device is in place, Amber climbs in my bed. She lifts me to a seated position while sliding behind me to brace me. Leaning over my shoulder, she crosses my arms and straps them in. She then puts on my back strap and climbs off my bed. After removing the block from under my lift, she lowers me down, and just like that, she can transfer me anywhere I want to go with very minimal lifting.

Like most people, I go to the bathroom right when I get up. I used to be able to hold it until after breakfast, but with the combination of an aging bladder and taking in more liquid?

Yeah, no.

I have kissed those days goodbye.

Once I'm in my wheelchair, my assistant helps me change my top half. We take my nightshirt off (did anybody else know there were pretty, cute, long shirts that are designed for sleeping in instead of old T-shirts from events that you didn't really want to attend in the first place?) and put on my deodorant and bra.

My shirt is almost always some kind of a loose-fitting but cute tunic.

Inside Sara? Probably still wearing tight-fitted V-neck shirts, because I wouldn't have bulges from my G-tube button or my pull-ups I would want to hide.

"I was going to text you last night." Amber grabs my hot pink brush and takes out my ponytail from the night. "But since I would be seeing you first thing in the morning, I wanted to tell you in person. Did you see the news about your husband?"

Even though she's brushing out my hair, I shake my head no.

"Grrrr to you and your social media ban!" She scoops my hair out of my face. "He's coming to Pittsburgh! Ed Sheeran is coming to Pittsburgh!"

I give her a big smile, because that's all I can really do without coffee.

"Maybe this is your chance to tell him he doesn't need another wife because he already has you as a wife!"

I smile again.

What can I say?

Sometimes I pretend Ed Sheeran is my husband.

Give a girl a break here.

Amber has put my hair in a perfect braided bun.

Inside Sara would probably wear her hair down most of the time. I just can't—I can't keep it tucked behind my ears.

After she washes my face and slips on my glasses, I go out to my kitchen. I don't put my communication device on until after breakfast.

I don't know how people do it today.

A screen. In front of my face. Right after I wake up. Before my coffee?

I can't do it.

At the spot where I eat, right off to the side of my galley kitchen, Amber asks if I want something besides my shake.

Ever since I got my G-tube button, my diet is 95 percent shakes that I make, even though I can eat by mouth whatever I want, whenever I want. My shakes include fruits, vegetables, yogurt, tofu, and some kind of a healthy juice. Before my G-tube button, I used to eat like crap, so huge improvement for me!

But 98 percent of the time, I just want a shake for breakfast. I was never much of an eater in the morning, so this didn't really change for me, but breakfast food for dinner?

Ummm. Yes, please!

Before my shake, I take a drink of water, take whatever meds I need, and vent.

Venting is the entire reason I have the button in the first place.

I swallow a lot of air, especially when I drink and, as I've recently found out, when I type on my communication device. Sometimes, it's so much air, I get a stomachache comparable to a knife stabbing me, and I have to go lie down on my bed until it passes. No pun intended.

Luckily, the G-tube button helped tremendously with these attacks.

This is why I don't drink my coffee through my mouth anymore, even though I absolutely loved it with just a dab of hazelnut cream.

So good!

So fricking good!

But definitely not worth the attacks!

Anytime, before and after I eat or drink anything, I have to vent, which is just a fancy word for burping through a tube. Somebody connects a tube to my button, leans my wheelchair all the way back, puts a syringe on the end of my tube, and a million and one tiny bubbles come out.

If this sounded confusing to you, don't worry about it. The logistics aren't really important. Just know that I have to vent several times a day. If

I don't, I wind up lying in my bed the entire day all because of a belly full of air.

After all the air seems to be out of my stomach, Amber asks me if I'm done. As soon as the words leave her mouth, another volcano of bubbles erupts in the syringe.

"Oh, your stomach answered for you yet again." She keeps holding the syringe up with a towel over it. "It always does that. It hears me ask you, and it's like, 'Nope. Here's your answer.'"

I smile and roll my eyes, wondering if I'm ever going to have this feeding tube thing down, or if it will always be pulling tricks on me.

A few seconds later, I nod my head, telling her I'm done venting, or so I think. She clamps my tube shut, disconnects the big syringe, and tilts my wheelchair back to its upright position.

She then heats up my shake and pours it and my coffee into a gravity feeding bag. Anything cold through my tube makes me sick.

Once my breakfast is in the bag, Amber hangs it on the portable IV pole that I was so resistant to get. I have never considered my disability to be "medical," but I finally caved in and bought the pole because everyone was getting annoyed when they had to move the coat rack around.

Yes, I was using a coat rack as an IV pole solely because I thought it looked cooler.

Probably would still be using the coat rack if it had been easier to move.

Amber hooks the tube from the bag to my feeding tube. She then unclamps both of the tubes and gently squeezes the bag, allowing my breakfast to flow into my stomach.

"Cool," she nods.

As my breakfast keeps trickling into my stomach, I start to spell to Amber, even though I don't have my communication device on.

A few years back, my friend and I invented a way for me to communicate without my device frankly because I wanted to be able to talk to him while we were lying in bed. Unfortunately, as soon as we had all the kinks ironed out to this totally amazing no-tech communication system, he told me he had gotten a girlfriend. Hence, no more cuddling occurred, and my totally amazing no-tech communication system was never used for its original purpose.

However, I use it with (almost) everybody else to say pretty much anything I want.

Silver lining to everything, I guess, right?

I have five head movements that means five different numbers.

When I look directly to my left, that is one.

If I tilt my head up and to my left, like where eleven is on a clock, that is number two.

Looking directly up is number three.

Looking up and to the right, like where one is on a clock is number four.

And directly to my right is number five.

So, five head movements.

There they are.

Now, enter the alphabet.

Each letter of the alphabet is assigned to two numbers. For example, 1.1 is A. 1.2 is B. 1.3 is C.

Now, put it all together and what do we have?

Whenever I want to spell, I just look to the directions of the numbers, and my assistant decodes my movements into numbers, and then the numbers into letters.

I have a chart with all the letter codes. I have copies literally taped up everywhere throughout my house. People only need the chart for about a month and then they start remembering the codes. It almost becomes a second language to some people.

I've included the chart on the next page. Feel free to use it with anyone who might benefit from it.

People don't even have to use it with their heads. Any body part that can communicate two different numbers will work: clicking their teeth, blinking their eyes, tapping their feet.

I start doing my head movements to Amber, slowly spelling out, "Did you have a good weekend?"

"Yeah, I did." She takes the empty syringes to the sink to clean them. "We just hung out. Took the dog for a walk. Did some laundry. And that's about it. I'm getting boring at my old age of twenty-seven."

I smile at her, happy for her. Happy she has a good boyfriend.

She deserves a good boyfriend.

I then want to smack myself for even thinking that.

Anyone should deserve a good boyfriend.

She may be boring in her old age, but I'm getting more judgmental in mine.

1.1	1.2	1.3	1.4	1.5
A	B	C	D	E
2.1	2.2	2.3	2.4	2.5
F	G	H	I	J
3.1	3.2	3.3	3.4	3.5
K	L	M	N	O
4.1	4.2	4.3	4.4	4.5
P	Q	R	S	T
5.1	5.2	5.3	5.4	5.5
U	V	W	X	YZ

I claim to be so open-minded. I claim I believe in equality for everybody. But the truth of the matter is that some days, I have moments where that is just not what I believe.

I think this is one of my flaws I'm most ashamed of.

And I'm definitely not like this with everyone. I'm not a little old witch with gray hair in a corner saying, "If I can't have anything good in my life, nobody should! I'm the only one in this world who deserves anything I want!"

This is absolutely not anything like that at all. Take somebody like Amber, for example. I finally understand my personal care and well-being are always going to be somebody's job most likely until the day I die.

My life is Amber's job, but Amber is one of the few people who understands her job is my life.

If I want to change shirts for the fourth time that day, I know she will not bat an eye.

If I want a snack an hour after I eat, I know she will not ask questions.

If I want to go to Wal-Mart to get new scented wax melts, I know she will not give me any attitude.

This is why I don't have a problem hearing about all the awesome stuff Amber is doing. I know she would do anything I want or need her to do. She deserves everything she's getting, because she's just a good person.

And if I dig a little deeper and am more honest with myself, I think the reason I feel like this is that people like Amber don't judge my life, even though they are helping me with it.

The less people judge me for the things that I do, the less I judge them for the things that they do.

Now, I've had assistants who tell me that I eat too much, tell me that I eat too little, get irritated when I want more to drink, suggest that I don't drink enough, get annoyed when I have to pee a lot, cop an attitude if I want to go somewhere just because, flat out refuse to take me somewhere because they didn't feel like going out that day, and question everything I want them to do.

Those are the women I have a hard time feeling happy for when they tell me they can't wait to go home to see their boyfriends.

Again, I really can't stand that I do this, but I think everybody does this to a certain extent. I think it's human nature.

Would Inside Sara be like this?

I don't think so, since I assume I wouldn't have as many people judging me so often.

I also think this feeling is intensified when you are with people all day, every day, and you see their true colors.

"Did you have a good weekend?" Amber leans against the kitchen counter.

I nod, happy she's getting my head out of that place it was going.

"Did you do anything?"

I hate answering this question. It's a yes/no question, and my initial reaction is to answer no, as in, "No, I didn't do anything that would be worth spelling out to you," but I feel like some people take it as, "No, I didn't do anything. Just hung out." And if they get that answer every time they ask me, I feel like they start to assume I really don't do anything but sit around and watch Netflix all day.

"Just write?"

I nod and smile, thankful she understands the way I communicate some things.

My breakfast and coffee have totally drained from the bag to my stomach. Everybody doesn't think I can be (and stay) full, but they're wrong. I'm not entirely sure why, but I'm actually fuller when I have a shake and not solid food.

Amber clamps both of the tubes shut and unhooks the bag. She then takes a syringe and flushes my feeding tube with hot water. Once she twists it off, I'm not attached to a tube anymore.

"Bathroom?" Amber asks.

She doesn't know how much that one-word question means to me.

Probably 99.999 percent of the time, I go to the bathroom every time after I eat. It's pretty much a given for any of my assistants. However, just because I do something 99.999 percent of the time doesn't mean I like anybody to assume that I'm going to do it. I would like to say it's because there's a slight chance I might want to do something different, and that's part of it, but the truth is that the more my assistants ask for confirmation of what they're about to do, the more I feel like I'm in charge of my own life.

Once I'm done in the bathroom and back in my wheelchair, Amber unplugs my communication device from the charger and slides it on to my chair.

My communication device is essentially a PC with software specifically designed to help people say what they need to say. My main screen is a keyboard with word prediction. The device automatically scrolls through each row, and whenever it gets to the word or letter that I need, I just hit the switch by my head.

I have also done a bit of customization. I have several pages of preprogrammed words and phrases that I can access from the main screen, such as "How's it going?" or "Can I have a drink?"

I love this device. I absolutely love this device. With it, I can say anything I want to say—if you're patient enough with me. Because I use my head and not my hands, I type about one sentence every two to three minutes. Obviously, the more I want to say, the longer it's going to take.

As you can imagine, this can be frustrating as hell sometimes. Unfortunately, with how society is getting with everybody being able to learn anything they want to know within seconds because of technology, people don't know how to be patient anymore. Unfortunately, my technology is not like that. Even though I am considered a fast device user, I cannot keep up with a conversation.

Luckily, Amber is extremely patient. Whenever someone is extremely patient, my feelings about communication change entirely.

I don't feel like I have to work to get my point across.

I don't feel like I have to rush to type everything out before they forget what they asked me.

I don't feel like I have to constantly watch what I say and how I say it in case they take it the wrong way.

I feel like I can just be myself, and after some of the experiences I've had with some assistants, and some people in general, I know the feeling of being yourself with someone is priceless.

9:15 a.m.

Every single day, the first official words out of my communication device are, "Thank you."

It doesn't matter if I love or strongly dislike the person. It doesn't matter if it's my mom, dad, or assistant. Whoever it is, they have been helping me for at least an hour, and I want to show my appreciation. Sometimes, I want to make those two words mean so much more, like "I know I asked for a lot today, so thank you!" or "I know my body was being a brat this morning. Thank you for putting up with it!" or "You've made my morning a good morning. Thank you!" but every day, those two words sound exactly the same, because it's coming from a computerized voice. I think it would be going a little too far, though, if I elaborated on what every "thank you" meant from me, since some people tell me I don't have to thank them at all.

"You writing today?" Amber grabs the teal laundry basket holding my towels.

I nod and head out to my living room where I can be by the big window and feel the sun shining on me while I work.

"Sounds good! I'm going to start the laundry and then hang out in the assistant room. Good luck! Keep at it!"

Oh, the assistant room.

So, I would say one of my top problems with my disability is that I'm simultaneously super independent and super dependent. Now, I've heard it all before. "What? You really have a problem with being independent? Are you serious? Girl, some people would kill for your independence! You could be so much worse off! What the hell is wrong with you?"

I can see where they're coming from, but to every problem, there's more than the eye can see.

Yes, with my communication device, I'm extremely independent. With my device and desktop computer, I can email. I can text. I can make phone calls. I can make video calls. I can read anything I want. I can write anything I want. Watch anything I want. Listen to anything I want. With sites like Amazon and Grubhub, I can have pretty much anything delivered to my house, including food.

Crap, I can even book a massage and have the therapist come directly to my house.

However . . .

And this is a *huge* however.

If I'm hungry, thirsty, or have to go to the bathroom, I'm totally dependent.

If my communication device freezes up or if it runs out of battery, I'm useless. I can't even call for help.

And, no! It's not like if your cell phone died for the day!

Yes, somebody actually made that comparison once, and I think I almost crapped myself at the stupidity of it.

If my arm comes out from my armband, somebody has to put it back right away or else my entire body will tilt to one side and my head will fling back, leaving me unable to breathe.

Oh, not to mention, if I want to go anywhere or do anything *outside* my house . . .

So, yeah. That's me. Super independent but not.

This is where the assistant room comes in.

Given the choice, I will almost always pick an activity that I can do by myself, whether it be reading, writing, listening, or watching TV. When I'm doing something by myself, I like to be by myself, no matter how much I like the assistant. I'm with them for everything else in the day. Plus, it's just awkward to be doing something by myself with somebody sitting there watching me do it (sometimes even commenting on how I'm doing it).

Just . . .

Very awkward.

The assistant room has a couch, a big comfy recliner, and a TV. Sometimes, I feel bad sticking people in a room until I need help, but until a miracle happens and I come up with a perfect solution to my situation, this will have to do.

I feel like my day has officially begun only when I'm out in my living room, checking my email. I'm trying to, on days I'm writing, just skim my emails right away and answer them later. That doesn't always work, but I'm trying to get in that habit.

Facebook used to be a part of every single morning. I've completely cut it from my life, except whenever I'm tagged in something, someone messages me, or I'm promoting a book. Since I was ten years old, I've had trouble with friendships, whether it be for one issue or another, and Facebook seems to amplify it. I'm so much happier waiting for people to come to me if they want to chat.

When I'm done checking my email today, it's about 9:20.

Perfect.

Today, I'm putting the finishing touches on the story of my birth.

I wonder if I would want a career in writing at all, if I were Inside Sara. Probably not.

I first decided I wanted a career in writing when I experienced total ignorance from someone strictly due to my disability. It made me want to share as much of my life as I could through my writing. It made me want to help change the world through my writing. If I didn't have a disability, that spark of passion wouldn't have been lit.

If I didn't have a disability, I could see myself doing something with psychology, sociology, or running a camp. Granted, I could do any of these things with a disability, but with the stipulations of my CP, I think writing is the most enjoyable job I could do right now.

When I started working on this book, I emailed both of my parents questions. In many ways, my birth changed my entire family. I wanted to get both of their perspectives.

To this day, my questions go unanswered.

My parents are amazing people. If I have any health problems, my mom is on the next flight that day. If I need anything physical done, like if I need to get out of my wheelchair to stretch my legs, or if my gutters on my house need unclogged, my dad will do it with no questions asked. Even my younger brother, who is extremely quiet and doesn't know much about my care, will help me, if I need it.

My family is just not the "let's make a playlist of our top fifty favorite songs and share it with each other" or "let's have a family game night just for the hell of doing something different" kind of family.

They would do anything for anybody. They are just very . . . unsentimental? I guess.

I'm pretty sure they only get excited about a book I'm writing when they see a physical copy of it, as if a book with my name on it just finally happened to fall out of the sky yet again.

Okay, they're not that bad, but you get what I mean.

Though I have a lot of questions that I'd love for them to answer, I did finally convince my mom to email me the story of my birth.

I was originally going to give you the short version, but after hearing the full story, I decided I can't not put it in this book. Once I read what my mom wrote, I decided I cannot rewrite this story in my own words.

I pull up the email again on my computer/TV. I'm not entirely sure why, but I've always been able to comprehend everything a thousand times better if I hear it rather than read it, so I have a program installed on my computer that will read anything I select.

Ironic, I know, since I'm an author, but hey! This book is all about not being normal.

With my communication device, I drag the computer mouse to the play button and click it. The TV starts reading the email.

Warning! This section contains graphic content. For those of you who are a little squeamish or get upset easily, I highly recommend you skip this section.

Tuesday, January 7, 1986, 5:23 a.m.

I woke up with cramps and thought I had to go to the bathroom, but . . . nothing. The cramps went away. I went back to bed.

5:50 a.m. Cramps again. Bathroom. Nothing. Went back to bed.

6:15 a.m. Cramps again. Bathroom. Nothing. This time I did not go back to bed. I realized I was having contractions and they were about twenty minutes apart.

I woke up Dad. We timed them for about an hour. Still twenty minutes apart.

I called the doctor's office and told them what was going on. They asked if my water broke. I said no. They told me to wait to go to the hospital until my contractions were closer together or my water broke.

I sent Dad off to work and told him I would call him when he needed to come home.

He was not out the door ten minutes when I went to the bathroom and the mucus plug came out. I ran and got my grandmother, Nunny, who lived across the hall. She told me what was happening and said it was the start of labor.

Now, we did not have cell phones in the eighties. I had to call Dad's work and ask them to tell him to come home as soon as he got there.

I called the doctor's office, and they told me to come in. Dad got back from work, and we went into the doctor's office, which was at the hospital. They did an internal exam to see if I was dilated and to check if my water had broken. My water had not fully broken, but I had a slow leak, so they told me to go to admissions.

On the maternity floor, I was barely dilated, so they told me to start walking the halls. It was early afternoon.

I walked, and walked, and walked. I was dilating very slow.

Around 9 p.m., they broke my water and started me on Pitocin, which is a drug that speeds up labor.

Now my contractions were coming every five minutes, but I was not fully dilated to start pushing.

Finally, around midnight, I was fully dilated, and my contractions were one minute apart.

I pushed for three hours. You would go in and out of the birth canal. (When you were measured later, you were 9 pounds 1 ounce, and 23 inches long—you were a big baby.) You were also posterior (face up), which means the biggest part of your head was trying to come out first. There was NO WAY I could have ever delivered you.

During those three hours, your heart rate dipped a few times. The doctor decided to do a test to check your oxygen level. He pricked the top of your head and drew some blood. (This test left you with a huge hematoma on top of your head when you were delivered). He put the vial in the machine to see if your oxygen level was okay, but the dumbass opened the door on the machine before it calculated your level. He missed several critical things that should have prompted him to do a c-section sooner.

Finally, after three hours of pushing, I said, "I can't do this anymore." He finally decided to do a c-section.

They unhooked me from the fetal monitor and wheeled me from the labor room to the operating room. They hooked me back up to a fetal monitor, and there was no heartbeat. Dumbass doctor said, "This can't be. Go get the portable monitor." They got the portable monitor, hooked it up, and still no heartbeat. (I still will never understand why they didn't use the portable monitor while they were transferring me between the two rooms. It would have shown major distress.) Things went into emergency mode.

Dad was with me, but they kicked him out. I remember I didn't want to let go of his hand.

They needed to give me an epidural to numb me for the c-section. They were pricking my stomach to see if I was numb. I could feel every prick. I was not numb yet. They could not put me to sleep because that slows down the oxygen to you, and you were already in distress.

I kept saying, "I feel that! I feel that!" But they had to get you out. So, they cut. It stung so bad. I screamed, "I feel that!" I had my eyes closed. But when it felt like you were out, I peeked out of one eye and saw a gas mask coming toward my face. I sucked that gas in as fast as I could so I could be knocked out.

In the operating room, you had no heartbeat. Your pupils were fixed and dilated, and your hands and feet were black. The anesthesiologist had to intubate you and use a bag to breathe for you.

They stabilized you. They had you in an incubator, and they brought you to my recovery room. They woke me up and said, "This is Sara. She is a sick little baby, and we are transferring her by ambulance to the neonatal unit at another hospital." I didn't get to hold you. And off they went with you.

You were at one hospital and I was at another. This sucked. I developed a uterus infection, so I had to stay in the hospital for eight days. Every day, Dad would go see you. They would take a picture, and he would bring it to me.

You had tubes everywhere.

Each day, though, the picture would show one less tube.

Finally, after eight days, I was released. I was finally going to get to hold you. The morning Dad came to get me, he forgot to bring my clothes. He had to go back home and get them.

The first time I held you, you had an IV in your head. Blood came out. It scared the crap out of me.

You stayed in the NICU for about another week. From there, we went to a facility for sick babies. At the time, you were on a heart monitor and antiseizure medicine. We stayed there for two weeks so Dad and I could learn how to take care of you. It was nice, because medical professionals were always there, so if I had any questions or concerns, I always had someone to ask. You were progressing very rapidly. They took you off the heart monitor and, since you had not had a seizure since birth, they stopped that medicine.

We finally got to bring you home on January 26. The first night, I put you to sleep with a baby monitor. After getting no sleep because I ran into your room every time you made a peep, the monitor was shut off.

You were like every other infant. You got up every four hours to eat, took naps during the day, and you started to sleep through the night at six weeks. However, your muscle tone was extremely low. The doctors had not given us an actual diagnosis. All of the receipts from visits would say "Low Birth Weight."

I remember thinking to myself when I read the receipts, "What are they talking about? Nine pounds, 1 ounce is not a low birth weight!" It wasn't until you were around ten months old or so that we found out. Dad and I were watching a telethon on TV that was raising money for disabled children. So many of the stories were hitting home with us. When I took you to physical therapy that Monday, I remember talking to your PT about the telethon and telling her that the stories reminded me of you. I asked her if you had cerebral palsy. She said yes. And that is how we learned you had CP.

I remember crying on the way home. But then, Sherry, my best friend, popped into my head. "Sherry has CP. She has a beautiful life. Sara will be okay."

To my surprise, I start tearing up this time at the part where my mom didn't want to let go of my dad's hand.

I have no idea what the hell is happening here. The speaker is reading off a story about something awful that happened to me—a story that changed the course of my life in so many ways—and tears are filling my eyes because my mom had her husband's hand ripped away when she needed it the most.

I distinctly remember someone asking me, "How do you feel about the whole thing? Like, are you angry?"

I was surprised by that question.

Actually, I don't think anybody has asked me anything serious like that before or since then. Sure, I've heard this story over and over throughout my life, and I think people have asked my mom a question or two about it, but they don't usually get past the wow-oh-my-god stage.

The truth of the matter is I don't feel anything toward my birth.

Now, I really can't stand that I have to rely on somebody for pretty much everything I do.

I get frustrated when I want to tell a story and, by the time I type it all out, people are usually three topics ahead of me.

I'm angry people don't see the adult I've proudly grown into but still see the childish teenager that I was.

But my birth? I'm not angry about.

To my mom, I think, it was something traumatic that happened to her and her child she was carrying. But to me, it's just a story of something horrifying that happened that I've only ever heard people talk about. It happened to me, but I didn't experience it.

I was just a newborn coming into this world. I did not know what was going on, nor do I remember any of it.

Plus, something was taken away from my mom that was not taken from me just yet: expectations.

Although I have to say my parents adapted to my disability pretty well, my mom was not expecting a daughter who would never walk, talk, and even sit up on her own. She never expected wheelchairs, communication devices, standers, and therapies would be a part of her life.

Me, on the other hand? My expectations were a blank page.

What's that saying? If you never had it, you never miss it.

I have never walked. I have never spoken. My parents made me get in my standers just like any other kid would have to clean their room. They would make me practice my communication device just like any other kid would have to do their homework. So, to me, wheelchairs, communication devices, standers, and therapies were my normal.

So, I'm not angry about my birth.

Since Amber can hear everything from the other room, I tell her that I have to go to the bathroom.

Forty-five minutes to an hour after I have a shake, I usually have to pee again. This is one of the things that sucks about having a feeding tube, but I'll take it over being dehydrated and having gas attacks every day.

Amber and I go back to my bedroom, she puts me in the transfer device, I do my business on the toilet, she puts me back in my wheelchair, and just like that, I'm back in my living room within five minutes.

I find myself hitting my head switch. I'm starting to type.

I type for forty-eight minutes straight. I basically get out everything I remember thinking that time someone asked me if I was angry about my birth, stopping with only a paragraph or two to go.

I save what I wrote today and check how many words I just put to paper: 263 words.

Forty-eight minutes.

And 263 words.

That's good.

I used to get extremely frustrated that I would type for forty, forty-five, fifty minutes and sometimes hit 300 words and sometimes not. Now, if I type for forty-five solid minutes with no stops, I try to be happy no matter how many words I get.

I would do anything, anything, anything to be able to type faster, but I'm slowly getting into a mindset where I consider *any* work I complete in an hour, a sitting, or a day to be good work.

It's not always easy, but I'll get there.

12:15 p.m.

I drive into my dining room and tell Amber I'm ready to eat.

"Do you want anything else besides a shake?" Amber walks into my kitchen.

I think for a second.

Do I want anything to eat-eat?

Nah.

Maybe later.

I shake my head.

As Amber is getting my shake ready, I tell my voice-activated speaker to play my Favorite playlist, which is mostly full of Taylor Swift, Ed Sheeran, and Broadway musicals.

"Ed Sheeran will never get old," Amber says as she hooks me up to eat.

I nod in absolute agreement.

After all, he is my husband.

He just doesn't know it yet.

"You good?" she asks once my shake is flowing into my belly. "I'm going to run downstairs to pee."

Giving her the go-ahead, I jump right into enjoying approximately two minutes listening to music completely by myself.

Inside My Outside

I used to listen to music a lot more. Kind of like every day, multiple times a day, the volume up as high as my ears could handle, letting my mind just be. It was one of my favorite times of the day. Sometimes I would get on my bed and rock out. Sometimes I just stayed in my chair, dancing around in my head. As long as the volume was up high, I was good to go.

Now, because I have somebody in my house all day, every day, I feel a little uncomfortable blasting my music just for the hell of it. I have a small house, where if somebody even just whispers, anyone can hear it in any room. Directly to the left of the assistant room is my living room, where I usually am most of the day. Directly to the right of the assistant room is my bedroom, where I could go, but my assistants can still hear everything I do.

A lot of people have told me to make my assistants go down to the basement and have them just come up when I need them. "It's your house," they tell me. "They're working for you. You make them do whatever you want them to do." I get what they're saying, but I just can't make myself require people to go sit in a cold basement with one tiny window all day.

It's just not in me.

I know any of my assistants would be totally okay with music blasting throughout my house or going out for an hour so I can have privacy, or even going down to sit in the basement for a few hours. They have told me this. But this *is* actually about me and what I want: I just want to make everyone who walks into my house feel like my welcomed guest, even if they are working for me just so they can get a paycheck.

What can I say? I care way too much about everyone.

Unless I can turn down the caring meter in my brain and get over everything, it's all on me that I don't blast my music anymore.

Amber comes up from downstairs with a basket full of clean sheets. "Chowing down?"

I smile.

The phone rings.

Amber puts down the basket, picks up the cordless, and puts it on speakerphone. (Yes, I'm aware I'm pretty much the only person in America who still uses a home phone. Just let a girl enjoy being old-fashioned without any comments, okay?) "Hello hello!"

"Hey, girls. How are you doing?"

I hit my head switch to type.

"We're good. Sara is typing. How's the weather there in Florida today?"

"Eighty-five and sunny," she says with a smirk in her voice. "I just got out of the pool, and I'm going to eat, and I think I might get back in. I'm off today, so why not, ya know?"

"Super jealous—it's gloomy here. Yeah, why not? Go for it!"

"You guys can come down! Any time! That would fix your gloomy weather!"

I nod, semi-telepathically telling Amber I'm up for that.

"We're in! Sara is nodding her head."

"Hey! I have an idea," my mom paused. "Amber, aren't you working four days in a row next week because Britney is on vacation?"

"It's two weeks from now, but yeah, I am."

"Here's something to think about. You don't have to decide today. Just think about this. Why don't you come early that Monday and leave late that Thursday? I know that's not a lot of time, but you could at least get some sun and go swimming for a few days? I don't know. Just putting it out there."

Amber switched the phone to her other hand. "That actually sounds good. I don't want to speak for you, Sar, but if you want to go down that week, I'm in! Whatever you want to do!"

I let out a little "Yeaahh" as I'm still clicking away with my head switch.

"Again," my mom started, "you don't have to give me an answer right away. You can talk about it without me."

I shake my head and Amber smiles in agreement. "No. I don't think we have to talk about it. I think we're coming down!"

"Okay. Cool. Awesome! So, do you want to look for plane tickets, and I'll look for the car?"

I nod, and Amber relays my answer.

"Kay. You go do that right now, because the sooner you book tickets, the cheaper it is, and I'll call you back when I book a van. Kay?"

I quickly gestured to my communication device.

Amber gets what I'm saying. "Oh, Sara is done typing."

"Oh. That's right. I forgot."

Just to be dramatic, I look up to the sky, smile, and shake my head.

Really?

Thirty-three years.

Thirty-three years!

If she didn't get it by now, God fricking help me for the rest of my life!

Amber quietly chuckles. She knows what just happened.

So, I just had an entire conversation with more than one person, where a pretty substantial decision was made while I was typing about something else. Right now, I find it funny more than anything, but whenever I'm with people I don't really know, especially people I want to impress, I can't help but feel defeated against my disability.

I finally say what I typed: "I finally finished editing your email today. I'm so excited. I think my readers are going to enjoy learning what happened to me."

"That's great! Okay, I'm going to call you when I get a van, or you call me when you book your tickets. Yay!"

"Sounds good!"

When we hang up with her, I remind myself that, sometimes, my mom has a one-track mind.

By the time we're done, I'm done with my lunch. Amber unhooks my feeding bag, flushes my tube, and unhooks it. After she cleans everything up, I make my regular stop to the bathroom.

Each time I'm done with a meal, I really like to clean my G-tube stoma. Around it, I have an absorbent piece of foam to catch all the mucus that comes out of the stoma.

I have my assistants take the foam off and show it to me so I can see how much gunk came out of it and if there was any blood. They wash it with soap and water. After it's completely dry, they apply a light coat of barrier cream around it and slip on the foam.

Back in my living room, Amber asks, "Okay, do you want me to help you look for tickets?"

I nod.

Yes, I like to do as much as I can on my own, but if I have to do a very mundane task that I know will have the exact results if somebody else helps me with it and it's going to be faster, I will pick speed over independence.

I try to think of how it would look like if I were to go to see my parents as Inside Sara.

First, I would never be able to go last minute unless I was a best-selling author, and my books were a smash, and I was making thousands and thousands of dollars every month. Like I said, I probably would have a typical job, where if I wanted to take a week-long vacation, I would have to schedule it with my boss weeks, if not months, before.

I would more than likely go by myself, if I didn't have a boyfriend. I would like to think Inside Sara would have a boyfriend, but with how guys are today, who the hell knows if I would.

That, or I would make my younger brother go with me. Due to the eight-year gap between us, we have never been really close. I'm not entirely sure if it would be different if I were able-bodied or if we would still be doing our own thing.

I would only have to buy one plane ticket.

I would be responsible for getting myself to the airport. I would probably take an Uber, and from what I understand, they say a time and stick to it. If they're early, nobody else would get stressed. If they're late, nobody else would get stressed. I could go with the flow and not have to worry if anyone else feels comfortable.

I could get on the plane by myself without having two to three people transfer me on.

I would sit by whoever and not worry if they try to talk to me, because I wouldn't be nonverbal and could respond like it was nothing.

Oh, I would absolutely *not* have to worry about any equipment getting damaged.

My parents wouldn't have to come to the gate so they could help me and my assistant; I would just meet them at baggage like everyone else.

We wouldn't have to rent a van; I could just go in their car.

Actually, they wouldn't even have to come get me, depending on how late I got in. I could just take another Uber.

My mom would probably still want to help me unpack, but she probably wouldn't feel as though as she had to so my assistant could take a break.

Likewise, she wouldn't be helping me with some of my personal care.

My dad wouldn't have to help me get in and out of the master shower, because I would be able to use the guest shower.

I would help keep their house neat with cleaning up after meals or straightening up after swimming.

Best of all, we wouldn't have this stranger-like-friend-but-not-type person in the house, and we could just be ourselves.

Amber kneels on the hardwood floor. Since I don't have to actually touch my computer to work it and it's hooked up to my TV, it lives in the corner on the floor.

This is not one bit of a problem for me.

For anybody else, it's kind of a pain in the ass.

She puts the keyboard on her lap. "Same airline as usual?"

I nod.

She opens up the browser and gets to work. "Okay. Round trip. Departing Pittsburgh on Monday. Arriving in Tampa. Departing Tampa on Thursday. Arriving in Pittsburgh. Any time. Two adults. Oh, you need to see the Special Accommodations section, don't you?"

I nod.

She clicks on the drop-down. "Let's see. You need assistance getting on and off the aircraft, and you will be traveling with a wheelchair that has a battery in it?"

I shake my head.

"Oh! That's right. You travel with your manual wheelchair, because the airline always messes up your power wheelchair?"

I frown and nod.

Multiple times, airlines have damaged my wheelchairs, but one incident made me just stop flying with my main wheelchair that I use every day.

I work, on and off, for the company that makes my communication device. Whenever they have a new product, I go into the office, test it, and give my feedback. They also have sent me to some pretty amazing places throughout the years to give presentations about using augmentative and alternative communication, or AAC.

They once asked me to go to one of the biggest assistive technology conferences in the country. I wasn't going to be presenting, but I was going to be demonstrating how I work the device. This was going to be my second time working the conference but my first time traveling out of state with somebody who wasn't my mom.

One of my first experiences with a personal care assistant, but that's beside the point.

Since it was my first time flying without my mom *and* my assistant's first time flying with so much equipment, my mom came to the airport with us. She had asked for a special pass to help us get through TSA and walked us right up to the gate. She explained to the gate agent about all my equipment and how the airline needed to be extremely careful with my wheelchair. I think the agent either took pity on her or was intimidated by everything, because they then let my mom actually go on the airplane to help.

Mind you, this was after all the 9/11 laws were passed.

God bless understanding people!

Once I was situated on the plane—they don't have spots for wheelchairs on the plane, so I have to sit in a regular seat, usually propped up with a million pillows—my mom went to work on my wheelchair. She took off any piece that could possibly break and put it in a duffel bag and then wrapped a towel around anything she couldn't take off.

The ramp manager, who had been in charge of getting the luggage on and off the plane, actually asked my mom if she would like to go down to help load my wheelchair into the belly of the aircraft.

"Are you sure?" she had asked, knowing most non-passengers typically didn't go as far as she already had.

Even to this day, every time she tells this story, "That was soooooooo illegal" comes out of her mouth at least twice, if not more.

Even though she had been extremely nervous about the legality of the whole thing, she took the ramp manager up on his offer—she wanted absolutely no problems when I arrived at the conference.

She rode with my wheelchair down to the tarmac, pushed my chair up the ramp to the belly of the plane, reclined it so it would fit, put on the heavy-duty brakes, and unplugged the power so it would not accidentally turn on.

My wheelchair was not going to budge.

Not on her watch!

As though she were afraid somebody was going to change their mind about her being down there, she blew me a kiss and scurried away as fast as she could.

Once the plane landed, my assistant reminded them again to be very careful. The flight attendant assured us she had called ahead to the airport and given them a heads-up.

After everything, that was still not enough.

Right before my assistant's eyes (I couldn't see out the window at the time, and honestly, that was probably a very good thing), my wheelchair came flying down the ramp and crashed onto its side.

My mom's beautiful, beautiful, illegal work had been all for nothing.

Apparently, somebody had taken the heavy-duty brakes off without holding it in place. Because it was on an incline, it had just started rolling. For whatever reason, the pilot of the plane had been down there at the time and had tried to catch it with one arm.

My wheelchairs come in at about four hundred pounds.

The pilot's arm was a human arm.

I'll give you a guess as to what won.

The poor pilot's arm was so jacked up, he had to be rushed to the hospital.

My wheelchair? Completely totaled.

The airline? Put my mom on the next flight to bring me my manual wheelchair. They also covered a new power wheelchair, which took about six months to get and left me at the mercy of other people.

The conference? Went surprisingly well, actually.

The moral of this story? I am never again flying with a power chair until they come up with a better solution.

"That sucks," Amber brings me back to the here and now. "I mean, I don't mind pushing you in your manual. I think you know that by now. I just know how much you like to be independent. It just has to suck having to rely on someone even more than you already have to just because you want to travel."

I shrug.

"So, you like to do nonstop, right? There's just one, both days, that leaves at 3:10 and arrives at 5:15." Amber reads from the computer what I'm seeing on the TV. "It comes out to be $453. That's really not that bad."

That's cheap, in my opinion. For two people, round trip, on a commercial airline, and last minute? That's cheap.

But I don't do this often, so what do I know?

I motion to the side of my wheelchair where my purse hangs.

"You want to go ahead with it?"

I nod.

"Cool." Amber scooches over on her knees to my side. "I know you don't really have a choice in taking me, and I know you pay for all your assistants' tickets whenever you go somewhere because that's your deal, but thank you very much for taking me! I appreciate this! We're going to have fun! Do you want to use your white card?"

I nod and hit my head switch to type.

She grabs my wallet out of my purse and crawls back to the computer. "Do you want me to enter all your information?"

I nod, still typing.

Once she puts in our information, hits "Purchase Tickets," enters my credit card information, and sends the itinerary to me, my mom, and herself, she exits the browser.

She stands and waves her hands, saying in a low-key but excited voice, "We are going to Florida! We are going to sit in the sun!"

I smile and hit SPEAK. "Thank you. I appreciate you appreciating going."

I really do appreciate it.

One of my deals with my personal assistants is if I'm traveling, I'm paying. If I'm traveling anywhere, I pay for their plane ticket, and, if needed, a separate hotel room for them. If I'm going to a concert or a musical, I pay for them to get in. The way I see it, they're going on my time, not theirs, and I wouldn't necessarily be able to go if it weren't for them, so this is my responsibility.

This wasn't always easy, and I didn't always see it like this.

Back when I hired some of my first assistants, two of my friends and I planned a trip to an amusement park. Obviously, I needed an assistant to go with me or else my friends would have to help me with everything.

We decided to go get our tickets in advance, because it was cheaper that way. When I was in line with the assistant who was going to the park with me, I told her I was going to buy her ticket. At that time, I was very naive.

I did not understand my relationship to my assistants.

I did not understand she was working for me.

I did not understand that, if it weren't for me, she would not be going to this park.

At that moment, I wanted to buy her the ticket just because I liked her and wanted to do something nice for her.

Her response when I told her the ticket was on me? A very flat "Okay."

Okay? I thought. *No, "Thank you"? No, "You don't have to"? She didn't even sound excited about it. How can she just say "Okay"? Well, you did this for her to show her how much you care. Hopefully, she got that. Maybe?*

Yeah, the younger me was not my best me.

The day of the park visit, I had asked my assistant if she was excited, embarrassingly, kind of like how a parent would ask their child to make them feel like what they were about to do was going to be the best day ever.

Her response? "No. I absolutely hate amusement parks."

Now that I have a fricking PhD in Having Personal Assistants, I know exactly what was going on here. She didn't like what she had to do for her job, but she was going to do it anyway, because it was a part of her job. She was not excited about it, but she was also not complaining, either.

A similar situation happened while I was still pretty new to figuring out how the hell to handle having assistants. I had asked a different assistant if she wanted to go see a movie with me. I remember specifically asking her if she wanted to go with me, because Naive Sara figured that would help. I didn't know I was supposed to say, "Hey. You want to go to this movie? My treat" or "Hey. I'm going to this movie. You can come, but you don't have to."

When we got to the theater, my assistant asked for two tickets. The guy behind the glass gave us the total: twenty dollars. My assistant reached into my purse, grabbed my wallet, handed him my credit card, and let him charge the entire twenty dollars.

Without asking me.

I. Was. Furious.

She hadn't asked me if I was going to pay for her ticket.

She had just given him my credit card and paid for her own ticket like it was nothing.

I had been so furious, I couldn't enjoy the movie. More than one person asked me if I saw this movie, and when I said I had absolutely hated it, they would do a double take. "Wait, what? Why? It's a chick flick with music!"

A year or so later, I finally watched it again, and I can now say yes, *Pitch Perfect* will always be in my Top Five, and I have a total girl crush on Anna Kendrick.

Looking back on it now, the poor communication went both ways. This particular assistant hadn't asked about the ticket, but I also hadn't told her I didn't cover the cost of movie tickets.

Still, assuming I would be paying for her without confirming it with me is a bit more of a problem, though.

One last situation made me finally realize I needed to change how I handled some of this. This was my tipping point.

I bought two tickets to go see one of my favorite artists. My assistant knew they were coming to our area and knew I had tickets. When I first got the tickets, she insisted she was the one I *had* to take with me. I figured she was just saying it to say it—she would eventually forget about it like a lot of people do when they make plans with me.

But, over the coming months, she kept reminding me she wanted to go with me. It was always in a joking way, but she always sounded super excited about it. Once, she even said, "You can't take anyone else! I'm the one who has to go with you!"

I always figured, if I really wanted to, I could have had an honest talk with her and been like, "Look, I'm sorry. I knew you really wanted to go, but I'm taking this other person, because they're my friend, and they're my tickets." I think she would've been a little disappointed, but I know she would've ultimately understood.

The week of the concert came, and she rearranged her entire schedule to make sure she was able to go. I'm not talking about just her schedule with me; she rearranged a pretty substantial event that was going on in her personal life. It was only then her seriousness smacked me in the face.

Just to reiterate, I knew I had a choice in taking this assistant, even though she told me I didn't. However, the two friends I had been thinking about potentially taking weren't really superfans of this artist like I was, so I figured, why not take someone who is just as excited to see this artist as I am? So, I took my assistant.

When we got to the venue, we found our seats, I got situated, and she went to the bathroom and to get something to eat.

Okay.

That's a pretty normal thing to do before a concert, so I didn't think anything of it.

She missed the entire opening act.

Okay.

That's also a pretty normal thing to do at concerts. Whatever floats her boat. But they were actually pretty good.

Surprisingly good.

I wish she was here to see them with me quickly flashed through my mind.

She came back with her food and a drink in her hand.

Once the main act was on, she was jamming right along with me.

By the second song, I was just as into it, but she started taking pictures. A lot of pictures.

By the third song, I was still singing as loud as I could (and by singing, I mean letting my voice make whatever noises it wants to, even if it's absolutely not coherent). She started posting pictures to social media.

By the fourth song, I was still going strong. They were one of my favorite artists, and they never cease to amaze me live in concert. She was completely engrossed in her phone, checking to see how many Likes she had received every two minutes.

I usually don't look at any of my assistants' phones. Sometimes, I'll get bored and curious and want to make conversation, so I'll ask what they're up to, but I would never go as far as snooping on their screens. This time, not looking at her phone was just impossible, because it was glowing in the dark not even a foot away from me.

I looked around at the concert, and in her defense, about half the girls there were doing what she was doing: showing off to everybody they knew and everybody they kind of knew that they were at this concert.

I guess I have a different perspective.

I absolutely love music. When I go to a concert, especially a concert of somebody I absolutely love, I don't mess around. I like to scream as much as I want, because everybody else is screaming. I like to sing as much as I want, because nobody can tell I'm not forming any words. I like to dance as much as I want, because nobody can see me in the dark.

Whenever I take somebody to a concert, I want the person to do the same, or at least, do whatever they feel comfortable with. I understand everyone enjoys entertainment differently, and I respect that, but when there is so much of a gap with how we enjoy it, I feel like there is judgement going both ways. When they're on their phone the entire night, I feel like they're bored and not interested, and when I'm happily dancing like a maniac, people have actually called me some version of a dork.

This was the night I decided I needed to change some rules, or, rather, have some rules.

I pretty much definitely need somebody to go with me to a concert because I dance a lot, and sweat a lot, so I need to be able to hydrate. I can't do that by myself. That, and the music is so loud at concerts, people never know when I'm saying something. If I needed help, a stranger wouldn't know to read my screen.

I think I would be totally okay going to a concert by myself, but for physical tasks, I will always need somebody to go with me, so two tickets it is.

Musicals and movies, there's not much physically involved, so I decided to have my assistants drop me off and pick me up. Unless somebody is super interested in seeing the show, I actually prefer going alone. I guarantee this goes both ways, but whenever I go to a show with somebody who doesn't share the same excitement as me, I imagine this constant pressure on them to show the right emotions at all the right moments.

When I go to a show by myself, there's no pressure on anyone. I can smile as much as I want to without being called a big fat cheeseball, and they don't have to pretend (or not pretend) they like a show they never actually wanted to see.

And I save a lot of money on unnecessary tickets this way.

With trips, though, I definitely, absolutely need someone to go with me, or else I'm not even getting out of the house, let alone to the airport, on an airplane, and to another state. I've come to the conclusion my assistants are either going to have fun or think of it as a work trip.

It is what it is, and I have to be okay with it.

I'm happy Amber is excited to go to Florida.

The phone rings. It's my mom.

"Hello hello!" Amber answers.

"I have good news, and I have bad news," my mom says. "What do you want first?"

"We have only good news here, so let's keep it going! Give us the good first!"

"You booked your tickets and are really coming?" my mom guesses.

"Yep!"

"Wooooohooooooo!" my mom says in a high-pitched voice. "You're coming to Florida! You're coming to Florida!"

Amber chuckles. "Yep. We're excited!"

"That's great, because my good news is I booked a van! Probably should've waited until you guys were definitely coming, but oh well. The bad news is it's not accessible. It doesn't have a ramp."

"Oh. Well, that's okay, right? You will just have to get out of your wheelchair whenever we go anywhere."

"Yeah," my mom answers for me. "I talked to Dad, and he doesn't have any problem lifting you. But here's what's going to make you mad. I almost don't want to tell you, because I know how mad you're going to be. The regular minivan without a ramp is eighty-seven dollars."

I nod, adding that to my costs of going down. I can manage that.

Amber translates. "Okay."

"No! Sara! Not eighty-seven dollars a day—eighty-seven dollars total! For all four days!"

Without thinking, I let out a scream.

What?

"I knew that would be your response. Yeah, it's sick."

I roll my eyes and shake my head.

This world.

"Amber, Sara is pissed because, like I just said, a regular minivan without any adaptations is about twenty bucks a day. An accessible van with a ramp is about a hundred and twenty bucks a day."

Now Amber is the one who's exclaiming "What?!" and not in her head.

"Yeah! It's sick. Her shower chair? Basically made of PVC tubing and fishnet? Sixteen hundred dollars. Her toilet chair? Again, basically made up of PVC tubing and plastic? Fifteen hundred dollars. It's absurd! Pretty much anything that's adapted and considered 'accessible,' they make the price ridiculously high. It's sick!"

"I still don't understand. How is that legal? That's discrimination! Why do they do that?"

"We think supply and demand. There aren't many people needing accessible things, so they can charge whatever they want, because they know the people who do need it can't live without it. And there's usually one or two companies who make accessible vans, and shower chairs, and toilet seats, so they aren't in competition with anybody else really, so, again, they can charge whatever the hell they want."

"Wow," Amber shakes her head. "You're right. That *is* sick."

"Yeah. It is. But it is what it is until we keep pushing for change."

I agree.

"You are coming to Florida," my mom sings. "You are coming to Florida! I'm so excited! I'm so excited!"

"Us, too," Amber chuckles. I could tell the cost of the van and this new information really bothered her, but she's trying to push past it.

"I'm going to cook for you guys, and you're going to swim every day, and we're going to just have fun."

"Sounds good!"

"What are you guys going to do for the rest of the day?"

"I'm not entirely sure. You done working for the day, Sar?"

I nod.

"We watching *Switched at Birth*?"

I smile sheepishly. It's my guilty pleasure show.

"Cool."

"What is it with you guys and this show? You're always watching it when I call. Is it something I would like? Would you watch it with me?"

I shake my head, and Amber, somewhat confused, translates. "No?"

In the last couple of years, I have really gotten into entertainment more than I have in my life. More so audiobooks and music but also movies and TV shows.

Whenever I like something, I don't just like it—I'm in love with it.

And sometimes, I will play it over, and over, and over.

When I'm in love with something, I stick with it and want to share it with everybody I love.

Naive Naive Sara makes a cameo again.

I would make whatever guy I was talking to at that time watch the cheesiest movies.

I made more than one of my very conservative friends watch *RENT*, a liberal as hell musical.

Ed Sheeran, my faux husband, has this video where he beatboxes, raps, sings, and plays the crap out of the guitar for eleven straight minutes. It gives me chills every time I watch it. I put it on for my mom, wanting to show her how talented this guy was. She had me turn it off within three minutes. She thought it was just obnoxious noise.

All the guys who didn't like my movies, all my friends who didn't like one of my favorite musicals, my mom not liking my favorite Ed Sheeran video—it upset me.

I was taking it personally, even though each and every one of them was taking time out of their day to watch or listen to something only I enjoy.

Okay.

Why was I getting so upset?

Why was I taking it so personally that somebody didn't care for something I wasn't even involved in making?

After some serious self-reflecting, I finally realized what the hell my problem was.

I can't make a guy dinner (not that I think girls have to) or even give him a hug without being like, "Hey, you. I want to hug you. Take my device off, wrap my arms around your neck, and make sure I don't smack you." I can't help my mom clean up the kitchen.

I think my way of showing that I care is showing them a video, a book, a show, or a movie I absolutely love in hopes that I can make them smile.

Sharing something that I'm in love with is like me giving them a little gift.

Now that I understand that is my instinctive way of caring, I don't take it personally if somebody isn't really digging what I'm showing them.

And if I'm just now understanding it, how in the fricking crap could I expect somebody else to know I was telling them how much I care for them by showing them something on a screen?

And now that I understand what's going on here, I don't just throw anything and everything I love at people. I try to get a good idea of what somebody will like and not like, and then I'll show then something we both will enjoy.

Switched at Birth is the epidemy of a teen drama. Even though I'm thirty-three, I love it despite all its cheesiness. Some of the characters are primarily Deaf, which I'm not, but I still feel like I can relate to it since it's the only show that captures the reality of what it's like to be nonverbal.

Truth be told, I would love to sit down and watch it with everybody I know so they could see some of the things I go through, but people like my mom? I think she would enjoy the nonverbal stuff, but the constant breaking up and getting back together, siblings fighting with siblings, and teenagers giving their parents attitude?

I think she's better off to sticking to shows like *This Is Us*.

"Is it because *Switched at Birth* is more for a younger audience?" Amber asks.

I nod. Exactly!

"Yeah. It can get pretty teenager-y."

"Then why are you two adults watching it?" my mom asks in a jokingly parenteral voice.

"Hey! Sometimes us girls need to watch a ridiculous teen love story just to zone out! Guilty pleasure!"

I agree.

Switched at Birth is definitely my guilty pleasure!

"Okay. Whatever," my mom's voice drifted out and back in. "I'm so excited you're coming! I'll talk to you soon!"

Amber lightly chuckles. "See you later!"

"Bye, girls! Love ya!"

Sara Pyszka

6:37 p.m.

I decide to sit in my big comfy recliner, something I very rarely do for multiple reasons, the main one being it's a little tricky for my assistants to get me in and out. I originally bought this chair because it seemed absolutely perfect for cuddling in with somebody else, since, I think, it's technically considered a chair and a half. Unfortunately, I haven't cuddled with a cute boy in it yet.

I decide to get in it tonight because Amber is tall enough to easily get me in and out, she never shows any frustration with anything I want to do, and she knows my letter code so well that I can be extremely comfortable without my communication device for a few hours.

And, hell! I just want to do something different for a change!

Once Amber puts me in the recliner with my transfer device and adjusts the chair to the exact position I need, she turns on Netflix without opening anything else up. She clicks on the episode where I left off.

"Oh, Emmett!" Amber takes a seat on the couch. "You are just adorable, even though you're a teenager and you're fictional! Why can't you be real?"

I nod a big nod and smile a big smile.

"Yes, I know you would date him! We all know you like adorable nerds!"

I give her a big cheesy smile to let her know she's right!

Adorable nerds?

I'm in!

Adorable nerds with glasses?

Sign. Me. Up!

One episode down.

Amber likes this show just as much as I do, and that's the only reason I feel comfortable enough to have her out here in my living room with me. She's on her phone, but she's still watching, and we're making comments to each other.

Two episodes down.

Still happy. Still loving it.

Still smiling like a goof, but Amber doesn't comment on it. She just lets me be.

Three episodes in, and I have to go to the bathroom.

Ughhh.

Why?

I don't want to get up, and it's not because I'm a couch potato.

I don't want to get in the lift, get up from this chair, go to the toilet, and come back to this chair. I was going to have my last shake in this chair. I don't want to go through the ordeal of getting up from this chair twice.

This is also probably why I don't sit in this recliner anymore.

Inside Sara would be in and out of the bathroom in fewer than two minutes.

I try to wait until this episode is over.

I only make it five minutes.

I have to go now before something happens.

"I have to pee," I spell out.

"Okay," Amber stands up. "Do you want to pause it or turn it off? Pause it?"

I shake my head.

"Turn it off?"

I nod.

Amber rolls the lift in front of me and stands it up. She comes over to the side of the recliner and scoops my back up more than she has to do in my wheelchair since I'm a little lower to the ground. Holding my arms in place, she comes around in front of me to strap them in. Because the lift is leaning more toward the recliner, Amber has to pull extra hard to get it to go down.

Yeah. Definitely can't do this with just any assistant.

Probably shouldn't have even done this with Amber.

Grrrr to always having to be careful and think about everything I do.

Luckily, Amber is cool and goes with any flow.

I pee and decide to just get back in my wheelchair. My original plan was to stay in the recliner and have my last shake while I finished watching the episode, but since I'm already up, I know it would be easier just to go back in my chair.

I could still finish the episode, but I go to my usual eating spot.

I don't really have a reason for doing this.

This is just what I do.

Amber heats a shake up and pours it into my bag.

Within minutes, all the liquid is in my stomach.

I feel full.

I now take my meds: Valium to calm my muscles from my CP.

Amber flushes my tube, twists it off, and I go back to my bedroom. I park my chair near the foot of the bed for the night.

"You showering?"

I nod.

Now more than ever, it's easier to give me a shower.

I had this one shower chair for over twenty years. I loved this damn chair to death. I was in a hammock-type position where I could sit and relax. Unfortunately, somebody had to lift me in it, and as time went on, my assistants understandably didn't feel comfortable with it.

And since I don't live with my dad anymore—he was the one who usually lifted me in and out—it was time to get a new shower chair.

Sad day.

I first ordered more of a general wheelchair-type shower chair. It had a headrest, and straps, and it tilted, but it was more like a chair you would find at airports.

Every assistant could get me in and out of it by using my transfer device, but never a night went by where I missed Ol' Blue.

I used that non-relaxing chair for about two years before I hit the jackpot.

Or so I thought.

One night, I finally decided I was over this shower chair. I was never comfortable in it. Why can't I be comfortable? I deserved to be comfortable again like I was with Ol' Blue, damnit! I went to the website of the manufacturer that made my old shower chair.

Jackpot!

Jackpot!

Jackpot!

They had an updated version of my old shower chair with a lower stand! I could probably get into it with my transfer device!

And it was pink!

Jackpot!

Jackpot!

Jackpot!

I ordered the thing right then and there!

Unfortunately, like a lot of things in my life, it didn't go exactly as planned.

The lower stand was still too high for my transfer device. To make a long story short, the chair could adjust in all kinds of different positions. I would have my assistants put it flat like a gurney, I would shimmy onto it from my bed, they would put me in a sitting position, I would shower, and they would put me flat again and roll me back on my bed.

Yeah, it was definitely not the safest thing to do, but what can I say?

I was happy!

We all do stupid crap sometimes to be happy!

This lasted about eight months, and then my mom came up from Florida again and became Super Creative Mom.

Basically, she took the bottom base of the first shower chair I ordered and wire-tied the pink seat to it.

Yes. Wire ties. Duct tape. Velcro. Essential parts of my life.

Two chairs became one chair, making the Ultimate Perfect Shower Chair.

A little creativity goes a long way!

Amber rolls my shower chair out of my bathroom and braces it against the side of my bed. She locks all four wheels. I turn my voice-activated speaker on to my Favorites playlist and shut my communication device down for the night. Amber takes it off and plugs it in its charger, along with my wheelchair and phone. She then proceeds to take my shirt and bra off.

I get in my transfer device and sit on the toilet for more than a few minutes. I like to try to get all the pee out of me before I go to bed for nine or more hours, even though I have the best diaper on the market. I have no idea if this actually helps anything or not, but if it helps, I'll do whatever I have to do.

Once I'm done, Amber leaves my pants down, wheels me over, and plops me down into my shower chair. She unbuckles me from the transfer device and straps my arms down at my side. She takes my pants and shoes off, reclines my chair just a little, and off to the shower I go.

Because I'm in love with my shower chair now, I've taken to sitting there and letting the hot water beat on my body. Not only does this help my body relax and make me a wet noodle, but it also opens up my mind and lets my thoughts rise up just like the steam filling the bathroom.

Sometimes I plan out the next day: what I want to do, how many words I want to try to write, what I'm going to do to relax after I'm finished writing.

Sometimes I think about a problem and iron out every little detail to make it better. I think about it so hard and so completely that I'm no longer upset about it and actually kind of looking forward to putting my solution into place.

Sometimes a random idea pops into my head, like a plot twist to a project I'm working on or another project I want to do in the future.

Amber peaks her head behind the shower curtain for a third time. "You want more time?"

I shake my head and she pulls open the curtain all the way.

I usually like to sit for ten or fifteen minutes, but I have my assistants come check on me every five.

Amber has her socks off and her leggings bunched up to her shins. She grabs the handheld and gets to work, starting with my head and moving down.

Having somebody not even a foot away from you in the shower is just awkward. There is no way around it.

Having somebody not even a foot away from me and not saying a word is even more awkward. Some people with disabilities definitely disagree with me about this, but for me, personally, I can't deal with the silence when someone is assisting me.

Making conversation is slightly less awkward for me, so most of the time, that's what I do.

We ask each other what we're going to do the next day.

A few more seconds and I nod at her to turn the water off.

Once I'm in my bedroom and drying off, I suddenly feel the weight of my eyes.

I'm officially done for the day.

Amber must've sensed I hit my wall, because she's not really talking anymore.

I seriously appreciate that.

It takes everything I have, but I get in my transfer device and flop onto my bed.

I be done.

I look at my clock and roll my eyes at myself.

A little past 10:30, and I'm this dead?

Getting old sucks.

Amber turns my body, cleans and dresses my button, throws on a diaper, and slips on a nightshirt. She turns me onto my stomach and puts my hair into a messy bun. She then places a pillow on each side of my body, covers me to my shoulders, and puts my big, heavy body pillow on top of my back.

The more weight I have on my body, the better!

"Okay." She turns on the portable fan—something I only have for white noise. "Do you need anything else, Sar?"

I shake my head no.

"Cool," I hear her grab my shower chair to take it back to the bathroom. "I'll talk to you soon! Have a few good days!"

I manage to make a little noise.

She chuckles. "Thanks."

She turns out the light. Within a few minutes, I hear my front door shut, and within another few minutes, I'm fast asleep.

Day Two

4:48 a.m.

SLOWLY FEEL MY BODY WAKING UP. *Ugh. Morning. No. Why?* My eyes keep fluttering until I realize it's still pitch-black in my bedroom. Yep. I'm awake, and it's not even—

Ow!

I feel the pain.

I know why I'm awake now.

I don't have to look at the clock to know that I'm screwed.

For the love of everything holy.

Not again!

And I can't do anything about it.

Eff.

Eff. Eff. Eff.

I gently turn my head to see the clock. I know I'm screwed, but I want to know how screwed.

Effffff.

I feel more pain while trying to move. It's the G-tube button. It's throbbing. However, even though the giant, gaping hole in my stomach is radiating with pain (okay, it's not giant, and it's not gaping. My mom says the stoma is about the size of the pencil tip. Just let me be dramatic here!), I'm more frustrated than anything.

I'm frustrated, because the pain woke me, and judging by the amount of pain, I won't be able to go back to sleep any time soon, if at all.

I'm frustrated, because I know what's wrong; I'm either growing unnecessary tissue around the stoma, which is called granulation tissue, or I'm just hungry and need to put something in my stomach quick, and I can't do anything about this, nor do I have anyone here at the moment to help me.

I'm frustrated, because I have this emergency button attached to the wall above my bed that will call three different people on my list and, if none of them pick up, send the police to my house.

And I'm frustrated, because nobody has clarified what an "emergency" is and what is not.

Seriously, does an annoying little pain keeping me awake warrant the emergency system calling my mom, having her call my assistants until she reaches someone who's willing to come, having that assistant drive anywhere from twenty minutes to fifty minutes just to be here for about ten minutes to fill my stomach up with fluid and put some numbing cream around my stoma? And, depending if they work in the morning, then they're supposed to drive back home?

I have no idea!

Now, if I was in excruciating, abnormal pain, or puking my guts out, then yeah, I would definitely hit the button, even though I don't know what good would that actually do since there is no guarantee any of my assistants would come and I wouldn't be able to communicate with the police very well.

But what is "I can't sleep because I have this annoying pain" classified as?

Emergency?

Non-emergency?

Suck it up and deal with it?

I have no idea, and at this moment, I'm mad nobody has explained what to do in a situation like this.

I may like to do my own thing and be my own person, but I definitely like some rules and guidelines, too.

I mentally curse the blue button above my head that's always proudly offering HELP in white capital letters.

I'm sure this emergency system works wonders for a lot of people.

Just not me.

Deciding not to call anybody, I start the process of rolling over.

It's the only thing that will help right now.

Picture this in slow motion—

Scratch that.

Picture this in extreme slow motion with jerky movements as though I can magically make this faster.

I move my arm above my head.

My other arm slides right beside my chest.

Oh, yeah—I've already made sure I'm not close to the edge of the bed, so I don't fall off, crack my head open, and die.

I shift all my weight to the side of my body that I'm rolling toward.

I'm almost on my side now.

I start with my legs, bending and turning them.

They get caught in my sheets.

Damn.

Of course.

Why not add some more drama to this?

I'm extremely careful of how I move my legs in the next couple minutes, because if I'm not, I could completely uncover myself, and that's all I need! To be in pain and be cold.

Sweet.

I manage to turn my legs over, very diligently, of course, without budging my blankets.

In my head, I give a little fist pump.

Crushing this.

Little victories, people!

Little victories!

Once my legs are sorted out, I use the arm by my side to push my upper body over as much as I can.

I am completely on my side.

Little victories.

Right.

Here we go.

Little victories.

However, the arm that I used to push myself over is sticking straight up in the air.

It will not go forward so I can go back on my stomach.

It will not go back so I can roll all the way back.

It's just sticking straight up in the air like I have a very important question for my bedroom.

If I wasn't supposed to be sleeping right now, and if I didn't know what lack of sleep actually does to me, I would be laughing my ass off just like I hope you are while reading this. This is so my luck. I get myself into stupid, ridiculous, absolutely insane situations, and somehow, everything turns out okay.

My luck even has its own name: P luck.

Again, I'd also like to point out that I'm fully aware of all the ridiculousness and crazy crap that can go wrong with living on my own. Nobody is making me do anything.

I'm choosing to have my own house with all the craziness that comes with it.

Why?

I'm not entirely sure. Hopefully that answer will come sometime in my life, but maybe I'm just a crazy person who attracts crazy situations.

I still don't know what time it is, so I have no idea how long my arm just chills above me.

It could be three minutes.

It could be five.

It could be eight.

Eleven minutes?

Fifteen?

I don't have the best concept of time when I can't see a clock, especially at night, so I don't have the slightest fricking clue.

I turn my head to try to see my alarm clock again.

Just like that, my arm flops to the side, and I'm suddenly almost on my back, laying on the pillow that's always beside me when I sleep.

Gahhhhh!

I'm a moron!

Of course my arm would flop to whichever way my head turned!

I knew that!

If I had thought of this earlier, my arm wouldn't have felt like a flagpole waving an invisible flag of surrender.

My brain really doesn't work when I'm woken suddenly in the middle of the night.

But I'm finally able to look at the time.

4:52.

Okay.

Okay!

That's frustrating, but it's not completely horrible either.

I've woken with this pain at four o'clock before.

I've woken at three, too.

The worst, I would have to say, is when I woke up at two and couldn't go back to sleep. Again, the question: should I have called the emergency system, or was I right to suck it up and go through the entire day as a red-eyed zombie?

For anyone in a situation like mine, I think it really depends on your circumstances, your standards, and your assistants.

Right now, it's 4:52.

And 4:52 is not two o'clock.

Nope—4:52 is only three hours away from eight o'clock.

I can do this.

I might be a bubble brain for the rest of the day, but I can do this.

Since I landed on the pillow, I'm not entirely on my back. I would stay like this, but it doesn't help the pain. I need to be flat on my back if there's any chance of it dying down, and now I have come too far to be like "You know what? It's all good. I'll just live with it." And because I'm already mostly on my back, it's all downhill from here.

Plus, I have three hours to kill with not a single sign of sleep ahead of me, so let's do this!

I bring my feet up to my butt.

With my leg strength, I flex my lower body upward. When I come down, I try to land more to the right.

It worked a little.

Okay.

Little victories.

Still remembering little victories here.

I do this three more times.

I'm halfway off the pillow.

Four more times.

And I'm off.

I'm completely off the pillow!

Oh, thank you, Sweet Baby Jesus!

I'm gasping for breath, and I don't even want to think about what I would've looked like if someone happened to video me, but I did it!

I'm off the pillow and flat on my back!

Screw little victories!

Just give me the entire damn thing!

I want to put my arms above my head and stretch, but they are currently under the covers, and I'm not about to take them out and chance them getting cold and being unable to put them back down.

I turn to look at the clock.

I blink, not sure if I'm seeing it right.

5:17!

Are you serious?

The entire process of getting off the pillow took more than twenty minutes?

No.

But . . .

I . . .

Little victories.

You can't screw little victories.

I feel immediate relief on my back, and I slowly slide the body pillow down away from my button by very carefully inching the covers down with my feet. This body pillow does awesome keeping me calm when I'm on my stomach, but when I'm on my back and it's adding pressure where it hurts?

Not so much.

I feel relief, but not complete relief. I'm still not sure if I'm starting to grow granulation tissue or if I'm just hungry.

My guess is probably both.

I close my eyes to see if there's any chance of sleep coming back to me.

Nope.

They just pop right back open.

I would say this is probably the most frustrating part for me, because I know what's coming, what today will look like. I will go around my house in a daze, getting nothing accomplished.

Oh, this button.

I silently curse the damn thing.

We have a love-hate relationship.

I should've known that this would be the case during the very first appointment when I tried to get one.

My mom had suggested, on and off for a few years at this point, that I get a feeding tube for additional nutrition. I could still eat by mouth whatever I wanted, she assured me, but I would be getting all of the nutrients I wasn't getting from eating Sara Pyszka style. I mentioned it earlier: I ate like crap. Partly because I was extremely picky, and partly because I can't really eat any food that's crunchy or hard. I liked the idea of being healthier, but I was not down with a twelve-inch tube hanging out of me.

Not that there's anything wrong with a regular feeding tube. If you like it, or if it's your only option, absolutely no judgment here. Again, it's all about your circumstances and all about your standards. Back then, a feeding tube was a choice for me, and my oh-so-proud standards were not ready to adjust just yet.

It wasn't until a friend told me about the button that I flew to the train and flung my entire body on board. She comes from a family that adopted a lot of children with disabilities, including her, so she's the woman I want on my side when it comes to anything disability related. She told me the size of it was comparable to a cap on a water bottle. She told me the tube didn't have to be attached at all times. Best of all, if I had any air in my stomach, I could just open it, and out it would come.

Well, hells bells!

No more gas?

No more air?

Sign. Me. Up.

Right now.

I'm pretty sure I called a GI doctor that day to make an appointment about getting one.

I met with three doctors who either didn't understand my need for the button, or who wanted to give me not one but *two* tubes, before my PCP recommended a GI doctor that was "absolutely incredible." *Alright,* I thought. *Let's give this another whirl.*

When I finally had my appointment with this "absolutely incredible" doctor, I met with his PA first. I had about a two-minute, very detailed spiel about what I wanted and what I didn't want.

I had done my research.

This was not my first rodeo.

I was ready to go.

I really wanted to give my mini presentation to the doctor. As far as I was concerned, this was my last GI appointment. If they couldn't do it, they couldn't do it, and I was just not supposed to get a button at this time, but I was not going to mess around and not explain what I needed. However, the PA insisted I tell her everything and assured me she would relay it all to the doctor.

Ha.

I presented my little spiel about how I wanted the button because I swallow a lot of air, and could not burp like everyone else, and I would get random attacks of pain from the air traveling down to my intestines. I said I wanted the button because it was low profile, and I couldn't have the longer tube because I was very active and I was afraid everyone would pull on it, including me. And, as an added bonus of having this button, I would be able to consume more nutritious foods.

The PA seemed to be listening, and she was taking notes, but . . .

Fail.

Epic. Fail.

The doctor came in and introduced himself. "So, you want a G-tube because you have a little air in your stomach, but you really want it for nutrition?"

I blinked at him.

I then shook my head and started to type.

"No . . ." my mom said, sounding just as confused as I had been feeling. I usually didn't bring my mom to my appointments, especially since she had moved to Florida. I can typically handle everything myself, if I have the right assistant with me. But this time, I was *not* messing around. I needed all the backup I could get. Because I had the appointment with this supposedly amazing doctor, I had wanted my mom to come with me. "Sara wants the G-tube for extra nutrition, yes, but she wants this button for getting the air out of her stomach. She swallows a lot. She told your PA this."

I spoke what I typed. "I have a message that I specifically wrote for you. I would really like to tell you personally."

"My PA already told me what you said. You want a G-tube button. You don't want a tube. I know what's going on."

Hmm.

Do you really?

Because it doesn't seem like you do.

But . . .

Okay.

"Unfortunately," the doctor started, "you will have the longer tube for about a month. That's just how the surgery works. We place a standard G-tube in for four to six weeks, wait for the stoma to heal, and if all goes well, you come back in for another surgery to replace it with the low-profile button." He shrugged. "That's just how the procedure is."

Well . . .

Crap.

I didn't know that.

Maybe that was what the other doctors had been saying—that I couldn't get out of having a longer tube *at first*.

No, they had seemed solidly against any low-profile buttons.

Grrrr doctors!

Communication. Good.

Knowledge. Good.

Communication and knowledge. Extremely good.

If I had to have a longer tube for only about a month, I could deal with it.

Right?

"So, you're okay with that procedure?" he asked.

I nodded. *I mean, if I didn't have a choice . . .*

"Radiology can do the procedure. They do a pretty good job, and they would be able to get you in faster than I can."

I immediately started typing. "I would really like you to do it. I just want to be safe."

Yes, I wanted the G-tube button right away. The pain attacks were really starting to get to me. But I didn't want to put my body in even more jeopardy. Since when did radiologists do these types of procedures?

"As I said, radiology does the same thing. They will do a very good job. I'm going to have my nurse come in and schedule you with them. It was really great to meet you, Sara!"

What the hell, doc?

The nurse came in. At that time, she was turning out to be more awesome than the doctor. She believed she could get me in with radiology within two weeks.

Two weeks!

For someone who wanted to be safe, but also desperately wanted this feeding tube as soon as possible, that had sounded amazing.

Okay, maybe this doctor did know what he was talking about.

Maybe radiology was going to be okay.

It was only until after I got my feeding tube that we realized Nurse Awesome wasn't really all that awesome, an absolute perfect match for this doctor.

The morning of the surgery started like every other Morning of Surgery, I assume. I can't say I've had too many operations to know the exact routine. We (me, my mom, and my assistant) woke up before the butt crack of dawn, I skipped breakfast, and we arrived at the hospital before the sun came up. Once I was checked in and registered, they gave me a bed and made me change into a hospital gown that was much too light for my CP's liking.

Now, obviously, because of anesthesia, pain meds, and sleeping meds, a lot of this adventure is a bit of a fog for me. Because I don't want to get anything wrong, I'm just going to give you some highlights that I definitely remember.

Inside My Outside

The doctor and nurse I'd met with to book this surgery were nowhere to be found. Not that I thought they would be around—this was not their floor. I met a surgeon whom I had never seen before and would never see again. This made me a little nervous, but again, what did I know? Feeding tubes were apparently so routine, people didn't need to know the surgeon putting them in. Apparently.

A typical stomach is shaped like the letter J. My stomach is shaped like the letter U. Why? I have no idea, but I'm guessing it's because I sit more than most people. That, or my body just likes to be as unique as possible. I would've thought the surgeon needed to know this detail before the procedure, but, of course, they did not, causing them to improvise and jerry-rig a tube that would fit inside my stomach.

The surgery was supposed to be outpatient; however, I was in so much pain. I didn't know what was going on. Was this normal? Was this not normal? Did they implant a baby alien inside of my stomach and not tell me? Nobody would tell us anything. Not to mention, neither my mom nor I knew how to work the damn thing. We didn't even know how to open it, let alone do everything I wanted it to do. I did not feel comfortable going home with this much pain and lacking so much knowledge. I demanded I stay in the hospital until we had some kind of a clue as to what was happening.

My little outpatient surgery turned into a four-fricking-day hospital stay

Yes, four fricking days!

P luck strikes again, everyone!

93

In those four days, after multiple tests, and X-rays, and even a CT scan, my new feeding tube was declared perfectly fine. There was nothing wrong with it. The tape pulling on my skin, however . . .

Mmhmm. Yes. A four-day hospital stay just to find out I'm allergic to a certain kind of medical tape.

I don't think my family will ever let me live that one down.

What can I say? I could feel the pain in my stomach, but I couldn't see my stomach, so I didn't know where it was coming from.

The Wonderful World of P Luck.

In those awesome four days, I waited, and waited, and waited for the "training" we were supposedly getting. New to feeding tubes, I thought they would have, like, a tube specialist come talk to us.

Yeah, I really don't think they exist.

Everything else I learned?

YouTube's the word.

When we got home, I wanted to try out my new feeding tube, which would later be named Tubie. If I'm being honest, I don't particularly like to eat. Of course, I love buttered noodles, mac 'n' cheese, and basically anything from Olive Garden, but unlike a lot of people, eating was never on my list as something to do for fun. Some people say they live to eat. I'm the opposite. I eat to live. Therefore, I was super excited to be able to fill up my stomach and not have to work to feel full.

My mom bought some of those nutrition drinks from the grocery store. I had received some formula in the hospital specifically designed for people who use feeding tubes and had tolerated it very well, so we didn't think twice about it. After all, they're sold in every grocery store for anyone to drink. I didn't have any dietary restrictions, and I had always been able to drink anything I wanted. We figured this would be fine.

Not so much!

Within minutes of my mom squirting the strawberry-flavored drink in my tube, I had started sweating, my heart had started racing, and then I puked my guts out.

We called the GI doctor's nurse. She said I was probably having an allergic reaction to a protein in the drink and she ordered me the formula I had in the hospital.

Huh.

So not only was I allergic to a certain kind of tape, I was now allergic to a certain kind of protein.

Alright then!

I learned so much about myself on this little feeding-tube adventure.

After I finally knew what I was doing and had a handle on Tubie, the Twelve-Inch Tube, the day that I had been waiting for came: I was going to get my low-profile button! Tubie had been living inside my bra for a month when he wasn't in use. Nobody could see him, but it still made me feel super unattractive. I was so unbelievably ready for this!

Oh, yeah, Tubie had also taken on a moldy scent after a few weeks. I tried having my assistants wash it with antibacterial soap, and then even my honeysuckle bodywash every night, but it didn't work. Tubie was going to do what he was going to do, and that included stinking up my nostrils with the smell of mold, probably because he knew how much I wanted to get rid of him.

Button Day came, and I was so excited I practically did everything but throw Tubie a goodbye party.

I was not going to have a twelve-inch thing hanging out of me.

I was not going to have the smell of mold wafting off of me, even though nobody else had claimed they could smell it.

Get this fricking thing out of me!

The day started like the first surgery day had: We woke up at the butt crack of dawn, I didn't have anything to eat, and we got there before sunrise. This time, I knew it would be different, though. It *was* going to be outpatient. It had to be. A hole would not be cut into my stomach. I knew now that hoping for any kind of training was useless, too. They were going to just swap out the tubes.

What could go wrong?

When I got out of surgery, I had a cute little button just like I had wanted for about a year. The surgeon, who was not the same as the first, showed my mom how to hook and unhook the tube from the button.

When I got home, I tried to vent like how I did with Tubie. Theoretically, a G-tube button should do everything a typical G-tube should do. The only difference should be the tube is not attached to the stomach 24/7.

Nothing would come out.

We then tried putting a little fluid through the tube.

It hurt.

Not like a sharp pain but definitely a crampy pain.

A little piece of advice to anybody who has anything at all inserted in them: Make sure it fricking works before you go home with it!

This should be obvious to everybody, but apparently, it's not.

Example. Me.

My mom.

My assistant.

My surgeon.

We decided the issue was that my stomach went through a little trauma that day and it just needed time to reconfigure. This would not explain why any air wasn't coming out, but it might explain the cramping. It was most definitely *not* the button's fault.

Like most shots in the dark, that was not it. The next day, nothing came out, and anything in caused more cramps. Taking the surgeon's advice, we called the GI nurse. By now, we could tell this nurse was completely over me and my ridiculous questions. They didn't know why the button wasn't working and told me to talk to the surgeon.

That's right.

The surgeon had told me to talk to the doctor if I had any questions, which, in this case, really meant the nurse, and the nurse then told me to talk to the surgeon.

Nice.

And I'm not making any of this up, I swear!

"Hey, Sara," my mom had said slowly, as though she knew the outcome of her question. "Do you happen to remember the name of the surgeon?"

I blinked at her.

I didn't even remember what they looked like!

"Can't you check the release papers?" I asked.

My mom bit her upper lip to keep from laughing.

That's right.

We had not received any discharge papers.

Or we left them at the hospital.

Or they were stolen from my apartment by a flying monkey.

However, I confirmed with my mom while writing this book, and she distinctly remembers not coming home with any discharge papers.

Not knowing what else to do, she called the radiology department. Luckily, they had been able to track down my surgeon, but unfortunately, we learned I would need emergency surgery.

Wait.

What?

Surgery?

Again?

That day?

But I just had surgery five days earlier!

Yeah, that didn't matter!

Even though I could still eat by mouth, it wasn't a true *emergency* surgery, but being that my mom was going back to Florida *that day* and that I couldn't get any air out of my stomach, we wanted to get it fixed as soon as possible.

We jumped into my van, hurried to the hospital so my mom wouldn't miss her flight, and I was transferred to a bed with all of my clothes on, including my shoes.

No time for gowns!

Or, more likely, it was just an oversight . . . by everyone.

Once I was in the bed, they told me they had to take out the button and showed me what they were going to replace it with.

Oh, no!

Oh, hell to the fricking no!

It was Tubie, the Twelve-Inch Tube.

He had been reincarnated, and he was going back inside my stomach!

"It doesn't have to be forever," the surgical technologist had explained at my protest. "You can talk to your GI doctor about trying a button again."

GI doctor, my ass!

Do you even know my GI doctor?

Because he's an ass!

"I know you don't want the tube, but we know it works," my mom had said, irritated. She was never one for sugarcoating, but when her patience is up, only facts come flying out of her mouth. "You can either take the tube or be in pain. Your choice!"

I gave my mom a dirty look because my patience was also just about up, and I finally agreed.

That tube.

That fricking tube.

That fricking, damn tube.

Ugggggghhhhhhhh!

Scowling all the way to the operating room, I just shook my head.

Stupid doctors!

Stupid tubes!

This is ridiculous!

Once they transferred me onto the table, they informed me that they weren't putting me to sleep because it was "just" a tube change.

Hold up!

You're doing what to me now?

Now, I know that, no, tube changes are not a big deal, and yes, people are very much awake for them, but back then, I might as well have been an art teacher substitute just told she would be teaching quantum mechanics.

Seeing how nervous I became, one of the guys on the team had suggested my mom stay with me.

Even though we swiped up that offer as soon as it came, I started sweating.

What the hell were they about to do to me now?

This feeding tube was a mistake!

I take it back!

I don't want it anymore!

Just take the button out and let the stoma close!

I'm okay with eating like crap! I survived on my diet of carbs and more carbs for thirty-one years. I'm sure I could survive it for, at least, a few more!

And my gas? I know how to manage it! If I'm lying on my back, it stops the pain. I've figured out a way to write in bed, and I'll just have everyone hang out in my bedroom when I have people over!

It's totally doable, and it would be totally better than having to deal with this crap!

I'll just live in bed on my back for the rest of my life, and everything will be okay!

Of course, that would never be totally doable or totally okay. That was just Nervous Exhausted Sara thinking.

Right before they began, my mom took my arms and raised them above my head. She held them there. Because I was so nervous, my CP was in overdrive, making my body even more tight and jerky than it usually was, which, in turn, forced my mom to hold my arms down with all her might.

And then some.

I don't know why they didn't just strap my arms down like they did with my legs, but then again, I seriously didn't know anything at this point.

All the research I'd done throughout the months leading up to this and I still felt like I had barely—barely—scratched the surface of the world of feeding tubes.

And I had been so damn proud of that research, too!

Oh well.

They started.

They pulled the button out of my stomach.

I don't quite remember, but I felt very little with the button coming out, if anything.

Okay.

Okay!

Maybe this wasn't going to be so bad.

I tried to focus on my breathing, which failed miserably, while my mom tried to get me to think about Ed Sheeran.

I didn't think I could focus on Ed Sheeran even if he had been in the operating room, holding my hand, singing to me.

"Okay, Sara," I heard the surgeon say. "The button is out. You're doing a great job! Now, we're going to insert the tube. You're going to feel a little pressure, but it's not going to be a big deal."

Guys!

When a doctor says, "You're going to feel a little pressure," in my experience, that's usually code for, "This is probably going to hurt, but I don't want to tell you, because I don't want you to freak out."

Again, just in my experience, of course!

Due to the blue paper curtain blocking my view, this next scene is drawn from what I felt and what my mom saw.

The doctor had tried to put the regular tube in me.

And it didn't fit.

Apparently, in a matter of days, my stoma had shrunk.

If the tube was going to go in, she would have to stretch it.

To do this, she had to use a tool my mom didn't even want to describe to me.

I'd like to point out I'm not a screamer. Whenever I scratch myself, or smack my hand off something, or twist one of my limbs the wrong way, I don't scream.

I don't even swear in my head.

I'm usually like . . . *okay* . . . and continue on with what I'm doing.

That. Day. Was. Different.

Since someone was literally making the hole in my stomach bigger with a steel tool, I screamed.

And not like a one-time scream.

Anyone outside of the operating room probably thought a tiny human was coming out of me instead of a tiny object going in me.

"A little pressure, Sara," the surgeon kept saying in a monotone voice. "Just a little pressure."

"Ed! Ed! Think of Ed!" My mom tried to be cheerful. "Ooh! Ed is singing to you! Ooh! Ed is holding your hand! Damnit, I wish I had a picture of him for you right now!"

Yeah, that didn't help.

I didn't stop screaming until it was done.

It. Was. Done.

The tube was in me.

"Okay." The surgeon had put a hand on my sweaty, sweaty shoulder. "You're good to go! You did a really great job!" she said.

Without even thinking, without even processing what the hell I was doing, I stuck my tongue straight out at her.

"Was that to me?" she asked in a quiet voice.

I gave her a very matter-of-fact nod.

That's how much I was not with it. I basically flipped off a surgeon and admitted to her face that I did.

Not my most mature moment, I know.

What can I say?

I don't think straight when I'm woken from a deep sleep or when I'm in severe pain.

I decided it was time to switch doctors, something that a lot of people were telling me to do for a while now. I'm not entirely sure what took me so long, but I emailed my PCP, asking for another recommendation.

They answered me back and recommended a trauma surgeon, who was also . . . wait for it . . . a tube specialist.

Ha. I knew it!

Tube specialists did exist!

I had no idea why they would be a trauma surgeon, as well, and this would've been nice to know a year ago, but hey! I'll take it!

I don't remember how quickly I got an appointment, but I will never forget that appointment.

I gave her a rundown of the previous five months: how I wanted the button, why I wanted the button, how it didn't work, and how I couldn't take Tubie anymore, because he was starting to smell. Again.

"Okay." She lifted up my shirt to take a peek. "Okay. I'll be right back."

Where are you going?

I looked at my assistant, confused. She verbalized my question. "Where is she going?"

The specialist came back with a mini pizza-looking box.

I knew that box! It was a button box.

What are you doing?

"Can her chair go back?" the surgeon asked.

"You can talk to Sara, but yeah, it can. What are you thinking?"

"She said she wanted a button, so I'm going to give her a button. I need her chair to lay back."

In a panic, I started spelling and my assistant translated. "But the last button didn't work."

"I know. It was probably the wrong size. I'm going to give her the right size now."

"Right now?"

After my previous experience, I definitely, absolutely wanted to be knocked out.

"Yes, right now."

What the hell?

"I would really like to be put to sleep," I spelled.

"We don't put patients to sleep for tube changes. Does she want this button, or not?"

If any of you watch *Grey's Anatomy*, think Christina Yang. 100 percent.

In a panic, I reclined my wheelchair.

Oh, my God! She was going to take the tube out and put a button in.

This was happening.

Today.

Right now.

When I was very much awake.

Oh, my God!

Remembering my last "tube change," I grabbed my assistant's hand and squeezed it.

"Holy . . ." she caught herself. "Grip! You're strong! And you're sweating! It's going to be okay."

"Breathe," the nurse in the room must've seen how nervous I was. "Sara! Breathe!"

Breathing is not on my list of priorities right now, okay?

But thank you for your concern!

I braced myself for the pain I knew was coming, but the tube came out without any pain.

And the button went in without any pain.

"Okay, you're done," the surgeon said, matter-of-factly.

What?

No. I can't be.

"Make sure it works!" I hurriedly spelled.

Hell if I was making that mistake again!

They attached the tube and pushed some water through.

No pain!

I then tried to vent. Air rushed out.

It worked?

It was working?

What just happened?

I had received my very first functional, low-profile button. That's what happened!

8:04 a.m.

I'm up.

My eyes aren't even open, but I am awake.

How?

Last I knew, I had been awake.

This doesn't make sense.

Oh, but as I come to and the sun bursts through my eyelids, I know what happened, even though it still doesn't "make sense" to me.

This has happened before. No matter how long I lay awake or how much I'm hurting, nauseous, hungry, anxious, excited, or want to have a dance party, I usually manage to fall back to sleep around seven o'clock. I have no idea if this has something to do with my circadian rhythms resetting or if it's something unique to my body, but seven o'clock always seems to be the magic time.

As I lift my very heavy eyes open, I finally register words hanging in the air that I need to do something with. The language part of my brain slowly revs up, and a few minutes after the fact, I process the scene I'm in.

Britney is here for the day, and she has asked me if I'm ready to get up.

She only asked the question once and only accompanied it with a, "Hello, Sara."

I find this to be a little frustrating, but I also think I understand where she's coming from.

It's frustrating, because she asked this when she first walked into my bedroom. I know this, even though I was unconscious, because this is what she does at the start of each of her shifts. I understand why she does this. This is literally what she's here for: to get me up out of bed. And normally, I don't really mind the dry routine since I'm usually ready to get going.

However, today, and occasionally some other days, I had just passed out (again) or am just waking up. When she asked the question, some part of my brain had to catch her words, hang on to them, and revisit them once it started functioning. While I'm processing, Britney just stands there, hands crossed, looking down at me, waiting for my answer.

She doesn't busy herself by straightening my nightstand.

She doesn't glance away.

She just stands there, looking down at me, my answer determining her next move.

I cannot tell you how frustrating it is to literally have someone standing over you, staring at you, waiting for you to tell them what to do.

This is technically my fault. Whenever I train a new assistant, I don't tell them what to do when I don't answer the question.

I should probably tell them to give me a minute if it looks like I need one.

I should tell them that if it looks like I'm still dead asleep, they can start getting my breakfast ready or throw in a load of laundry.

Even though I'm accepting the blame for this completely weird and incredibly awkward situation, I can't help but feel a little disheartened that

Britney, and some other assistants, for that matter, can't think of anything else to do *on their own* other than to watch me come out of my nightly coma.

It makes me feel nonhuman.

I can't be mad at her, though. She's just doing her job.

I make a mental note to figure out how the hell I want to handle this when I train future assistants.

Okay, Sara. Say something. End this awkwardness.

I start to nod my head but quickly began to spell. "I need to do something different today."

"Okay." Britney places one knee on my bed.

"I need to eat right now."

The pain is back, and it's definitely hunger pains, and I could probably make it the thirty or so minutes it takes her to get me dressed, but I'm not entirely sure, and I don't want to risk it.

If I were Inside Sara, the moment I woke up after a bad night of sleep, I would make no effort to get up, let alone string words together to tell someone about it.

Actually, I would never have woken up in the first place, because I would never even think about paying a person to come into my house at eight o'clock to get me out of bed.

Actually, the bad night would never even have happened, because I would've hopped right up and shoved my face full of food. Who the hell knows if I would've gone back to bed or not, but at least I wouldn't have been in pain.

"You want to eat in your bed?" Britney's face is pure confusion.

I nod. I'm not awake enough yet to try to explain.

"You're on your back. Was your tube hurting?"

Or I could explain with a nod. That works.

"Oh. Okay. Do you want your meds in here, too?"

I nod.

"Ibuprofen?"

Another nod.

"Okay." I feel her take her weight off my bed. "I'll be back."

Even though I really don't have a good enough reason, I look up at my ceiling and shake my head. *God, fricking help me today!*

Britney is a decent assistant. She's almost always on time, rarely calls off, and although she has given me one too many what-the-hell faces when I want to do something that's out of my routine, she always ends up doing what I ask.

She's just not very personable.

Better put, she thinks of me as a job.

A lot of people say this is good to have, that I should want this in every assistant. "Your assistants shouldn't be your friends," they tell me. "You can't work with friends. You want people who are able to do the job right. That's all that matters."

To a certain extent, I see where they're coming from, and I agree. But they don't wheel around in my shoes; they only imagine footwear as something to walk in.

When you're just a job to somebody, they only think about getting your tasks done. They don't think how it gets done or how it feels when it's done.

When you are just a job to somebody, you might be thinking, "This is going to be so much fun. I'm so excited about this!" while they might be thinking, "Ugh! She really wants to do this? I can't believe she's making me do this!"

When you are just a job to somebody, they are not in your house, helping you live your life. Instead, they are at their work, doing things they need to get done.

Now, along with the people who tell me I shouldn't be friends with my assistants, a lot of people with disabilities actually prefer it like this. They want it to stay professional. They don't want anything to get personal. They strictly want an employer/employee relationship. There is absolutely nothing wrong with this. However someone feels the most comfortable, I think that's how they should live their life.

I'm just not one of those people. I'm not entirely sure, but I think it has something to do with me being nonverbal. Because I can't talk, the closer I am with my assistants, or, more accurately, the more frequently they're on the same brainwave as me, the more comfortable I feel communicating with them.

And, granted, not everyone who works for me just for the paycheck treats me like something they have to do. Some do ask me how I'm doing and try to get to know exactly how I like everything done. Whenever I get a reminder that I'm just a job to someone, I can't help but feel a little pang inside my stomach, because I know this is going to be part of my life forever.

A few minutes later, Britney comes back with an arm full of my tube, syringes of medicine and water, and pulling my IV pole with my bag of breakfast with her other arm. She unloads all of my supplies onto my nightstand and rolls the IV pole right next to me.

"Can I see the foam from my button?" I spell out.

"You want me to change it now?" She sounds a little confused, probably because this isn't our usual routine.

I don't necessarily want her to do the entire thing now; I just want to see the foam from it, as I literally just spelled out, but I'm too tired to clarify or really, in this case, repeat myself.

Besides, cleaning it might actually help.

Britney pulls the comforter to my waist, which immediately makes my arms go above my head. I'm grateful to be able to stretch, but I'm now afraid since I don't have anything holding my upper body down, I'm going to hit her. She gently takes off the beige foam and holds it right in front of my face, as though it were a permission slip I need to approve.

Through my blurry vision, I don't see the blood I was expecting.

Huh.

That's good, at least.

But that's also nuts.

No blood means I was just really hungry.

Alright then.

I asked Britney just to make sure. "Do you see a bump starting to form?"

Before I knew it was granulation tissue growing out of my stoma, I called them bumps. Very technical, I know, but that's what they were to me. Little, red, evil, angry bumps. Once I found out the actual medical term,

I tried using it with my assistants, and it just didn't work. It completely threw them off.

Little, red, evil, angry bumps they are then. Forever and always.

"Can I throw this away?" Britney asked.

Oh. Right. The foam. Still in my face.

I nod, and she tosses it into the garbage can beside my bed.

She proceeds to turn my button in a slow circle and dabs it with a freezing washcloth.

I suppress an arrrrrggghhhhhhhhh face.

Why is it hurting so much while she's moving it? This is not normal!

And why is this water so cold?!

She must've gotten it when she first came in and didn't warm it up.

Why didn't she warm it back up? This is making my entire body tense!

Britney stops twisting it, and I silently thank everything and everyone I've ever known. "It actually looks really good, Sara." She shrugs. "Do you want Lidocaine?"

Gah!

How can it look really good?

How can there not be a bump?

I don't understand this button!

The numbing cream would be nice, but it's not the outside that hurts. It's the inside, which doesn't make sense to me.

Maybe I get so hungry, my stomach tries to digest the balloon that holds the button in place.

I have no idea!

All I know right now is that I just need food, or else I'm going to take this pain and shove it somewhere!

Instead of spelling, I just look at my breakfast in the bag, figuring that would be quicker.

"You want to eat now?" she guessed.

I nod.

"You don't want me to finish your button?"

Confusion is back on her face, plain as day.

I summon all the patience I have.

She doesn't know how exhausted you are!

She doesn't know how much pain you're in!

She doesn't know that if you don't get something in your stomach now, your body might possibly very well explode before her eyes!

I shake my head.

"Okay. Do you want to vent first?"

Probably be a good idea. That's all I need today—a gas attack.

Britney grabs my tube and hooks it onto my button. I typically don't feel this, but today, it feels like she's twisting a bullet that's been lodged in my stomach.

Oh, my God!

Why is it hurting so much?

This. Is. Not. Normal!

Britney puts the venting syringe on and opens up my tube. Because I haven't had any liquid in hours, the air coming out of it sounds like somebody flattening a beach ball.

This goes on for more than ten seconds.

Holy crap!

So. Much. Air.

Probably from turning over.

The more I move, the more air I seem to swallow.

And the more my stomach deflates, just like a beach ball, the more pain I'm in.

Ow! Oh, my God! Okay, it's definitely because I'm hungry. But why? I didn't eat anything different yesterday. Ow! Oh! Okay!

I nod at Britney to tell her I'm done.

Even though it hurt, I'm so glad I vented. That was a lot of air, and seeing how today is already going, it would've probably led to my intestines feeling like they wanted to explode.

Britney takes off the venting syringe and connects my breakfast bag. Within seconds, I'm getting the grayish liquid I so desperately needed all this time.

This better work!

Within a minute or two, the pain dulls.

Are. You. Kidding. Me?

I scream in my head.

By the time the shake is gone, no more pain!

I mean, like, 0 percent of pain happening in my stomach right now!

Ahhhhhhhhh!

Alright then.

I was just hungry.

No "emergency" here, kids! I really was just hungry.
Ahhhhhhhhh!

Britney starts gathering my supplies in her arms. "I'm going to go clean everything out. When I'm done, do you want to pick out what you want to wear?"

I nod.

When she leaves, I look up at the ceiling again and shake my head, this time, at my stomach.

God, fricking help me!

Even though I ate breakfast in bed, it still takes Britney another forty minutes to get me ready for the day.

This is one thing that's challenging for me to accept about having many different people help me with my life.

Some people go at the speed I would go, if I were Inside Sara. Not too fast but not too slow.

Some people rush as fast as they can to get everything done, which makes me wonder if they are unconsciously showing their anger or frustration toward me. These are the people who tell me it's not about *how* it gets done but *if* it gets done, so I then wonder if it's less about how they feel and more about how detail-oriented they are (or are not).

And some people, like Britney, like to make sure everything is *just right*, which leads them to be a lot slower than everyone else. Yes, I'm a very detail-oriented person, but some people are more so than even I am, which makes me feel like the fly on the wall has pushed the slow-motion button for his enjoyment.

Obviously, I know every assistant is not going to be like me, nor do I expect anybody to change their personality to fit what I'm feeling that day. What makes this challenging is when I have three different assistants working for me at the same time, who have three different personalities and go at three different speeds.

A lot of my family tell me that I should desire diversity. "It will change it up for you," they say. "If you aren't really crazy about one assistant, you know you're going to have someone else the next day. It will give you a nice balance."

My family doesn't understand many, many, many things about my life. This is one of them.

Love you, family! I don't mean anything by talking about you in this book! Promise!

I'm all about diversity. Seriously, all about it. I don't think we can get enough.

However, whenever I'm doing something so routine—eating, drinking, showering, getting dressed—I generally want to do it the exact same way every day. I don't want to do anything differently. If someone is a little faster, I have to prepare myself not to take their rushing hands personally. If somebody likes to take their time or be gentle, I have to prepare for them to move a little slower and have to keep that in mind if I want to schedule anything that day.

I know my assistants don't mean anything by this. In fact, I would guarantee none of this would even cross their minds if someone were to ask them, "So, what is one thing that annoys Sara about having assistants?"

I genuinely know in my heart that my assistants would never do something to intentionally annoy or frustrate me.

I say this, because I'm human. I get frustrated. I get annoyed. Sometimes, I need to vent about something or someone. Sometimes, all I need to hear is, "Yeah, Sara. I get it. That would be annoying." That's really all I need. Instead, I usually get some kind of response like, "Sar, they don't mean anything by it," or "Oh, Sara. You're so sensitive. Don't take it personally." Or, my favorite (not!), "Hey, just be thankful they show up."

During past vent sessions, a lot of people have told me I seem depressed or anxious. Some people have actually suggested I talk to a therapist or even go on medication. I assure you I don't take this lightly and appreciate so many people are worried about it. However, I know my body enough to know it's not a serious issue.

What I'm feeling is purely frustration. Once I have my *I hate people!* moment, I'm perfectly fine.

Think of the people who get extremely frustrated with weathermen. "I can't believe how wrong they were about this storm," somebody says. "They said there was going to be rain, and sleet, and we were going to be snowed in for seventeen days, and look at it outside! It's sunny, and warm, and rainbows are shooting through the sky! I can't believe they still get paid!"

"I know!" their friend replies. "I bought five loaves of bread and twenty-two cases of water! It's ridiculous!"

Not even thirty seconds later, they're planning where they want to go out that Saturday night.

Now, the weatherman didn't mean to frustrate everyone. They were just doing their job. They were doing what they thought what was right. I would like to think everyone knows this, but they still growl about it anyway.

This is what I'm usually doing when I'm venting about an assistant. I know they're a good person. I know they're not out to get me. I know whatever annoys me about them is just a part of their personality that doesn't match up with mine and nothing more. Still, though, I'm only human—a human who is around other humans 365 days a year. Steam is bound to come out of these ears every once in a while.

I just wish more people understood it's just natural steam and not downright hatred, or depression, or anxiety.

Another thing I can't seem to get used to with having many different people helping me is that everyone has their own way of doing my routine. Of course, I have a guidebook I wrote with detailed, step-by-step instructions, but everyone eventually adapts small little details to what, I guess, they would do.

I don't mind people making minute changes to details if it's easier for them or if it feels more natural to them, but let me explain why this is such a challenge for me sometimes.

Whenever I'm in my chair and dressed for the day, I like my assistants to, in this order, brush my hair and put it into a braided bun, wash my face, and slip on my glasses.

That's how I like it, but more importantly here, that's what I'm used to.

Let's say I have three different assistants in four days.

Day One. Assistant One. Does it how I prefer. Hair. Face. Glasses.

Day Two. Assistant One. Again. Hair. Face. Glasses.

Day Three. Assistant Two. Hair. Face. Glasses.

Day Four. Assistant Three. Even though I'm aware she does a lot of things in her own way, when she starts to do my face, I start to shake my head just because I'm so used to doing it my way. I don't think she's doing anything wrong per se; it just takes me some time to remember she does things a little differently.

No big deal, right?

Yeah, not so much.

Before I catch myself and remember who I'm with, she's going to see me shaking my head. She's either going to be really confused like, "Why are you telling me no?" To that, I'm either going to have to explain myself or tell her never mind. Or, she's going to think I assume she's forgetting to do my hair and might even get a little offended like, "Yeah, Sara. I know I have to do your hair. Just give me a second."

Again, this is not a big deal, but neither of these situations are particularly fun to be in.

Why don't I tell them to speed up, slow down, and do everything exactly how I want it to be done?

For the most part, I do.

If someone is taking the straw out of my mouth before I'm done drinking, or taking their time getting me to the toilet when I really have to pee, or shoveling food into my mouth like it's a garbage disposal, I will absolutely speak up. Because these things are important and kinda-sorta involve my well-being, I have no problem asking someone three, four, five times to do it differently.

However, I really don't like asking for something more than twice. Some people can ask for something fifty times without any problem, and if it's appropriate, I think that's great. I'm just not one of those people. Like, seriously, to the depths of my inner core, I really can't stand asking for something twice. So, for the important stuff, I will ask someone again, and again, and again, but if someone washes my face before they do my hair, I will say something, but if they somehow fall back into the same routine, I'm probably just going to go with it.

10:06 a.m.

It may take Britney a little longer to help me with my morning, but today, it doesn't really matter. Not only don't I have enough sleep to fully function, but I also had to move my body a lot more than usual. My energy level is just about at E. I'm not going to be able to accomplish anything that requires even moderate thinking. I might as well be a sack of potatoes.

I'm in the process of turning on my TV to check my email when I hear a familiar sound: Britney, in my kitchen, turning on my stove, warming up a skillet.

She's going to make pancakes.

Not for me, but for her breakfast.

I try not to roll my eyes, even though she can't see me in the living room.

Rules, Sara, I shake my head. *You gotta make some more rules and reinforce them.*

Ha. Make some more rules? Reinforce the rules?

I sound like I'm running a military boarding school and not living in my own house.

Make no mistake: I have absolutely no problem with any of my assistants eating whenever they want if I don't need help at that moment. If I do need help, they are all usually okay with pausing their meal for a minute. They technically don't get a lunch break or a dinner break, which I know is not conventional for a workplace, but they eventually figure out the best times to eat. In the interview, I even tell them they're welcome to use my stove or my oven.

I'm not delusional. I know my assistants are humans, and I know humans need to eat.

Breakfast, however, is a little tricky. This is just my opinion, and I know there are about seven billion opinions in this world, but I think that if someone likes to have breakfast, they should have it before they come to work or on their way to work. If they really need to have something a little after their shift starts, I think it should be a quick food, like a bagel or a yogurt.

Besides, what other job would be okay with homemade pancake-making an hour after someone clocked in?

I think I would be more chill about it if it were once in a while, but Britney makes and eats her breakfast at the start of every shift. I think what really did me in was the morning I had a doctor's appointment. I had to leave as soon as I was ready for the day. Once Britney found out, she looked at me, frowned, and said, "Aw. But I was going to make bacon and eggs right now. I really don't like to be rushed in the morning."

Uh.

What?

You were going to make bacon and eggs right now?

I'm sorry for the inconvenience. Let me call and reschedule. Can you help me with this now, or do you need to go make your full-on breakfast first?

Okay, I wasn't that mean about it, but I definitely didn't let it go, either. I just said something like, "Hey, I'm sorry, but like I tell everyone in my interviews, some days are going to be busy, and some days are going to be chill. I suggest you come in prepared to help me with anything, but if it ends up being a quiet day, you can be relieved."

Actually, now that I think about it, I really, definitely didn't let it go. That was a decent correction, in my opinion.

However, it didn't actually correct anything.

Her response to my response was cocking her eyebrow and saying a disappointing, "Oh." And because I didn't say anything specifically about *all* breakfasts, she continues to make herself something every morning without asking me if I have to go anywhere.

I guess I could put something in my guidebook like, "Make sure I have everything I need before you make yourself a nine-course meal," but that would break my heart. That, and I feel like, "There will be downtime but not all the time. Please respect that. If all my laundry, errands, cooking, and cleaning is done, then feel free to relax until I need your assistance" should cover it.

Apparently, it doesn't.

I try to push Britney's pancake-making out of my head. I'm probably not going to need much from her today, so it doesn't really matter at the moment. I do, however, make a mental note to figure out how to handle this situation in the future. Does her breakfast-making bother me so much that I want her to stop completely, or should I wait until I have to go somewhere again and she gives me pushback?

What's the right thing to do?

That's a thought for later when I'm more coherent.

Right now. Email.

I open up Gmail to eleven junk emails; some for local news stations, some for coupons to online sites, some to newsletters I don't read anymore but am too lazy to unsubscribe to. One email catches my eye and actually makes me excited. It's a New Contact Entry Form from my website.

I absolutely love it when I get these. It either means one of three things:

Someone wants me to come present at an event. I typically don't do presentations anymore, due to the time and expenses it takes to get to and from the event, but it's still unbelievably flattering to be invited to share my experiences and my advice with an audience.

Someone, normally a parent with a disability or someone with a disability themselves, is asking for my experience about something they are going through. They usually want to know exactly how I handle the situation myself and ask for any advice I have that could make their situation go smoother. This is unbelievably flattering, as well. To have a stranger come to me (a person who's not certified in anything) for help with something they're going through? It's almost hard for me to comprehend.

However, to give them the email I want to give them, to type a detailed answer, it usually takes me one to two hours. Sometimes, it's even more than that. Even though I want to help as many people as I can, whenever I write a long email like that, my body gets so exhausted that I don't want to do anything else that day. So, it always comes down to this question: Do I want to chinse out on my answers, which I don't think anybody choosing to email me deserves, or do I want to tire myself out?

This is mostly why I decided to write this book. I want to help as many people as I can. If I answer all the email I received, I would be too tired to do anything else. If I book every presentation I'm asked to do, I would actually lose money, which has happened before. I figured if I took all my answers to the frequently asked questions and put them into a book that was very detailed and, hopefully funny, it would be a win for everyone.

Of course, I absolutely don't mind answering the occasional question. I don't want you to be sitting there, reading this, and be like, "Man, I really want to ask her this, but I really don't want to bother her." As I mentioned before, I'm always happy to see a question come through my inbox. I just can't answer multiple questions several times a week without it becoming my full-time business.

Lastly, and definitely my favorite reason for a New Contact Entry Form, is a reader telling me how much my books affected them. It could be a teacher telling me how much their student connected with them. It could be someone with a disability who doesn't feel as alone anymore because they read about a character who is like them. I even received an email from somebody from Hong Kong; they wanted to know where they could get my second novel because they found the first one in the local library.

If I get one of these emails, I go around my house with a big, goofy, unshakeable smile all day. These emails will never get old, and I will never take any of them for granted.

This new email is from the mother of a son with a case of cerebral palsy just like mine. I don't know her, nor do I know how she found me. She is asking for any advice I have about my schooling, and after reading her reason for asking, I feel like I want to puke.

Her son is going into first grade. Like me, he uses a communication device and a power wheelchair. From what I'm understanding, he pretty much needs help with everything. The school doesn't want to take him, because A, they would have to hire someone to be with him one-on-one, and B, they don't know how much he will be able to learn since he's nonverbal. They think "he would benefit more from a specialized school that could better fit his needs."

That's right. A school doesn't want to pay extra to help a student, because they don't know what good it would do, if any.

This kills me from the inside out for more than one reason.

This is downright illegal. Turning down a child requesting an education is illegal.

I really can't stand to compare anyone, but we're talking about a school that doesn't want to take a chance on a child because they're unsure of how far he'll go. I know of this kid who had straight A's and was an athlete. He took his first hit of heroin while he was a sophomore, and his life took a turn for a worse. He was in and out of juvenile detention several times and flunked his senior year. He did not graduate high school, but he was still able to walk with his class at commencement.

He just didn't get his diploma.

I'm not saying this is right or wrong. I'm just posing a very important ethical question: Where is the line drawn when giving children chances?

If I'm not extremely, extremely careful with how I explain the biggest reason this situation guts me to the core, some people might take it the wrong way, so I'm going to try to make my words match my exact feelings. If I were to take this situation and replace the child with a disability with a child who is gay, a child who is transgender, a child of a different religion, or a child of color, it would be a totally different story.

There would be a lawyer involved—possibly more than one. You would never hear the end of it, because it would be on the news. It would probably be national news. There would be a Twitter campaign. The school would be sued, and everyone in the community would shun the place.

Okay, I'm not entirely sure if all of that would happen, but I think you get the point.

Here's why I'm always a little hesitant to talk about this.

If another minority gets discriminated against, I definitely think there should absolutely be consequences.

Bring on the lawyers!

Bring on the media!

Bring on the community coming together!

Justice for all!

However, justice for all sometimes doesn't mean justice for *all*. It sometimes means justice for the minority/minorities someone is familiar with.

I would never want to downplay anybody's discrimination. It saddens me any minority still faces it in today's world. However, I am going to say people with disabilities deal with a greater amount of discrimination and prejudice. For example—and I'm sure this happens occasionally, but it's hard for me to see—in today's world, another minority being told they should go to a more appropriate school just because they fall into a certain group.

Why?

Why, when interacting with people with disabilities, do people think it's still acceptable to treat them as less than?

I fight the urge to tell the mom to hire a lawyer.

And then I question if I should actually fight that urge?

I'm not entirely sure, but it doesn't matter. Days when I'm too tired to type, I just think about what I'm going to say, which is what I'm going to do today.

I try to imagine someone asking Inside Sara about her educational background, and I can't. Even if I were an author, I could see someone maybe wanting to know where I went to college, but that's it.

And even if I worked at a camp with kids and teenagers, like I think I would, I could see some parents asking about other kids' experiences but definitely not mine, as a counselor or a director.

But let's pretend someone did ask.

I would probably have attended the same public school from kindergarten through twelfth grade.

I would like to think I'd meet my best friend in kindergarten or first grade just because I think that's adorable, and we would still be in contact to this day.

I have no idea what my personality would be like if I didn't have a disability, but if I were still an introvert, there would be no extracurriculars for me!

I could see myself being a bookworm, and I could see my small circle of friends lovingly making fun of me for it.

Academic wise, I think I would just be okay. Not super amazing but not completely horrible, either.

All in all, I think I would be a typical student. I don't think I would stand out in anything.

As far as college, my heart always wanted to go to California. I would like to think, if I were able-bodied, I would've gone to a school there, but I think the same thing would've happened: the price would've been too high, and the distance would've been too much, and I would've ended up going to a school in Pittsburgh, majoring in something like psychology or sociology.

Okay, my *actual* school experience?

Here we go.

This could be its own book, but my parents would've had to keep detailed notes, and I would have to do multiple, in-depth interviews, so for now, you're going to get the typical memories of school from someone in her thirties.

Starting when I was six weeks old, I went to Early Intervention one or two days a week. They pretty much stretched me and worked on my range of motion. I'm not entirely sure if this is technically considered "school," but whenever my mom talks about my experience, she always starts with this, so I guess, in this case, it is.

When I was two years old, I started going to a preschool for people with disabilities. It was more of the same; physical therapy, stretching, range of motion, along with a little academics. I obviously don't remember any of this, but my mom told me this was where they first realized I was going to be cognitively okay.

One of my exercises consisted of me lying on my back and rolling to each side. The therapist had plastic alphabet letters that spelled my last name on one side. She would have me roll to one side and pick the letter to spell my last name. They realized I could spell my last name at a very young age, which pointed to the idea that my mind was okay.

My mom was present during this. She always tells me she had never questioned my cognitive state, because I was a very alert baby, but it was at this moment that she thought, "Yeah, she's there. She's going to be okay."

After preschool, they enrolled me in a specialized school that was, again, for children with disabilities. Today, I really can't stand the word "special," but back then, that's what it was to me.

My Special School.

Gah. Can't believe I'm calling it that, but it is what it is, and it was what it was.

I don't remember every little detail, because A, I don't have the best memory in general, and B, that was twenty-five years ago, so I'm just going to list the things I do remember.

My mom drove behind the bus my first day of school, because I was four years old, nonverbal, and the school was an hour away.

Throughout the five years I rode that bus—

The driver would literally come into my house and help my seventy-five-year-old great grandma put me on the toilet when she babysat me. Don't worry, there was another adult on it while the bus was just chilling on my driveway, but seriously! Who would do something like that today?!

I would make my first "best friend," who could not have cared less that I couldn't talk, because she knew what I was saying. I would later drift away from that friend, because sometimes, that's just how it goes.

I would feel for the first time what it was like to be cared about by a peer when they caught my wheelchair from tipping over. They would then make sure I felt safe the rest of the ride by never taking his hands off my chair.

I would come to know that although seizures are extremely scary, they are a part of some people's lives.

I would have to stand up for myself for the very first time to a student who was annoyed at me for having my communication device, claiming that I talked too much. To some students, I would forever be known as the girl who loudly stated, "If you can talk, I can talk, too."

Sometimes, I desperately miss the seven-year-old version of me.

Oh, yeah, we had a radio, too, and whenever a good song would come on, the volume would go up with no questions asked.

So, that was my bus. I'm not going to put any of this in the email I'm going to send to the mom asking for advice, but it was sure fun to just think about how much I learned and felt just from the rides to and from school.

Now, onto the actual school.

Because of my disability and the questions I've been asked throughout the years, I feel like I was a guinea pig, paving the way for people like me. Unfortunately, I didn't realize that at the time. I don't want to say I didn't pay attention to what was going on around me, because I did, but I didn't pay attention intently. I didn't ever think I'd need to remember these days later on. I think my parents felt the same way. To our family, I was just going to school like anyone else.

That said, I'm just going to list what I remember or what my parents have told me—

This school didn't have grades, per se. The classrooms were broken into learning ability.

My first year or two was spent getting me "up and running," as my mom puts it. I received my first power wheelchair at this school. To prepare me for this, my mom said my teachers and my therapists would push me in whatever direction my head was going. For example, if I looked to the left, they would turn my wheelchair to the left. If I looked to the right, they would push me to the right. I'm sorry to say I don't remember actually doing it, but I do think this is a genius creative idea.

Props to whoever came up with that!

This is where my story becomes even more unique. Most people remember when they got their first power wheelchair. They remember where they were and how they felt. Unlimited. Free. Independent.

Here's what I remember:

The first few times, I put holes in multiple walls, leaving me with a fear of getting in it again.

I was also afraid of driving in front of anyone watching me. I still don't like driving in front of an audience today, but I don't stop dead in my tracks and make one of my parents push me until I've passed the crowds.

Yeah, that happened. A lot.

One example of this happening: my First Holy Communion.

What can I say? That church was packed, and I was a seven-year-old!

The last thing I remember about my very first wheelchair was it was pink.

As an adult and several wheelchairs later, my wheelchair has become a vital part of me. I cannot imagine my life without one. Yes, I like somebody else to push my chair occasionally, but if that were my life? If I had to rely on someone else for, literally, every move I make?

Yeah, no.

Not cool, man.

Not cool.

The other thing this school did for me right away was set me up with a communication device. One would think I'd have a totally different reaction to getting this device than my wheelchair. I always say the hardest part of my disability is being nonverbal, so you would think I would've been in love with this device, that I'd never want to take it off.

"How did it feel when you finally received your first communication device?" people ask me. "Do you remember what your first words were? How frustrated were you before you could say whatever you wanted to say?"

Again, I was not the typical child, so not the typical response.

Although, I'm not entirely sure what the typical response of a child getting a communication device would be, so who the hell am I to say if I had a typical response or not?

I absolutely hated this device.

Like . . .

Hated. It.

Like . . .

With. A. Burning. Passion.

Like, in the one class, we would have an individual goal of the day. We had a huge chart with everyone's goals on it. From what I remember, the goals were always something we needed to work on. Some examples would be "I will look someone in the eye when I'm looking at them," or "I will share my toys at playtime." If we met our goal of the day, we would get a big, bright star from the sharpie. If we didn't, that sharpie was going to give us a big, fat X.

My goals were always about my communication.

"I will say two sentences today."

"I will give somebody a compliment today."

Finally, the subtlety of my teachers wore off. "I will not use my eyes to talk. I will use my communication device to say what I need."

Every week, I would end up with two X's, if not more.

The first reason I hated this device? I already had a system I used to talk. It wasn't a fancy computer, but I could get my point across. Everyone around me knew to ask me yes/no questions. When yes/no didn't work, I used my eyes to look at whatever I wanted, just like my "goal" said not to do. When that didn't work, someone would go through the alphabet, stopping at each letter I nodded at until I spelled out a word.

I was five years old when I first got the device. I didn't know the meaning of *independence* yet, so I didn't crave it.

The second reason I absolutely hated this device? I had to use my entire body to operate it. One lone red light continuously blinked in the middle of the screen. Think of it as a mouse to a computer but always resetting to the center of the screen after each click. To make this blinking light go up on the screen, I would have to hit the switch directly behind my head, my forward switch. Left and right were easy; it was just my left and right switches. To have the curser move down, I would have to hit a switch by my left knee. To select what button I was on, or, really, to click, it was my right knee.

I have no idea who came up with that method, but if you happen to be reading this, really, dude? Really?

Unlike my communication device today, that device did not have words and letters to type out what I wanted to say. It had symbols. That's right, the display was filled with pictures that fit into half-inch bubble-like buttons. To select just one word, I would have to select two or more buttons. For example, if I wanted to say the word *red*, I would have to hit the rainbow icon and the apple icon.

And I believe that was one of the easier combinations.

With the help of my friend Google, I can recall that the sun icon and the thumbs-up icon would produce the word *smile*.

Okay, I guess in a roundabout kind of way, that sorta-kinda makes sense, if I really think about it, but if that device were in front of me today, that sequence would never even cross my mind.

A less obvious sequence: the elephant icon and the thumbs-up icon producing *lift*.

I'm sorry.

What?

How?

I am absolutely not bashing this device. Like I have said in my presentations, some people like Coke and some like Pepsi. Neither one is better than the other, but everyone generally prefers one over the other. I'm sure I could've come up with a better comparison, but I've been using this one for so long, I figured I might as well bring it along for this book.

I know a lot of fabulous communicators who still use this device, and they do a really good job; they're even quicker than I am with my current device. It really is a matter of preference. However, my younger self was not having it. With the combination of making multiple sequences with multiple switches, that device just wasn't for me.

Except, apparently, when I was on the bus. I only remember telling someone off, because every once in a while, I'll see my friend who witnessed it, and they'll bring up my infamous quote, "If you can talk, I can talk, too."

Now that I have the right device with the right setup for me—a word-based program operated by a single switch—I can't imagine going through life without it. Sometimes I do feel extremely limited not being able to talk, but this device and the alphabet chart take some of the sting out of my disability.

Once I was "up and running" at my Special School, academics was supposed to be my focus. I'm going to be totally honest here, because, ya know, it's my memoir, and I should be honest: I don't remember anything about my academics, other than my favorite classes were Music and Art. In Music class, we had a chorus that actually performed concerts for the parents. Although I was 100 percent nonverbal, I was in that chorus every year I could be. I'm not entirely sure if I was young and oblivious or if that was really what the school was about, but me being in the chorus class was just as normal as cars driving down the street.

I attended a school filled with people with disabilities, but the really incredible thing is that I didn't know what anyone's disabilities were. To me, they were just my classmates.

A classmate could walk, but he didn't talk. That was just Michael.

Another classmate used a device like me. That was just Justin.

Another classmate was in a wheelchair, but she could talk. That was just Dee.

I think this amazes me now because, back then, nobody had a disability in my mind. We were just kids. We did what we could, and that was that.

Nothing more.

Nothing less.

I haven't been anywhere like it since.

One question people ask me when the topic of my education comes up is how I learned to read.

Not *if* I can read.

Not *how well* I can read.

No, they want to know *how* I learned.

At first, I thought this was a really fricking weird question. *How did I learn to read? I don't know! How did you learn to read?*

But now I know that people who are nonverbal usually have a difficult time learning to read, because they can't sound out words.

Facepalm.

Duh, Sara!

You're such an ass!

Luckily, I never actually got sarcastic with anyone!

Just in my head.

Still, though!

I'm an ass!

Because this was such a weird question to me, I polled my readers on Facebook, asking if they remember how they learned to read. To my surprise, a lot of them did. In fact, most of them did.

Alright then.

Looks like the question isn't weird, but I am.

I have no idea how I learned to read. I do know my teachers leaned books in front of me and told me to look at them when I needed the page turned. I remember sitting on my dad's lap at night, having him read to me. One night, he held the book in front of me and said, "Okay, now you try by yourself." I remember whenever I had a reading homework assignment, my parents would put the book in front of me and wouldn't remove it until I said I was done. So, I don't know. Maybe it was a combination of everything.

I'm sorry I can't give people more information about my reading education. Sometimes, I feel like I've gone through most of my life in a bubble like, "Okay, this seems to be working, so this is what I'm going to keep doing. They say I should do that, and it seems to be going okay, so that's what I'm going to do. I don't know why I do that, but it works, so I'm going to keep doing that." It's only recently that I started thinking about everything I do, how I do it, and why I do it.

I may not be able to remember how I learned to read, but I definitely remember the first book I read entirely by myself, probably because how I did it was totally out of the ordinary.

That's usually how my brain works. Anything routine I do, my mind switches to autopilot, but when I do something out of the ordinary, my brain eats that crap up like it's candy.

I read the first Harry Potter book completely by myself on my kitchen wall. Literally.

Not even kidding here.

Once again, my mom broke a lot of laws to be able to help me.

The first book came out when I was in middle school. Before it exploded and everybody and their sister needed to read it, my friend could not put it down. She thought I would like it, so she suggested it to me. Knowing how big the book was, my mom knew she was going to have to get creative. She didn't want me to have to rely on anyone else to turn the page. This was, of course, before ebooks and Audible. If I were growing up today, my childhood would probably be so different.

"I know I'm breaking every copyright law known to mankind," my mom said to the Kinko's employee as she photocopied the first fifty pages of Harry Potter, "but I'm not going to sell it. This is for my daughter. She can't use her hands to turn the page."

I'm not entirely sure what he said back to her, but he didn't have her arrested, so that was a good thing.

When I came home from school that day, I found about ten pages of black and white photocopied text taped up along my wall.

What the hell?

"We're going to try something different today," my mom started.

She explained what she came up with.

I think because I was so curious, I began reading right away.

Now, I'm not the fastest reader. That has never changed. I would say it takes me three times as long to read something as it does the average person. I'm not entirely sure why that is. Now that I'm an adult and can choose how I want to read, I will always either do an audiobook or have my computer read it. Not only is this faster, but I comprehend it a thousand times better, which I still don't understand. However, back then, extremely slowly, page by photocopied page, I conquered the first Harry Potter.

Although I didn't read at the typical pace, I seemed to be doing okay.

Actually, more than okay.

Once I was in third grade, the school said I had maxed out of the curriculum. I had a handle on my wheelchair. I had a handle on my communication device, although I still didn't even like it. I could (somewhat) read. I could write in sentences when I would actually use my device. I could do (very) basic math. The school felt like they couldn't do anything else for me. They suggested to my mom that I try going to our public school.

Naturally, I don't remember how I felt when I found out (do you see the trend going on here?) and neither does my mom. However, some moments from the time have popped into my mind.

Once we or, rather, my parents and teachers, decided I was going to change schools, our local school district had three different paraprofessionals come to my school and observe me. I was going to have a one-on-one aide—something that was going to be totally different for me—since the classrooms I was used to had two aides who helped everyone, plus the teachers. The school wanted to see who I matched with the best.

Spoiler Alert! None of them got the job.

Due to budget cuts, seniority won, and I ended up assigned to someone who hadn't come to observe my other school and only took the job because she was going to be let go.

Yeah, that was a mess and a half.

More about that later.

I call for Britney. Bathroom break.

10:59 a.m.

Ten minutes later, I'm back reminiscing, clearly caught up in my own educational experiences and backgrounds as I think more about what my email back to this mother will say when I have the energy to write it.

I remember what I was wearing the first day of public school, which is weird, because outfits are usually the last thing I remember. It's probably because my aunt had taken me shopping. She knew it was going to be a big day for me, and she wanted to get me something special. Together, we picked out a pink and white–striped terrycloth jumpsuit.

It was very, very unSara like, which is also probably why I remember it.

I also remember the embarrassing comment I made to the entire class on my very first day.

Let me set this scene with some background:

My communication device at the time only had certain phrases preprogrammed in it. If I wanted to say something other than a preprogrammed phrase, I would have to type it out, letter by letter, which took even longer. This device was so not for me! One of the wonderful preprogrammed phrases was, "Please talk to me."

Let me think for a minute on how I want to explain this. . . .

I've recently realized that, throughout most of my life, I've been matching my thoughts to the words I have in front of me instead of matching my words to my thoughts. For example, in my current device, I have, "Can I have a drink?" preprogrammed in a button that is fast and easy to get to. So, I never say, "I need a sip of water" or, "I'm so thirsty I could drink the entire gallon." It's always, "Can I have a drink?" because it requires very little of me.

This way of thinking has gotten me into too many misunderstandings, but that's beside the point.

On my very first day, with my aide right beside me (and, oh, God! I totally forgot! My first few days, they had the fricking school nurse sitting in with me, too, until they realized CP was just CP and I wasn't going to die), the teacher had given everyone a little break. Wanting everyone to know they could talk to me, I embarrassingly—embarrassingly, *embarrassingly*—hit the sequence to make my device loudly announce the oh-so-pathetic phrase, "Please talk to me," thinking that would break the ice with my new classmates.

Yeah, I don't know when I became so introverted, but no amount of money would get me to do that again with a room full of strangers.

Like a lot of things we do when we're younger, it's only embarrassing now that I think about it.

Another thing I remember—my last day at my old school, the morning was like any other morning, completing Math and English handouts. Come afternoon, different people started to trickle in. Teachers I had in previous years. Some of the aides who'd assisted me. A few of my friends from different classrooms. As soon as someone brought in a cake, I knew what was going on.

They were having a surprise going-away party for me.

I then proceeded to cry.

Back then, if someone were to ask me why I was crying, I would've said I was sad because I was leaving, but thinking about it now, the crying, I believe, was from all the gratitude I had for each and every person who came to send me off.

Along with cake and crying, there were some gifts. There were two gifts that vividly stand out to me, one being a photo album. Sure, inside were a few pictures of me doing activities and me with my friends, but most of them were just polaroids of important people in my life at that time. It was like the person put it together had gone around the school, saying, "Hey. You were a part of Sara's time here. You want to pose for a picture for this album?"

It was just a simple gift, but it meant the world to me. I will never forget it.

At the time I was changing schools, *The Lion King* had just been released. I was obsessed with it. Obsessed with it, I tell you! Whenever I'm obsessed with something, everyone knows it, although I'm getting better with that. My second favorite gift was from my Art teacher. It was a two-foot-tall hand drawing of Pumbaa, my favorite character. It was so fricking awesome, it lived in my bedroom for a good year or so.

So, that was my big transition between schools. I don't know if I'm going to tell the mom who emailed me every little detail, but I'm definitely going to tell her how going to a public school had a drastic impact on my life.

At first, I spent most of my time in public school in the learning support classroom. I was participating in one or two subjects in the regular education classroom, but for the most part, I went to the learning support room, a.k.a., the Special Ed classroom. Now, contrary to popular belief, there's nothing wrong with being in Special Ed. Everyone learns at different paces, and if a child needs a little more help, it's awesome schools have that. Students shouldn't be ashamed if they have to take a learning support class. However, as the years went on, the fewer Special Ed classes I needed to take, and I was actually really proud of that.

Come my sophomore year of high school, the only learning support class I had was Math. When it was time for me to pick my classes for the next year, my Math teacher suggested I take a regular Math class. I accepted that challenge, thinking it would feel really great to close out my high school experience without any Special Ed classes.

I signed up for Algebra I.

I have no idea why I did this. I am *so* not math- and/or science-brained.

Being that most people take it their freshmen year, I was the only junior in the class. I was a little embarrassed about that, but I kept remembering it was my first regular math class, which was a huge step. My teacher understood that, too, along with the fact that I type with my head, something that doesn't mix very well with math since I had to show my work by writing out everything.

All in all, I ended up receiving a low B in the class.

I'd never been so proud of a B in my life.

I think what really made this work was my aide at the time. No, she didn't give me the answers or anything like that. Can you believe a lot of people thought she did? Of the three aides I had in public school, I could communicate with her the best.

Like I mentioned before, my first aide only took the job with me because she was going to lose hers. She hadn't wanted to work with somebody with a disability; she had only wanted to keep working for the school district. I truly wish I could say she didn't have a problem with disabilities and that she just had a problem with human interaction. Unfortunately, that was not the case.

Being in the care of someone who didn't want anything to do with a disability, I experienced things that would forever destroy my self-esteem. She complained I was going too slow. She rolled her eyes at me when I needed something adjusted. She would get annoyed whenever I brought specific things for lunch just because she would have to feed me a little differently. She would not wipe my mouth, leaving the saliva to crust over. When I would get a cold, she would not wipe my nose, leaving the snot to drip down my face to dry. When I hit puberty, I overheard her tell another teacher she didn't want to take me to the bathroom anymore.

As if that weren't enough, one day my wheelchair stopped working. Immediately, she found a phone to call my mom. When my mom suggested, the most obvious solution of pushing me, she started waving her hand and said, "Not an option!" When my mom protested, my aide protested even more and kept saying, "Not an option! Not an option!" until my mom was forced to pick me up.

Yeah, Algebra I with her?

Just. No.

Finally, enough was enough. I drove right down to the principal's office, almost crying, and announced that I couldn't do it anymore.

Three cheers for self-advocacy!

The next year, I had a new aide waiting for me when I got off the bus.

This aide was a thousand times better. She was nice. She was positive. She had previous experience with people with disabilities; she understood the craziness that sometimes comes with having a disability. She wanted me to do well in school. She was *willing* to help me do well in school. She knew what happened with my other aide, so she made sure to be as positive as she could be.

What more could I want, right?

My family has drilled into my brain with every imaginable tool the idea that there is no such thing as a perfect aide.

Once I get to know whoever is helping me, I tend to talk to them as though they are one of my best friends. I'm extremely proud to say I am so much better with this today, but back then, I had absolutely zero boundaries with any of my aides. I was a young teenager at the time. My conversations consisted of boys, and friends, and boys, and friends.

If I talked about a boy too much, she would tell me I was obsessing.

If I talked about a friend too much, she would tell me I was obsessing.

It got to the point where she would just sing the word *obsessing* like a little reminder, and I would feel guilty and change the subject.

Mind you, I was not saying anything more than what my friends were saying on these topics. I just used a communication device, so any conversation took me five times longer than everyone else's, so maybe, to others, it seemed like I talked about these things—boys and friends—a lot more than my peers. Today, twenty years later, I still feel the need to watch how much I say about something for fear that I'm "obsessing" about it.

It's something that I still have to get over.

Something else my second aide would do is give me the cold shoulder whenever I did something she didn't like, or when my friends would do something, or, frankly, when I was in a flat mood where I didn't really want to talk that much. She would just not talk to me.

I would ask what was wrong or try to apologize, and she wouldn't have it.

I'm just going to say it: what kind of *adult* does that to a *thirteen-year-old*?! Especially when they're a school employee assisting a student!

I think that's why I feel very awkward with assistants who don't talk much.

Oh, childhood! How it can haunt one in mysterious ways!

So, yes, I could probably have taken Algebra with her, but it probably wouldn't have been as tolerable as it was with my third aide.

My third and final high school aide was definitely my best. Again, I really don't like to compare people, but in a situation like mine, it happens constantly. Some people can just communicate with me better, while with others, I have to be a little more patient. Now that I realize this, I know it has a lot to do with my disability and less to do with the actual person. I wish I would've learned this early in life; I know for a fact I destroyed a few perceptions of me just by saying "I absolutely love this person" or "I really can't stand that person" without any explanation.

I would say the reason my third aide and I clicked so well is she understood that I was a teenager, and having four of them herself, she understood teenagers are far from angels. I believe this helped tremendously. One awesome thing she did was notice I was having trouble understanding innuendoes my peers were using, because I was essentially in a bubble all day long. An adult was always by my side, warding off any dirty jokes. She asked my friend to make her a list of the most frequently used innuendoes. When I gave her a questioning look, she simply said, "You deserve to be in the know. I'll help you. No judgement here."

Nobody will ever understand how much that meant to me, even though my friend, of course, didn't follow through.

Similarly, when I received my very first devastating, earth-shattering heartbreak, she looked right at me and asked, "What do you want to do?"

What? Again, I gave her a questioning look.

"You heard me. What do you want to do to him? Do you want to tell him off? Do you want to toilet paper his car? Tell me, and I'll help you do it."

Together, we decided to put hundreds and hundreds of packing peanuts in his locker. Hello, major mess!

Even though it was the result of one of the most traumatic times of my life, it felt amazing to have someone offer to help me with something silly rather than just personal care and schoolwork.

Okay, back to the Math class.

I think what really made Algebra work, along with my less-than-mediocre math skills, was our ability to communicate. By then, we knew each other pretty well, so we started to make up codes. If I looked up, I wanted her to write a positive number. If I wanted a negative number, I would look down. For any number from one to five, I would blink to it. If I had a lot of homework that day, she would tell me to do everything else with my homework assistant and she would help me with my math assignment in the morning in my study hall.

For anyone reading this, I hope this illustrates how the quality of communication can really affect the quality of my life.

Okay, onto graduation.

In a meeting with my guidance counselor my junior year, I learned that if I took one extra class in the beginning of my senior year, I could graduate a semester early. I was starting to loathe high school more than anyone has ever loathed anything, so I jumped on that idea before they finished explaining how it would work.

I've heard people say middle school was hell and high school was a breeze.

Nope. Not the case for me.

As usual, I was the opposite.

In middle school, along with telling the principal I needed a new aide, I also told her I needed to go down the hall without being stopped if I didn't have my aide with me. I had an amazing group of friends who I actually attended a week-long summer camp with. I was in the school play and made a few friends from it. I was madly in love with a guy who was my "best friend" until he wasn't anymore.

I would seriously say my middle school experience was perfect.

High school, however, was my own personal hell. It was an open campus, meaning there were eight different buildings. Students had to walk outside every forty minutes. Because of this, the district didn't want me to be without an aide. They were afraid my wheelchair was going to tip, which is absolutely insane when I think about it—there is a much greater chance of someone who could walk tripping and falling between buildings than my wheelchair tipping. Also, did they really think my aides were going to stop my four-hundred-pound chair from tumbling over if it was on its way?

Along with being babysat all day and not being able to leave my aide's sight, I was dropping friends left and right. I naturally drifted away from one friend, which I still regret to this day. One had gotten into partying and boys, which I don't really have a problem with, but it just wasn't my style. One moved away, again, making us naturally drift apart. One friend took my heart, slammed it on the ground, ran over it with a truck, backed over it for good measure, and drove off without ever coming back to try to fix it. Another friend didn't think the aforementioned friend had done anything wrong and chose his side over mine. And anybody else who didn't already know me wouldn't make eye contact with me, let alone take the time to talk to me.

I just want to say this: We were all teenagers. We all were figuring everything out. We all didn't know what the hell we were doing. Today, this is all water under the bridge for me, but back then, it felt like my world was crumbling.

Around the same time I discovered I could graduate early, I found out that my summer camp, which was for people with disabilities, had a program for people who were transitioning into adulthood. I'd been attending for a few years at this point, not only for a month in the summer but also for one weekend a month, and it had become my safe haven from the hell that I was going through in high school. They had a personal care home right on campus, where people could go for six months to learn how to be independent.

Once I found out that was an option, the decision made itself.

I was going to graduate early and go live on my own for six months! As an added bonus, it was going to prepare me for college.

Hey yo!

This should not surprise anyone at this point, but honestly, I'm a little shocked by this: the only thing I remember about my very last day of high school was that it fell on the day before Christmas break. I can remember the night before and the night of, but for the life of me, when I try to think of the day that I'd been looking forward to for three and a half years, absolutely nothing comes to mind.

I can't decide if nothing particular happened that day or if I was just so ready to be done, I blocked the entire thing from my brain.

The night before the big day was like any other night for Teenage Sara. I closed out of my conversation in AIM (if you don't know what AIM is, I'm seriously dating myself! Think DMs in Instagram or Facebook Messenger, but without the Instagram or Facebook parts and on a desktop computer—literally just a messenger service) and put up an Away

Message. Because I am a giant cheeseball, I picked my favorite verse of my favorite song of the musical, *Wicked,* that talks about how flying solo means flying free.

Yep. Giant cheeseball. Right here.

I cried the entire time typing it out.

Not because I was sad, but because I had done it.

I had made it through high school without committing any acts that would land me in jail!

Go me!

That night, I had a small get-together with just my friends, who were from the camps I'd attended throughout the years and *not* from school. (I still had a typical graduation party in June, which I didn't want but my parents insisted I have, after I walked at commencement, which I also didn't want to do but my parents were too proud of me to not let me.) At this little get-together, I just remember being surrounded by people I loved, and exchanging gifts because it was almost Christmas, and genuinely just hanging out and being happy.

The day after New Year's felt totally different, and weird, and strange. I was going to a place where I felt safe, a place where I would be encouraged to be more independent, a place that would accept me for me. This would be the absolute opposite of high school.

My parents and I packed up everything I could possibly need for six months, and off we went.

When we arrived at the house, my parents started to unpack everything while I talked to everyone. Some people I knew and some I didn't. I already knew my good friend was doing the program at the same time, and he gave me a hug when I saw him. I was so excited I was going to get to live with him. In my room, I found my new roommate sitting on her bed and smiled at her. I recognized her from camp.

Wait.

Hold on a second!

I didn't just recognize her from camp.

She was from my school!

Are you serious?

Was I being pranked?

Here I was, at a house I came to because I wanted to get away from my school and everyone associated with it, and my fricking roommate was from my fricking school!

F luck again, everyone!

Once I got over my mini meltdown (seriously, I think I almost cried there for a hot second, embarrassingly), I knew that everything was going to be okay. She was very nice, and very quiet, and she went home every weekend, so we didn't get to hang out that much, but, most importantly, she wasn't like anyone from school.

That night, after my parents left, I was asked a question that both made me crazy and also informed me that I was no longer in my parents' care. Call it my introduction to having personal care assistants.

A staff member, one of the night assistants, came into our dorm-like bedroom. "Hello. I hope you're getting settled. What time do you want to get up tomorrow morning?"

Huh?

"I can get up by myself," my roommate answered. "I don't need any help."

"Sounds good. They just want everyone to be ready to go by nine o'clock, so just make sure you leave yourself enough time. Sara, what about you? What time will you be awake?"

I'm sorry. What? What the hell kind of a question is that? I don't know what time I'm going to get up. I just get up when I get up. Granted, school was different, but on the weekends, I get up whenever I get up, call for my parents, and they come get me. How am I supposed to know when I will get up?

Oh, Sara!

How dumb you were!

I don't know what I said to her, and I don't know what time I actually woke up.

All I remember is being really fricking confused.

Over the next few years, I realized this was not only a routine question for any and every new assistant, but it was an essential question. My assistants were not going to come if I didn't tell them when to come. I have gotten so used to the question, it doesn't even phase me anymore, but back then, for a good two to three years of having assistants, whenever somebody would ask me that question, I would think back to that night and be reminded of how completely and utterly confused I had been.

For the first few weeks, we were encouraged to take the classes the house offered. The classes were stuff like learning how to do laundry, money management, cooking, and cleaning. Unlike the other residents who were still in wheelchairs and could use their hands, they taught me how to talk somebody through everything. This might seem a little unnecessary, but in my opinion, this is vital information, and every person who is nonverbal should have a few classes like this. For example, I had previously had speech therapy where I worked on having basic conversations, but I had never had someone teach me how to give specific directions for how to feed me or give me a drink.

This was something I struggled with a lot but eventually taught myself to do. It would've been *so* nice to have continued guidelines on this until I nailed it.

When we were done with the classes, we were required to get a job, volunteer, or take a class at the local community college.

I chose to take a class and get a job, because why the crap not?

To be fair, I already kinda-sorta had a job. I was working on and off at the company that made my communication device. Since the house was encouraging me to have a steady job, I decided to ask the company if I could come in steadily one or two days a week. They were happy to have me and even expressed how helpful my work was because I actually used the device from day to day and wasn't just working to develop it.

I'm even hesitant to put this part in this book, because people with disabilities have an extremely hard time getting jobs, let alone a good job. However, I feel like I have to put it in to show that I, along with a lot of people with disabilities, are not perfect.

Like I said, employment for people with disabilities is a messy, messy, messy subject. A lot of people either can't get the job they want, because the company won't look past the disability (even though that's against the law), or they can't make above a certain amount of money or else their Medicaid benefits get taken away. This is a huge, crappy, and downright unfair problem that a lot of people with disabilities face, and I don't want to downplay it.

That said, I absolutely loved the company I worked for.

I'm so incredibly grateful that they chose to hire me and create a job that was just for me, an advanced user of the device.

I felt so useful when they told me I had found a software bug that no other employee had found because the others didn't use the device all day, every day, like I did.

For somebody like me to get a job that I could do independently when I was literally right out of high school is unheard of, and I know that. I appreciate every opportunity I have been given.

Knowing what I know now about employment, and people with disabilities, and society in general, I don't have the words for the two employees who became my friends and who volunteered to feed me lunch every day I was on-site. It's beyond astonishing a workplace would be okay with that.

I don't have anything negative to say about the company.

My job, however, was a different story.

I was responsible for finding bugs (problems) in the software updates, making sure they were consistent, figuring out how they happened, and reporting them to someone who could fix them. This involved sitting at a desk by myself, which I was not a fan of but eventually became okay with (I had to be to write), looking at a screen for an extended period of time (which, again, had to get used to later for my writing anyway), and repeatedly hitting the same five buttons until the bug appeared again.

I think that's what did it for me. Doing the same thing over, and over, and over is not my jam, but again, I'm so thankful for the opportunity, and I would've definitely picked that any day over being back in high school.

As far as my community college class, I chose to take Intro to Psychology. I always had a deep fascination with the subject. I still do. I even debated majoring in it at Wright State. When I decided not to because they say nobody can do anything with just an undergrad psychology degree, I regretted not taking more classes in the subject, at the very least. I just love learning how people think and trying to figure out why some people think the way they do.

Because I couldn't take notes by myself or even set up a tape recorder, and because this was before professors put notes online, I had two house assistants alternate attending class with me. Since they were only a few years older than me and not a few decades older, like my high school aides had been, I became really close with both of them. Another cool thing about the house was they understood I comprehend better if I heard things rather than read them, so someone would record all my assignments, and whenever I was ready to do my homework, someone would just set me up with the tape recorder.

All in all, the class went pretty well, but unfortunately, it didn't count as anything at Wright State.

Despite the house seeming incredibly busy, I would have to say one of my favorite times was hanging out in the kitchen on weekend nights. A few of us would just migrate there—I'm not entirely sure why—and we would just talk. We would laugh. We would have snacks, if we felt like it. We would make silly inside jokes that I guarantee nobody remembers today.

I distinctly remember my friend thanking a weekend staff member for not making us go to bed at a certain time.

I don't think I'll ever forget their response: "Why would I? You should be able to go to bed whenever you want. It's your house!"

All assistants should have that attitude!

Once my six months were up, I moved home just in time for my high school graduation. As we gathered in a single-file line in the hot heat on the football field, I felt more out of place than I did while I was attending school. These people went to prom together while I refused to go, despite my aunt begging me to go and even offering to help me find a date. These people still bonded with each other while I was busy making my own unique bonds.

As the music started and we made our way to our seats, I grew nervous. Here I was, driving in a crowd in front of another crowd of onlookers.

Not my thing!

Not my thing, at all!

But hell if I was going to have a repeat of my First Holy Communion. I could just imagine my mom running down to the football field, ready to push me.

I can do it!

I just have to get to my spot without hitting anything or anyone!

I can do this!

I made it to my spot without incident (go me!) and the speeches started. All I remember is, "Blah blah blah. Blah blah blah. Blah blah blah blah blah blah blah blah." Then, out of nowhere, I heard, "I personally would like to welcome back one of our classmates, Sara Pyszka! She has been gone for six months, and now she's back. Sara, it's so nice to see you. We missed you."

I. Wanted. To. Die.

What?

What the hell is going on? I don't even know who's talking right now! Someone must have told him to put that in his speech, or he looked up facts about our class, or something like that!

I had made it a point not to talk to anyone other than my quickly dissolving five-person circle of friends! Granted, including me in his speech was a very nice thing to do, and I don't want to take that away from him, but what the hell? This class and I are like ketchup and peanut butter, Ohio and California, toilets in kitchens! We just didn't go together, and that was that.

Bull crap they actually missed me!

Not only was his comment out of left field, but he'd said it in front of a class of 519, all the faculty, and everybody in the bleachers, which definitely doubled, if not tripled, the size of our class.

I have sung the national anthem at a Pittsburgh Pirates game and at a Cleveland Indians game. After I graduated college, I started giving presentations to teachers and students about how they don't have to be afraid of people with disabilities. If I have to, I can mentally prepare myself to be in front of a crowd and be the center of attention, especially if I'm spreading a message I firmly believe in. However, if attention is unexpectedly being called upon me in a group, I basically have a panic attack, and my CP starts going, and I can't get my body to stop moving.

If I had been an active member of my class and had participated in a lot of school activities, it would've probably been different. I would've been more okay with it. However, when I was in school, especially at the end, I had just wanted to get through a day without any incidents. This comment, albeit a nice thought, was just from outer space.

I tried to calm down.

I tried to get my body to stop moving, so I didn't distract anyone.

I tried to focus on the other speeches. This was just the beginning.

I still had to drive up on stage and get my diploma without dropping it. Oh, God.

At the end of the day, I managed to go up on stage without hitting anything or anyone (score!), the teacher knew to put my diploma on the side of my wheelchair so it didn't even have a chance to touch my hands (double score!), and commencement was soon over after that. (Triple score!)

Overall, the morning had been decent for something I didn't necessarily want to do.

It was time for the party.

Because my mom was extremely proud of me, she wanted to have a blowout of a party. While I was writing this book, I asked why. Her response? "You could not walk. You could not talk. You graduated from an open, eight-building campus. I thought that was cause for a celebration."

Alright then. I'm not going to argue with that.

She rented the big party room at the community center, decorating it with my not-so-flattering school colors of orange and black. Two hundred people came to this massive event, including but not limited to, my entire family, all my camp friends, all the people who lived with me at the house the six months prior, a few school friends that I still half talked to, some of my teachers, family from out of town, some of my coworkers, all of my mom's coworkers, and her best friend's friends. One of my favorite restaurants catered it, and there was even a DJ. I believe someone eventually took me out of my wheelchair so I could dance for a little.

It was absolutely insane. That's for sure.

Me plus two or more people doesn't really work. I can't keep up with a conversation, because, ya know, me typing with my head doesn't really compare to talking with a mouth. I want you to imagine two hundred people wanting to talk to me in a span of a few hours. The only way I survived involved me abandoning my communication device, except for saying, "Thank you," nodding at whatever was being said to me, and smiling for a lot of pictures.

I remember asking my friend to help me to go to the bathroom. When we got inside, I admitted I didn't have to go and just needed a minute of peace. Seeing I was completely overwhelmed, she leaned against the door so nobody could come in. Once I caught my breath, she took a cool paper towel and wiped the sweat off my face and neck. One more deep breath, and back to the party we went.

True introvert right here, folks.

Only wish I knew that back then.

I don't want anybody to get the wrong idea—I did enjoy myself that day. I'm so grateful I have parents who were so proud of me for graduating high school that they wanted to throw me the biggest party they could give me.

I'm just not a party person.

My absolute favorite part of that day was at eleven o'clock at night. We were home, everything was done, and I was sitting at the kitchen table with my mom and two friends from camp, opening my graduation gifts. And no, the gifts were not my favorite part. It was sitting with a few people I absolutely loved, sipping on green tea, laughing, and chatting about the day, chatting about the house, chatting about the future.

Ah, the future. Which brings me to college.

I'm not entirely sure if the mom who wrote me is even thinking about college yet if her son is in first grade, but I'm going to tell her a little about it anyway when I write her back.

I attended Wright State University in Dayton, Ohio. Although I don't like to admit it, because I really don't like my cerebral palsy to define who I am, I chose Wright State because they had one of the best disability services in the country.

I first heard about Wright State very early on in high school. My family and I were on vacation in Myrtle Beach. I met this guy with a disability and hung out with him and his brother because they were around the same age as me. He told me about this college he was going to apply to. At that time, it was one of the best universities for people with disabilities because they had a program where students with disabilities could hire students without disabilities to be their personal assistants.

From that moment on, even though I was far from applying to colleges right then, I knew I was going to Wright State.

Sadly, the guy passed away before he had a chance to attend college. I'll never forget him. Despite only knowing him for a few days, he had a *huge* impact on my life.

I always am fascinated when a stranger interferes with someone else's life in a positive way. I think that's one of the coolest things ever.

This is where I don't suggest anyone follow in my footsteps.

When it came time to consider colleges, I only looked at Wright State, and I only applied to Wright State.

Now that I'm older, I know that, as with anything, having a backup is a good idea.

A backup to the backup. Even better!

A backup to the backup backup? Winning.

Luckily, this little overlook didn't bite me in the ass, but if I had to do it again, I would definitely, at least, see what else was out there.

I still remember the day I found out I had been accepted. It was very Pyszka style. I was still in school, getting ready to go to the house. For some reason, I was home from school, in my bedroom, working on my computer. My dad came in, holding the opened letter. I slowly read, "Congratulations! You have been accepted to Wright State University." He placed the letter on the desk, kissed my forehead, congratulated me, and went back to work in his upstairs office.

Back then, I was just a privileged, oblivious little idiot. I thought everyone went to college. I thought that was just the thing to do after high school. I didn't know everyone had a choice. I didn't know some people didn't go to college, especially a lot of people with disabilities. So, even though I was smiling and looking at the letter, in my mind, I was like, "Oh! Cool!" and went back to whatever I was doing.

Yeah, I know. Privileged, oblivious little idiot!

I didn't mean to be oblivious, though!

I just was, okay?

Along with having a two-day orientation earlier that summer telling us everything the office of disability services, or ODS, could do for us, students with disabilities had to get there a day or two earlier than all the other freshmen. Not only to get all our equipment moved into the dorm (if you are a person with a physical disability, chances are you come with *a lot* of equipment), but we had to meet our personal care assistants.

Each year, ODS would assign us four assistants. If we needed more, it would be our responsibility to find and hire more. My first semester, I made it through with only four. I have no idea how I did this, but I did. Going forward, that number grew. By the time I graduated, I was up to eight or nine assistants each semester.

The first time I entered my dorm, one of my new assistants was waiting for me. "Hi!" she walked right up to me. "Are you Sara? I'm going to be one of your assistants. My name is Mia. Nice to meet you! Do you need help unpacking?"

"That would be really great," my dad had said. "Thank you! Nice to meet you, too!"

Just then, a girl came flying down the dorm stairs. "I'm sorry! I'm sorry! I'm sorry! I slept in! I'm sorry! I'm here now! My name is Emily. What can I do to help?"

I don't believe it was me, but I'm sure someone in our group was thinking, "Yeah, she's not going to last a day as an assistant."

Actually, Emily became one of my good friends and longest assistant ever, staying with me from that moment she slept in that morning until I was literally getting in my van to go home for good five years later.

The other assistants were okay.

Well . . .

When I look back on it now, I can see all of us were freshmen in college, just eighteen and nineteen years old. Stupid, ridiculous crap was bound to go down. One night, one assistant was helping me with dinner. Her friend popped his head in my dorm room (my assistants and I would go get food from the Student Union, but I was never a fan of eating there) and asked when she would be done.

"I don't know!" she loudly exclaimed. "I don't want to be doing this! I want to go get drunk!"

Her friend laughed and popped his head out of my room, never actually acknowledging me.

I don't remember getting angry.

I don't remember getting upset.

All I remember is pure shock.

Ooooookaaaaay.

So, that just happened.

And . . .

Yeah.

That just happened.

Okay.

That assistant and I never really talked like my other assistants and I did, so I believe she just kept feeding me and I just kept eating.

As I write this, I'm laughing to myself, thinking of how unbelievably odd it is to recall that situation and be like, "Yep. This happened to me. Okay. Moving on."

Needless to say, she didn't even last the semester. I ended up hiring Emily's roommate in replace of her.

Luckily, all freshman with disabilities were required to take a Managing Personal Assistants class. Unfortunately, it didn't help with that assistant; I believe I just had to wing it with her. However, in the class, we went over hiring someone, letting someone go, and everything in between. We had homework assignments like making up mock ads and figuring out how to handle unusual situations. This was a great class for freshman, and in my opinion, they should offer another class for seniors going out in the real world.

The main difference in having assistants at Wright State was they didn't stay with me throughout the day. They would come do my morning routine and leave. They would come give me lunch and leave. If we had to go to the bathroom, we could go to the personal assistant station, which was a giant bathroom with people there to help. The PA station was a totally amazing idea, but for me personally, I didn't really like to use it. A, they didn't have my lift, and B, there was a good chance I would have a guy helping me, and I was just not down with that. If I had to randomly pee, I would text all of my assistants, but they weren't required to come since they weren't scheduled.

There is one moment that distinctly stands out in my brain. A few days into college, I realized I needed to buy one or two more books for class. My assistants weren't always with me. They would only come when I needed help. I was by myself, and I realized I was going to have to go by myself. While I was driving to the bookstore, I realized I was actually nervous. Even though I was getting what I wanted, I was nervous about it. I remember being extremely mad at my high school. I had always wanted to be able to go from class to class by myself, and here I was, doing it, and I felt like I was doing something wrong! I felt like I was going to get in trouble for doing what I dreamed of! This was so screwed up! How was this preparing me for anything? Why, if they really didn't think I should be alone, didn't they try to talk to me about it or help me figure it out?

Oh, I was so cursing them up and down in my head!

However, I managed to get my books without getting in trouble.

Fast-forward five years, and I had finished college. I had moved home. My parents worked, so I needed a personal assistant. Not only had I gotten over the anxiety of being alone, but having assistants come in and out of my apartment had become second nature to me. I thought this was how it was like to have assistants wherever I was. I very quickly learned my personal care was going to be a job, and people, who were not on a college campus, don't want a job where they work for an hour, and leave for two, and come back for an hour, and leave for two, and then come back.

This is where I sorely wish I had something or someone to walk me through this transition, but I eventually figured it out and learned everything I needed to learn.

Rewind now, back to having assistants in college.

One of the hardest things to get used to my freshman year was having assistants the same age as me. It's weird, because that was all I had wanted in high school—to have assistants who were more my age and not some teenager-repelling adult. In college, I finally got that, and I absolutely hated it—at first, anyway.

One night, my assistant came in my dorm room to give me a shower and to put me in bed.

I started sobbing.

Uncontrollably sobbing.

"Oh, my!" the assistant was, naturally, in shock by this unexpectedly blubbering mess. "Sara! What's wrong?"

I started typing. "You don't want to shower me. You want to go out."

"I'm going to go out. But first, I'm going to shower you like we have scheduled."

"But you want to go out."

"Right. But first, I'm going to give you a shower. Or, don't you want one?"

She wasn't getting it, and frankly, neither was I.

Now, I realize this was the very first time I was feeling like just a job to someone. It was also the start of a crackle in my brain—a crackle that would eventually tell me I was not like everybody else.

She was a freshman in college, having to give me a shower before she went out at ten o'clock.

I was a freshman in college, having to take a shower and get in bed before ten o'clock.

It was the very first time I'd noticed how different I really was from my peers.

Okay, onto academics.

Along with the personal assistant program, Wright State also offered some extremely useful services for students with disabilities. Each semester, I would take my books to ODS and they would scan them into the computer. We had the option of getting an audio version or a text version. At first, I, of course, went with the audio version, but after realizing it was a computerized voice that talked too fast and was barely understandable, I opted for the text version and found a program with a much better voice for my computer that would read to me.

Along with dropping my books off at the beginning of the semester, I would also go to the test proctoring center to give them my syllabi. Students who needed help writing down answers could take all their exams there if we scheduled them early enough. My first few exams, I had a proctor with me, but then I found out they could scan my tests into the computer. From then on, I started taking all my exams by myself, which was something I could never do before.

The last service I used quite frequently was the note-taker service. We could either have someone go with us, which I only did for Math, otherwise the class would've been impossible for me to get through, or we could ask someone in the class to give us their notes. This was right before it became commonplace to take a laptop to class, so the note-taker would have to take their notes to ODS, scan them into the computer, and email them to me. If they did this throughout the semester, ODS would give them a gift card to the bookstore.

It truly is the little things in life that help me tremendously.

If Wright State wasn't just a college campus, I would move back in a heartbeat. It seriously had everything I needed.

When I first started at Wright State, I was going to get a degree in English with an emphasis on Creative Writing. Nothing else makes me happier than when I'm writing something that's either going to make somebody think a lot or feel a lot. However, back then, I didn't know this about myself. I just knew that Creative Writing had been my favorite class in high school, and it just sounded like a fun major to have.

Ah, youth.

In my sophomore year, I decided to change majors. "You can't do anything with an English degree" eventually got to the core of me. I wanted a degree that I could get a good job with. I thought about a degree in Psychology, but I would have to get advanced degrees to be able to do anything with it. School was never my cup of tea, and I did *not* want to do more of it. I then thought about Sociology, but again, more schooling.

At the time, I really, really, *really* wanted to start a camp for people with and without disabilities. I still do, but back then, I wanted that to be my career path. One would think I would want to major in something business related, but that was not how my brain worked.

I decided to major in Rehabilitation Services so I could learn more about different disabilities. I really wish I would've talked to my adviser more, or did more research, or met a magical fairy that would've pulled my head out of the clouds. Rehabilitation Services, I slowly realized, had a strong emphasis on helping people with disabilities find jobs.

If I could do it all over again, I would stick to Creative Writing and just load up on psychology and sociology classes.

But hey! At least I have a degree!

11:37 a.m.

So, that was my educational experience. I'm not going to put it all in the email to the mom; I'm going to pick and choose what would be the most helpful to her.

I'm also not going to answer her right away. Writing a long email with a lot of details doesn't go over very well if I haven't had enough sleep. I usually end up skipping words while I'm typing and totally forgetting entire things I had wanted to say.

I close out of the email, fully intending to come back to it later in the week when I have had my normal amount of sleep.

I can't help but wonder, if I were able-bodied, would I be able to pump out an email on very little sleep?

My guess? Probably.

I imagine that I would think about what I want to say for a few seconds and type out a paragraph within one or two minutes. A few minutes later, the entire email would be ready to send, regardless of how much sleep I'd had the night before.

Actually, come to think of it, I don't know anyone else who completely shuts down when they have a bad night.

I'm not entirely sure if this makes me feel lucky or makes me feel like a loser.

A little bit of both, I'd say.

I think my problem is that I think about eight times faster than I can type. I can plan out what I want to say, but once I'm about a sentence or two in, the perfect paragraph I had planned is in the past. I'm not always like this, obviously, or else I wouldn't be a writer. It's just that when I don't have enough sleep, things tend to come and go out of my brain even faster than I can type.

Even though all I want to do is stare at the ceiling, there is something I need to do today. I start a new email to my service coordinator.

The state I live in offers several different waivers to people with disabilities to assist with their needs. Because I'm in a unique situation, I qualify for one waiver and one waiver only. It gives me hours so I can hire personal care assistants, and they can get paid through the state. This waiver is a game-changer. I absolutely could not live independently if I didn't have it. Unfortunately, my waiver is only available in my state, so as far as I know, I won't be moving anytime soon.

With this waiver, I have the choice of using an agency model or a consumer model. With the first model, I would have an agency find the assistants and do all the scheduling. This sounded wonderful to me, since hiring and scheduling are two things I don't like about having assistants.

But wonderful, it was not.

The agency I used had a lot of rules. Now, I'm actually a big fan of rules (I know, you can call me a dork; it's all good), but when it comes to my personal care, a lot of rules need to go out the window. For example, they had someone come to my apartment every two hours for two hours. If I needed someone longer, they couldn't really make it happen that day, since the assistants were helping other people at other specific times. This means if I needed to go somewhere, even somewhere as close as the mall, or the grocery store, or meet up with a friend, I would have to schedule it two weeks in advance. The other thing I had a hard time with was, if I didn't particularly like an assistant, I would be stuck with them. Even if what they did was moderately dangerous and wrong, the agency would have to find evidence of this before they could take action.

I understand why they were like this. They had to accommodate every client, it was really hard to find and keep employees, and some clients would complain about everyone and everything. I know for a fact they tried to accommodate me the best they could, but ultimately, the agency and I mutually decided it wasn't working for me. Just as I was about to tell them I was going to move on, they "strongly suggested" I move on, saying my situation was a little too unique for them.

Besides, most agencies won't take anyone with a feeding tube, not that I would want to try it again.

Consumer model, on the other hand, makes me the showrunner. I hire. I train. I schedule. I tell them what to do and what not to do. I attempt to correct them despite wanting to avoid confrontation at any and all costs. I let them go, although I usually make my mom sit with me for that, if need be. Even though I don't like a lot of things about being a boss, it's so much better to be in the driver's seat of my care rather than in the back seat.

Inside My Outside

Although I'm in charge, if I need to change my hours, such as overtime hours or an increase of hours, I have to email my service coordinator, which is what I'm doing now.

I start typing and send my text to the computer, checking to see if I had any typos.

"Hey, I am just going to ask this because I am just curious. I had a completely horrible night. What is the max hours you can get on my waiver?"

She must've been at her computer, because she responded right away.

"Hey Sara. Oh no, I am sad to hear you had a bad night. There really isn't a set limit that I know of, but I'll check. Some people have round-the-clock care sometimes; it just depends on your needs and what you need help with throughout the day. We could complete another assessment to see how many hours more you could get if you'd like. How many extra hours are you thinking you need each week?"

I think for a second.

I don't like what I'm about to do. I already can't stand having someone else in my house the amount that I do, but what if something worse happens than last night's event?

What if there's a fire?

What if I get sick and puke everywhere?

What if I have to roll over, and I fall out of bed?

A few years ago, I had to realize something that was hard for me to swallow:

I'm not independent.

I'm responsible.

In middle school, my motto was, "I'm independent."

High school . . . "I'm independent, I'm independent, I'm independent."

College . . . "I'm independent, I'm independent, I'm independent."

After college . . . "I live with my parents, but I'm independent."

When I was in my first apartment, I was in bed one night when my wheelchair started making noise. I was five feet away from it, and I could not get up to check on it.

This moment made me realize that I'm not independent.

I'm responsible.

I was not independent enough to get out of my bed, but I was responsible enough to know to call for help.

It's time to put away the independence pride and take responsibility.

I emailed her right back.

"Honestly, I really need overnight care. If you need me to describe my night, I can. I cannot do anything for myself."

She wrote back: "Yes, there is no limit. So, we could probably do overnight care. I agree. You do need it. I don't know why you don't already have it. I would just need a doctor's script along with an explanation from you about your needs and why you need the twenty-four-hour care. Just email me the explanation. I just need to visit with you for a couple signatures next Tuesday and then I can put the plan in for review!"

I stare at the screen for a good minute.

Holy crap.

That was so easy.

I had emailed her about something I needed, thinking the worst she could say was no, and it looks like I'm going to get it!

Or, at least, she's on my side, which will help.

Sweet!

This is huge!

Just as I exit out of my browser, Britney comes out of the assistant room. "Hey, you only have two shakes left, and you're out of bananas and yogurt. Do you want me to go to the grocery store?"

"I will go with you," I spell out with a smile.

"It's easier to go without you, but if you want to come, you can."

I'm not smiling anymore.

What. The. Hell?

Did she really just say that?

Yep.

She did.

For a hot second, I'm not entirely sure what to say.

Way to make me feel awkward for telling you what I would like to do!

If I say I still want to go, I'll feel like I'm putting her out and don't care about her feelings. If I say I don't want to go, I'll feel like I'm letting her tell me what to do, not to mention not doing what I want to do. That's her job! It's her job to help me live my life, even if that means going to a simple grocery store for thirty minutes. Now, if I say I want to go to Ohio for a day to meet my friend for coffee, I'd expect any assistant to give me minimum to major pushback, and I'd never expect anyone to actually take me, but going with me to a grocery store that's, literally, one mile from my house? How much easier is it to go without me?

Her comment, in my opinion, was just unnecessary.

That's her job.

Taking me places is part of my assistants' job!

That's what I hired them to do!

Britney hears my wheelchair turning on. "Are you eating now?"

I know this is not the end of it, but I nod.

I know I need to address this situation, but I need a distraction. I need to walk away from it and come back to it, or else I'm going to say something I regret.

I drive to my usual spot in my dining room. Wanting to change the subject for a second, I start typing. "I'm so excited. I think I might get overnight care."

Britney takes the shake out of the microwave and pours it into my bag. "You mean you would have us stay the night?"

Ummmm.

I haven't really thought about how I would do it yet; I was just telling her my good news.

I give her a half nod and spell to her. "Maybe, but I probably would hire another person."

"Oh." She holds the straw and towel to my mouth. I take it. I start to sip. Water is going down my throat. "I really don't like to sleep here."

I try not to choke.

I succeed.

I wait for a follow-up to the comment.

There has to be a follow-up.

Britney leans my wheelchair back and puts my tube on.

No follow-up.

She vents me, letting all the air out of my stomach.

No follow-up.

She puts my wheelchair up and hooks the bag up to me.

No follow-up.

Just very awkward silence.

Granted, I could say something, but what?

Oh, I'm sorry you don't like to sleep here?

Did something happen the last time you slept here that made you uncomfortable?

Oh, that's good to know. I won't put you on nights?

I just found out about this minutes ago, and I told her because I wanted to share the good news with someone. I don't even know if I will get the extra hours, nor do I know how I will schedule people if I get them. My plan of putting one awkward conversation aside for a moment turned into another awkward situation.

Okay, I can look at this one of two ways:

I can take this personally, like she doesn't want to sleep at *my* house. Even though I have two places someone could sleep—downstairs in the finished game room that I made into a giant, cozy, guest bedroom with a queen-sized bed, a giant TV, a recliner, a desk, a table and chairs, and a bathroom with a shower, or my living room with the most comfortable pull-out couch I could find. Even with these options, she's still feeling like that's not good enough for her.

Or, I can think about this in a professional way, which I should always do but totally suck at. I told her I might be getting more hours. Despite the "I'm so excited" and the "might be getting," there's a good chance Britney is probably thinking, "Okay. She's getting more hours. There's going to be more work for me. I don't want to be doing more of what I don't like to do."

Still, though, did she really have to say it like that?

There's a third way I could look at it that's probably more accurate.

Britney is just Britney. She states her opinion like it's nothing. She doesn't do it with malice, and I don't think she's ever *intentionally* putting me down. She's just very extremely blunt.

For example, one day I was watching *Switched at Birth*. Britney came out of the assistant room, rolled her eyes, and matter-of-factly said, "This show is absolutely ridiculous." Without even looking at me, she continued on into the kitchen.

Wh-wha-what? Did something offend her? What does she want me to do? Not watch my show in my own house? I didn't ask her to watch it with me. Should I turn it off? Should I turn it down? Should I ask her about it?

I was so confused.

This was before I realized she's the type of person who is just very blunt, to the point, and says whatever she's feeling.

Before I had time to decide what to do, she had gone back into the assistant room with a drink.

Alright then.

Everything is okay, I guess?

Ughhh. I'm a terrible boss.

Inside My Outside

Actually, no.

I think I'm a good boss.

I'm just terrible in awkward situations.

As my food drips into my stomach, Britney sits down at my dining room table, setting her phone down on it. For a quick moment, I hear the familiar music of the game she likes to play, but then she silences it.

Even though I'm looking at her, she doesn't look at me.

After one too many assistants whipped out their phones while I was in the bathroom, actually doing my business, I made a rule. "Please don't use your cell phones while you're working directly with me." A lot of assistants seem to stretch this to their advantage, acting like, "If Sara doesn't need my hands, I guess I'm okay to check my phone."

I have mixed feelings about this. On one hand, I'm old-fashioned. I don't particularly like when someone is five feet away from me looking at a screen. I would prefer it if we made small talk or they busy themselves doing something that needs to be done. For example, right now, she could load my dishwasher. On the other hand, I get it's today's culture. The second someone has a moment of down-time, the first thing they do is take out their phone, even if it's just for ten seconds.

What's the right thing to do here? She obviously doesn't want to talk, so I'm not going to make her, and I know she will clean up everything once I'm done.

To try (again) to make this situation less awkward, I tell my voice-activated speaker to play some music.

The first song comes and goes.

Still, no follow-up response from her.

I give up.

If I get overnight hours, I'll ask her why she doesn't like to sleep here. No need to worry about something that might not happen.

Another song comes on.

Out of nowhere, I hear, "I hate this song."

I immediately look over at Britney. She's still looking down at her phone, playing her game. I continue to look at her, but she never glances up.

Ummmm.

Okay.

What am I supposed to do with that information? Should I skip the song? Normally, if I know someone doesn't like a song, I will skip it, but frankly, I don't want to do that. I'm a little annoyed with her right now. I just want to eat, and listen to my music, and not worry about anything else. I know I could ask her why she doesn't like this song, but she's not even looking at me right now, so what's the point?

I'm very much aware my thought process is not professional, but what can I say? I'm not perfect.

Confused about me eating in bed? I get that. It's not normal for me.

Saying it's easier to go to the store without me? I get that. It's easier to go without me, because they can just run in and out. But "easier" isn't what I hired them to do.

Saying she doesn't like to sleep over? I understand, if I think about it. I was saying I might get overnight hours, so she's probably thinking I'm going to make her do some nights.

Stating that she "hates" the song I'm listening to and that I'm clearly enjoying? It seems just unnecessary.

If I were Inside Sara, listening to music would never even cross my mind as being a potential issue with anyone else.

If at work, I'd wear ear buds.

If at home, nobody would know.

If I had a boyfriend, he might say something like that, but maybe it would be in a loving way.

If I were listening with a friend, maybe they'd give me a reason why they didn't like it and ask me to skip it.

Eh.

Maybe she really is just a very blunt person.

Maybe she's having a bad day, although her comments aren't that out of the ordinary for her.

I never know what someone is actually thinking. Maybe that's why I never know what to say.

My shake is done draining. Britney stands and unhooks everything. "Do you want to go to the bathroom, and I'll pull up the van after you're done, and we'll go?"

Oh? Okay?

I guess I'm going?

I would've gone anyway. I guess now I don't have to get assertive with it.

Sweet. Okay.

Here we go.

1:08 p.m.

I drive down the wide sidewalk I put in when I first moved into my house. At the end of it, a ramp into my van waits for me.

This is the best van I've had so far, in my opinion. Most accessible vans are just minivans ripped apart to put the ramp in and lower the floor. This van was built from scratch and specifically designed for people in wheelchairs. My favorite part of this van is that it didn't come with a passenger seat, enabling the person in the wheelchair to sit right up front— something I had never been able to do.

This van seriously looks like it was shipped straight from Europe, so every single time I go somewhere, people ask whoever is driving, "What's the van? Who makes it? Where did you get it?" Once they find out it's for people in wheelchairs, they usually go about their days.

I joke and say if I had a dollar for every time someone asks about it, I'd be able to buy another.

Only I couldn't.

Unfortunately, the manufacturer doesn't make it anymore, so when this one bites the dust, it's going to be a sad, sad, sad, sad day in the world of Sara Pyszka.

I roll up the ramp and turn right into my spot. I turn off my wheelchair as Britney puts all four heavy-duty hooks on my chair so it won't move around. She pushes the button to make the ramp go in, climbs into the driver's seat, and off we go.

Britney doesn't say anything on the four-minute ride, but honestly, I really don't care at the moment. It is what it is, Britney is who she is, and who am I to say anything about it? Now, if she were putting me in danger or doing something wrong with my care, I would definitely, absolutely speak up. But whenever it's something that has to do with an assistant's personality, I don't feel like I have the right to say anything.

I may get super annoyed with someone in my head, but I like to respect everyone as they are.

Is it still respect if I treat someone with kindness but am secretly annoyed with them?

I would like to think so, but I'm not entirely sure.

We pull into an accessible parking spot and Britney turns off the van. She puts the ramp down, unhooks my chair, and I descend to the parking lot. She's closing up the van when a woman about my age comes up to us.

And here we go again!

Someone else wanting to know about my car.

Another imaginary dollar for me!

"Excuse me." She halts her cart full of grocery bags. "Can I ask what happened to her?"

My head snaps up.

Huh?!

Britney looks at me, and I look at Britney, feeling the fear spread across my face.

"I'm sorry," Britney says. "I don't know what you mean."

"I'm pregnant, and I don't want my baby to turn out like her, so can you tell me what to do so my baby doesn't turn out like her?"

The first thing I notice is yes, she's pregnant.

The second thing I notice? Cold.

Cold starting in my feet.

Cold spreading through my entire body.

We're outside, so I can't see my screen. I don't even know what I would say if I could see my screen.

I look at Britney, pleading in my head for her to provide a decent answer.

"She just has cerebral palsy." She shrugs (shrugs!). "It happened to her at birth."

"Okay. What can I do to make sure my baby doesn't turn out like her?"

Cold.

Everywhere.

Cold.

"I don't think you can do anything. It was an injury at birth."

"Oh. Okay." The mom-to-be sounds relieved. "Thank you. Have a good day!"

As she's walking away, Britney turns to me with her confused face and shrugs.

I manage to spell to her. "I need a minute."

I can't even breathe. There's no way I can go into a store right now.

"Okay. I guess I'll grab a cart and wait for you in the front?"

I nod but barely.

As she disappears behind the van without saying anything else, a small part of my brain remembers that she didn't particularly want me to come, and now she has to wait for me to gather my feelings, which were just shot across the parking lot.

Another small part of my brain feels guilty/embarrassed that I proved her right. It would have been easier for me not to come, although for reasons she would've probably never predicted.

The majority of my brain, though, is focused on the conversation that just happened.

How do I make sure my baby doesn't turn out like her?

How do I make sure my baby doesn't turn out like her?

That question keeps repeating in my mind.

Not only do I feel cold, but I also feel like I'm going to throw up.

How do I make sure my baby doesn't turn out like her?

There are so many other ways to ask someone about their disability, if you really need to know.

Of course, it's always, always, always more appropriate *not* to bring up someone's disability if it doesn't come up naturally. For me, personally, my disability is not always in the forefront of my brain. However, if you really need to know, just be as polite as you can be.

How do I make sure my baby doesn't turn out like her?

That question is just wrong on so many levels, but I think the part that's bothering me the most is she doesn't want her baby to "turn out" like me.

She doesn't know how I turned out! Yes, she saw my wheelchair, and she probably saw the computer in front of me but probably didn't know what it was, but she doesn't know how I turned out!

She doesn't know my education.

She doesn't know my accomplishments.

She doesn't know my personality.

She doesn't know my success with writing.

She doesn't know how much I learned from my mistakes, so I make sure I don't repeat them.

She doesn't know my passion for treating everyone with respect, even if they do get on my nerves.

Damnit, she doesn't even know my fricking name!

All she saw was my disability and probably thought, "I don't want to deal with that, and I don't want my child to go through that."

This makes tears prick my eyes.

I would never, ever, wish my kind of cerebral palsy on anyone, because it does come with 101 frustrations, but at the end of the day, all those frustrations turn out to be not a big deal, at all.

This conversation can't help but beg a bigger question:

How bad does a situation have to be to cancel out all of the positive things?

I blink my eyes to try to make the tears go away.

I know the mom-to-be probably didn't mean anything by it, but damn! The question was like a needle injecting poison right into my veins.

Okay, Sara!

Get your crap together!

You're sandwiched between two cars, having a meltdown! You probably look ridiculous! If you don't get yourself together, someone will probably think you need help! Not to mention, you need to go grocery shopping! It was just a stupid question! Get yourself together, and let's go!

Only it wasn't just a stupid question.

As I'm driving toward the entrance, I already know that question will stay with me for the rest of my life.

I breathe in.

I breathe out.

I breathe in.

I breathe out.

I breathe in.

I breathe out.

Okay.

I'm ready to go.

As I go in, Britney is waiting with a cart. This time, I don't care that she's looking down at her phone.

I mean, what else was she supposed to do?

And besides, I just took a major blow. Nothing else will phase me at the moment.

"You good?" Britney simply asks.

I give a little nod. What good would it do to say I'm not okay right before I'm about to grocery shop?

"Don't worry about it." She shrugs. "People suck."

She can say that again fifty times over.

Even though it's only six words, I know she's trying to comfort me the best way she can. I appreciate that.

Before we head into the actual store, I spot a huge display of scented wax. I manage a small smile.

Scented wax is like crack to me!

Almost everyone I know says I have a serious problem, because I have two big baskets full of it, and I'm always getting more whenever I have the chance.

What can I say? I like things that smell good, and I like my house to smell good.

"You want some?" Britney asks.

I nod.

"What ones do you want?"

Confused, because I can't just grab wax and go without smelling it, I spell out, "Can you read me the names? I can't see from here."

"Okay. Berry Applesauce?"

That sounds good. I nod.

She picks it up and throws it in the cart.

Ughh.

Of course. I didn't specify.

I spell again. "Can I smell it?"

"You want to smell here?"

Well, where the hell else am I going to smell it?

I can feel this distraction disappearing and my mood returning.

This is not good.

I need to keep my cool.

I nod, and she puts the plastic to my nose without actually opening it.

Yeah, this is just not working.

Inside Sara would stop the cart with one hand. After reading all the names, I would open what I think would smell good and take a quick whiff. If I liked it, it would go in my cart. If I didn't like it, it would go back on the cardboard shelf.

Moments later, the plastic is still squished under my nose. I have to nod for her to finally take it away. "You want it?"

I think it smells good, but I'm not entirely sure.

I nod anyway.

Why not?

She throws it back into my cart. "You want anymore?"

I shake my head. This was supposed to be a fun little detour, and it's turning out to be more work. Granted, it's mostly my fault—I didn't explain what I wanted her to do. I know I still could, but honestly, I don't have the energy for that. It's slowly ticking away. Food is a necessity, and wax is a luxury, and I need all the energy to focus on getting what I need. Still, though, I can't help but feel like wax shouldn't be this hard to pick out.

Britney lets me go in front of her and the cart. I normally don't like to lead when we're out just because it's a little hard to navigate where I'm going and drive my wheelchair without taking anyone out, but the grocery store is an exception. I know everything I need, so I just zip to it, look at the item, my assistant grabs it, and off we go.

What makes it easier to go without me, especially when it's someone's *job* to take me places, I will never know.

First, I make a stop at the bananas. Britney knows I like one green bunch and one yellow bunch.

Next up. Apples. I tell her I want two bags.

I like to stock up, so I only have to come about once a week.

A quick stop to the gourmet cheese department to get my five-cheese ravioli.

Don't judge. Guilty pleasure.

So good!

Onto the deli.

"You want your usual?" Britney asks. "A quarter pound of Colby-Jack?"

You got it.

I stay with the cart a few feet back while Britney goes to the counter.

I let my head fall for a second.

This day.

Oh, this day!

I look up to a man tossing some type of meat into my cart.

Huh?

My mind clicks into gear.

Oh, crap.

He threw it in my cart thinking it was his cart.

I think fast while keeping an eye on him. He seems to be waiting for another order, so that's good! I have time!

Okay, if I start typing to him right now, there's a good chance he will move on with his shopping. If I finish before he moves on, there's no fricking way he will be able to hear my device. It doesn't get that loud. Even if I drive in front of him to get his attention, more than likely he'll be like, "What the hell is this chick doing?" He will not know to read my screen. Communication devices are not a commonly known thing. I could go get Britney, but I don't want to lose him.

I want to cry.

I really can't stand not being able to talk.

Things would be a thousand times easier.

If I were Inside Sara, I would take the meat to him and politely explain what happened. If, for some reason, he started walking away, I would make sure I never take my eye off him until I catch up with him.

Britney is back, but the man is walking away.

I quickly spell. "A man left his ham in our cart."

"Oh." She picks it up, not knowing what to do. "Do you know where he went?"

I search the direction he went in, but before I can answer her, she's putting the ham on the counter.

Wait. Seriously? She's not going to even tell anybody?

It's going to spoil.

As I'm debating telling her to say something to someone, she's pushing the cart and walking away from me.

What should I have done?

I look at the bag of meat one more time, feeling totally helpless.

This day needs to be over.

6:02 p.m.

It's after dinner, and Britney just finished helping me make twelve shakes.

I need to chill out.

I did not sleep well, and I took one of the biggest verbal gut punches of my life.

Not to mention, it was a Britney day, and I was reminded of how much me being nonverbal can really affect everything around me.

I think about going to bed right now, but that would throw off my entire schedule, and I really don't want to wake up at four o'clock in the morning again.

I drive into the living room just as Britney goes into the assistant room.

I've said it once, and I'll say it again: It's super awkward to have everyone in my house only to help me with my basic needs and not have them be a friend-like person, especially when I'm going to watch a show I know they don't particularly like. I don't see myself getting over this. However, I know I'm going to have to.

I need to go to one of my happy places right now. I turn on my TV, wake my computer, and put on *Switched at Birth*.

For the record, I don't always sit around watching *Switched at Birth*. I would say I'm definitely, definitely a binger in everything I do.

Inside My Outside

If I feel like listening to books, chances are I would probably listen to four or five that week.

If I'm in a movie mood, I'll watch all of my favorites in just a few short nights.

If I want to listen to music, I'll probably not do anything else for that hour or so.

I feel like this is not the typical way people enjoy entertainment, but it's the way I enjoy it.

I start the show and tilt my wheelchair all the way back. Immediately, I feel relaxed. I'm being transported to an imaginary world where everyone supports everyone's differences.

Daphne is the character I can relate to the most out of any TV show or any movie. If you haven't watched the show, which sadly ended a few years ago, Daphne, along with Bay, were switched at birth and lived with the wrong families for sixteen years. The show opens with Bay and Daphne meeting their biological families. Along with not fitting in with her biological parents, she also does her best to try to fit in with society. At her school, everyone understands her and uses sign language. Outside school, she has to work twice as hard just to be able to understand what's going on around her.

I'm not Deaf like Daphne, but I feel like I sometimes have to work twice as hard just to be understood.

She adapts to situations, which I also have to do.

She overcompensates by almost being too nice to people, which I sometimes do.

She makes mistakes that echo more than if anyone else would do the same thing, which happens to me.

She sometimes doesn't want to try harder than most people, which I can definitely relate to.

All in all, even though it's because of a different disability, it's just nice to see a character on TV that's going through what I have to go through on a daily basis.

In my opinion, the more characters with disabilities in entertainment, the better the world would be.

That's why I started writing.

Actually . . .

No.

I can't lie.

That's not why I started, but that's why I keep writing.

I first started writing when I was at the camp's house, after I finished high school. This was right before everything could be done online. Whenever I would come home from class or work, I would check my computer, which just consisted of checking my email and instant messages. At the time, there was no Netflix or iTunes. I had just started to discover Audible, but I wouldn't fall in love with it and want to have its babies until a few months later.

If I wanted to listen to a CD or watch a DVD, I would have to ask a staff member to physically put it into the computer for me.

I could have gone out to the common area and chatted with the staff and other residents, but most of the time, I would sit beside my bed, and I would just think.

Sounds boring, but I enjoyed it.

One day, words and sentences started forming on my communication device screen.

A story was forming in my head.

That story was then forming on the screen in front of me.

Since I had my communication device on me all day, every day, I started to write a sentence or two, whenever I could, wherever I could, almost like how people are today with cell phones.

Waiting for someone to get my meals ready? I'd be writing.

On the bus going to work or class? I'd be writing.

Down-time in my room, whether five minutes or an hour? I'd be writing.

It just felt incredibly good to be able to do something completely by myself.

I would also read it to everyone and anyone willing to listen. If I read it to a staff member, and if I wrote another scene between their shifts, I would read it to them once they came back to the house.

I probably embarrassed myself and annoyed a lot of people, but again, it just felt so good to share something I did completely and utterly 110 percent by myself.

Once the story was finished, I transferred it to my desktop. Even though it completely, utterly suuuuuuuucked (really, the story was based on my first time going to a camp that was for able-bodied people with characters as flat as pancakes and plot holes as big as potholes), I was like, "I think I want to do something with this. I think I want to try to get this published."

And so, I started the second draft.

While writing my second draft, an experience happened to me that changed my thoughts from "I like to write because I can do it by myself" to "I have to write because I need to educate as many people as I can."

One night, I was out to eat with my assistant and my friend, who was also in a wheelchair. To be honest, I'm not entirely sure if her wheelchair played a part in this, since it was a manual chair and much less visible than my chair, but it very well could have. This assistant didn't feed me well, so a little food kept coming out of my mouth, but it wasn't as bad as it could've been. I didn't feel like I wanted to stop eating, because I didn't feel that gross, if that says anything.

An older gentleman came up to the table, handed my assistant a twenty-dollar bill, and said, "Thank you for doing what you're doing. I appreciate it."

Surprised but smiling, my assistant took the twenty dollars and cheerfully thanked him.

We were in the middle of the restaurant, and for me, everything froze.

I remember glancing around the room, looking for a bathroom I could escape to.

I then realized I couldn't move, or I was going to have a meltdown. Shit!

I was in the middle of a very crowded restaurant, and a waterfall was about to explode from my face.

What the hell do I do?

That man might as well have grabbed a knife from our table and stabbed me in the gut.

My assistant tried to give me another cheese fry.

I shook my head.

I was barely keeping my crap together and still breathing; there was no way I could keep it together and still eat.

"It's okay," my friend said in a quiet voice. She never let anything like that bother her. "Just try to let it go."

"What's wrong?" my assistant asked, innocently.

"The money," my friend clued her in.

I could see her face changed from confused to insulted.

Yeah. She was definitely, definitely insulted I was feeling terrible that some guy would give her money for just being with me.

They finished their dinner in silence. I could not eat anymore.

In the van, my assistant finally spoke: "I'm sorry. I don't understand why you're so mad. It just felt so good to be appreciated by someone other than you and your mom."

How can I not be angry right now?

By giving you the twenty dollars, he was basically saying, "I don't know how you do this," or "I could never do that," or "You're such a good person for helping the disabled girl." Of course I appreciate you, but he was basically saying he didn't know how you were doing it, because he couldn't do it! He was basically saying that because I needed a little more help, I was less than everyone else! This has nothing to do with you, but everything to do with him!

I think that's basically what I said to her, but I made sure to say it in a nicer tone.

"I still don't understand. That man was giving me a compliment, and it made me feel really good about myself. What's so wrong about that?"

Because he was giving you a compliment at my disability's expense! I wanted to scream.

I tried to explain it again, rearranging the same words and adding that he didn't know if she was my sister. He didn't know if she was my friend. He didn't know if she was my partner.

He didn't know anything about our relationship. He just assumed that she didn't want to be with me, or she had a crappy job, or she was just volunteering to take me out, even though it was not the easiest thing to do.

She still didn't understand, and my friend finally texted me that she was probably not going to get it and suggested I just drop it.

That's probably one of my biggest frustrations in life that I don't think I will ever get over.

I almost always understand where everyone is coming from, even if I don't agree with them, even if it hurts me, even if it pisses me off.

I actually take a lot of pride in that.

If someone has different political or religious beliefs, I understand. There are seven billion people in this world. How could everyone have one single belief system?

If someone I really like doesn't want to date me, I understand. I may be upset. I may cry. I may spiral into a "I'm going to be alone forever" funk. But I ultimately understand. People can't help who they are or are not attracted to.

If someone even has a problem with my disability, for example, say, my flying limbs make them nervous, or if helping me in the bathroom makes them squeamish, I understand. Everyone is different, and everything is not for everyone. If they tell me in a polite and respectful manner, I will understand.

Hell, I understand where that assistant was coming from, even though I wanted to break down crying. Someone randomly walked up to her and gave her twenty dollars just for doing her job. She was excited. It made her feel good. Under any other circumstances, I would be like, "Wow. That's awesome."

What's so frustrating is that, if you turn it around, people don't understand *my* side or, generally speaking, the side they oppose, and I'm not talking about at first glance, without explanation. In my experience, when I try to explain what I'm thinking or feeling, people typically don't want to hear it, or they tell me that I'm wrong, or get defensive, or tell me that I don't understand.

I'm definitely understanding. I'm just explaining my take, and you're the one who's not understanding!

Of course, not everyone is like this, but when someone is, it just kills me.

However, I think this is human nature. I guess I have to understand everyone is not going to understand.

I love one specific lyric from one of my favorite bands, Bowling for Soup:

"What is the obsession with always being right? It's not always win or lose; it's not black or white."

Amen to that, BFS!

In conclusion, I think if everyone tried to understand one another more—really, actually tried to truly understand—the world would be a much better place.

And that's a wrap on my rant about being understood.

Back to the night the stranger insulted me while I was just trying to enjoy my cheese fries.

I can't see something happening quite like this to someone able-bodied, but for the sake of this book, let's insert Inside Sara in a few scenarios like this.

I wouldn't have an assistant with me, obviously, but let's say I was out to dinner with two of my friends. A guy comes up to one of them, looks at me, hands her twenty bucks, and says, "Thank you for doing this. I really appreciate it." At first, we would probably be like, "What? What the hell? Did that really just happen? Was he drunk?" We would then wonder if he was hitting on my friend. After thinking about it some more, we would probably come to the conclusion he wants something to do with me, and my friends would watch my back for the rest of the night.

Let's say I'm out to dinner with a guy or my boyfriend. Following exactly what happened to me in real life, he hands him twenty bucks and says, "Thank you for doing this. I appreciate it." We would be like, "What? What just happened? Really?" I would start to wonder what was wrong with me. *Do I look okay? Is there something in my hair? Is there something in my teeth? Am I doing something wrong? Talking too much? Talking too little? Am I being boring?*

However, that's probably not what would really happen if a man gave another man money for being with me. If I was really able-bodied and something like that happened, I'm going to say it would mean something gross, and disgusting, and wrong was about to go down.

Am I upset that a gentleman gave my assistant money just for being with me? Absolutely.

Am I happy he only gave her money for being with me and didn't try to actually do anything else to me? Absolutely.

So, in this situation, was my disability working for me or against me?

I'm not entirely sure, but I thoroughly enjoy thinking about these kinds of questions.

Again, I should've been a Sociology major!

After that night, all my feelings changed about writing.

I didn't want to write just for fun anymore.

I wanted to write to educate the world!

There were two reasons for this.

The obvious reason was to educate people like that gentleman. Not knowing anything about our relationship includes not knowing how my assistant treated me. He only saw a snippet of the whole picture. He had assumed, and I'm obviously just speculating here, that I was the one who was hard to deal with here. That assistant was a decent assistant, but it probably never even crossed his mind that *she* might've been the one who was hard to deal with. She might've been lazy. She might've had a temper. She might've, God forbid, been abusive.

He probably didn't think about any of this, and so, after that night, I discovered I really wanted to educate people who were just like him.

Of course, the best way to do this would be to speak up right when a situation like this occurs directly to the person who's uneducated. I never seem to be able to do this, and no, it's not because it takes me some time to type out what I want to say. When a situation like this happens, I never know what to say in the moment. I usually want to go hide somewhere and cry. I'm ashamed of this, because I say I want to educate the world. I should've said something to that gentleman. I should've said something to the lady who didn't want her baby to turn out like me. However, sometimes I don't process a situation for a few days. Sometimes, I don't even process a situation until I'm writing about it.

The other reason I wanted to write is less obvious but more fun to think about. In fact, I enjoy thinking about it and talking about it so much that when I do, people assume I'm obsessing over something I'm mad about and tell me to let it go.

I'm not mad whenever I see this happening. I'm actually completely, utterly, totally, 100 percent fascinated by this.

That night at the restaurant, we had one single situation with four entirely different perspectives.

The gentleman, again, purely speculating here, who wanted to do something awesome for someone else and more than likely didn't want to do any harm.

My assistant, who felt awesome that a stranger would do something like that for her.

Me, who felt like I required so much help, a stranger wanted to give another stranger money for doing it.

My friend, who liked to focus on the positive and wanted me to let it go.

One situation.

Four different perspectives.

And probably a lot more now that it's published in a book.

How could people think so differently about the exact same situation?

It's incredible.

It's just fascinating.

When I started on my third draft, that night was with me. A switch had flipped in my brain. My main character, Brynn, originally could talk and use her hands. She was just in a wheelchair. In my third draft, I wanted her to be more like me. I wanted her to use a communication device. I wanted her to rely on someone else for everything.

I wanted her to have my disability.

Because if I didn't tell my story exactly through my eyes, who the hell would?

I also wanted to have characters with all different perspectives, which any author should do regardless, but this time, it was definitely in the back of my mind more.

I have characters who totally accept Brynn.

I have characters who downright don't accept Brynn.

I have characters who want to accept Brynn but don't really know how.

I even have a character who used Brynn to make herself look good.

As long as I'm writing books, I'm always going to make sure I have characters with a wide variety of perspectives just because I think it's so important.

Plus, that's just real life. Everyone doesn't agree with everyone else.

When I was finally done and had a polished manuscript, I started to email literary agents. To get in with a big publishing company, you basically need a literary agent. I put on Facebook that I had started looking for agents, because I was just so excited. Somebody messaged me whom I met at Wright State. She has a son who uses a communication device. She told me she had a niece who worked in the publishing industry, Nicole. She told me to email her. Being the big shot I thought I was, I didn't want to email her. I wanted to do this by myself.

I emailed about fifteen agents.

Ha.

Looking back on it now, fifteen agents? That was a joke. They now say if you want to work with an agent, you should contact as many as you can (who represent the type of work you're writing).

I didn't hear back from any of the agents. Surprise, surprise. It was then I was like, "Okay, maybe I will email this Nicole. Maybe she will know of some agents." She did. She also worked for a small publishing house and wanted to see what I had. I sent it to her. She loved it. And to make a long story short, it made it to the person who had the final say. He really liked the idea, but he said it needed some developmental work. He gave Nicole permission to work off the clock with me.

Nicole and I worked together for six months. She would revise a chapter, email it to me, I would make a few more changes, email it back, and we would move on to the next chapter. I cannot say enough good things about Nicole. She is one of those people in my life who represented a turning point. I will never forget her. I can only hope I can hire her for my next books.

Unfortunately, Nicole's company did not take my novel. I'm going to be honest—I cried. I really wanted to work with her company. I really wanted to work with Nicole. After emailing another forty agents with no reply, I said, "Screw this!" I didn't want somebody else to tell me my book wasn't good enough to publish. I didn't want to wait around anymore for permission to publish my work. I decided it was time to self-publish.

Self-publishing was kind of controversial at the time, because along with being the writer, you have to hire your own editor, do all of your marketing, and all of that good stuff. But after doing a lot of research, I decided self-publishing was right for me. I knew I had a good piece of work. I knew I had an audience, somewhere. So, I decided to just do it. And so far, I could not be happier.

I also self-published my second novel, and as far as I can see for the foreseeable future, I'm going to stick with self-publishing.

Even though at the time, I desperately wanted to work with a traditional publishing company, I think it was a blessing in disguise they didn't take me. For one, I wanted to have Brynn go through a series of books, where readers would see her go from an unsure teenager to an independent-thinking young adult. This was so important to me, because this is rarely seen in people with disabilities in entertainment. This company, like many others, didn't consider full book series right off the bat. They would offer a one-book deal to start. If the book did well, they would consider possibly giving the author another deal for another book, but I think this is very hard to come by, especially for a new author.

Another reason I like self-publishing is that I have total control over my work. When authors sign with a traditional publishing house, they are essentially selling the book to that company, and the company is selling it. This means if the company doesn't like the title, the company can change it, even if the author isn't okay with it. If the company doesn't like a plot line, they can suggest changes to it, add to it, or delete from it—depending on that company's contract.

Now, I personally love when my editor tells me what's wrong with my manuscript and how to fix it. It's just nice to know that if I don't necessarily agree, I don't have to change it.

The biggest reason self-publishing is right for me is that I am so incredibly horrible with meeting deadlines. Seriously, I'm going to say this is one of my worst habits, and I'm going to make a sincere effort to break this. My problem is that I see the entire book played out in my head, but I overestimate my typing speed. I have no idea how I still do that after twenty years with this communication device, but there you have it! That's what happens.

When I miss a deadline now, I tell my editor, who understands, and I go online and tell my readers, who definitely understand and encourage me to take as much time as I need. If I were with a traditional publishing house, I think they would be okay with me missing one deadline, but I don't think they would be down with constantly pushing it back because they sell books so far ahead of their release dates.

Obviously, a million authors have been traditionally published, and it worked for them.

For me, I like self-publishing.

I'm going to be writing for as long as I can.

I love coming up with an idea for a project.

I love ironing it out.

I love starting it.

I love forming words into sentences, completely by myself.

I love forming sentences into paragraphs, and paragraphs into chapters.

I love when I have so many chapters, it becomes a first draft of a book.

I don't particularly love editing just because it's kind of a pain in the ass to do with my communication device and the computer, but I love when I'm done editing.

I love sending my manuscripts to my editor.

I love getting them back from my editor with suggestions and ideas to make them better.

Again, scrolling through entire documents is a little difficult with my communication device, but I love making those changes so that people will love my books even more.

I love when I have my completed manuscripts.

I love when I send them to the print-on-demand service.

I love when they format the files.

I love seeing the final cover designs.

I love getting the very first hard copies in the mail to proof.

I love hitting that PUBLISH button.

I love seeing them up on Amazon.

I love selling my books at events.

I love that I'm the one who's driving the reader to the story.

Most of all, I absolutely love hearing how one of my books impacted a reader.

So, yeah. I think it's safe to say I really like writing.

Anyone want to try to talk me into changing careers?

8:25 p.m.

I've watched four episodes, and my mood has elevated, even though this show is fictional.

I don't care what anyone says—fiction can make someone feel, heal, and learn just as much, if not more, as real stories can.

That's why it's my favorite thing to write.

I love making up an awesome story that will emotionally affect a reader and have them take away something they can apply to their life.

Just as I turn off the TV, the doorbell rings.

I jump out of my skin.

That's a CP thing. We can't take sudden, loud noises.

If you're ever in a room full of people with CP, you never want to randomly scream, or pop a balloon, or slam a door, unless you want to be hated.

But more importantly, who the hell is at my door after eight o'clock at night?

Inside Sara would absolutely not open the door. If I were by myself in this house, I would hunker down in my big, comfy recliner until they left.

Maybe I would even call someone and have them stay on the phone with me until I was sure the visitor was gone.

At that moment, Britney shuffles through my living room and says, "Sorry. It's my food."

Oh.

Her food.

Okay.

Sometimes, my assistants order food. I'm okay with it. Sometimes they tell me, and sometimes not.

I guess today was a "not" day.

As she takes the brown bag and closes the door, I do a mental double take.

Wait.

Her food?

At eight-thirty?

I usually eat at eight-thirty.

I blink.

I can't believe what I'm seeing.

She's sitting at the dining room table, unpacking the bag, getting ready to eat.

Now, let me try to explain exactly what I'm feeling right now, because a lot of people usually misunderstand my side of a situation like this.

I'm not annoyed that she ordered food without telling me.

I'm not annoyed at the pure fact that she ordered food pretty late and at the same time I usually eat.

I'm annoyed that I now have a situation on my hands, where I'm basically like, "Hey, you. You can't eat right now, even though your food just came, because, uh, I need to eat, or else you're going to be here after your shift is supposed to end. You should know this by now."

I'm annoyed I'm in a position where I now have to be the bad guy, even though I know I'm technically not the bad guy for saying that I need to eat and just doing what I always do every night.

I don't know how she's going to react.

She could get huffy.

She could get an attitude.

She could be okay with it.

I'm annoyed, because this entire situation could've been avoided.

I slowly inch up to the table, hating that I feel guilty. I've already typed what I'm going to say. "I'm sorry. Can I eat?"

I know I don't have any reason to be sorry, but my communication device voice doesn't show any emotion. A lot of things come out rougher than I actually mean them. Putting "I'm sorry" is my way of lessening the tone.

Britney pops a French fry in her mouth, stands, grabs a shake out of the refrigerator, sticks it in the microwave, and comes over to give me some water.

Alright then.

Good thing I don't want anything by mouth.

This is where I would love to ask if she's okay, but in my experience, assistants don't like when I do. Of course, all assistants are not like this, but most of the time, they either say they're okay but keep acting as though they're not, which is extremely awkward for me, or they get defensive like, "Why? Do you think I'm not okay?"

One assistant got downright sarcastic with me like, "Yes, Sara, I'm okay. Are *you* okay?"

Woah, dude! You really seemed upset, and I was just worried about you. Honest! No need for sarcasm!

That's when I decided it's better to let someone be if I notice they're having a bad day.

After I take a drink, Britney vents me and hooks me up to the shake. She then goes back to eating.

I want to put on music, but I don't. I don't feel like hearing a comment about how she doesn't like my music.

People often think I'm too scared to ask an assistant to do things or that I don't want to inconvenience them. This is incorrect. A lot of the time, if I don't do something I usually want to do, it's just because I know they'll make a comment about it. I would be okay with a negative comment every once in a while, but when comment after comment after comment keeps coming at me, it's like a wall automatically pops up around me to protect my likes and wants.

I want to be like, "Ahhhhhh! I know you think that this is ridiculous/cheesy/lame/stupid/not what you would do, but this is what I enjoy."

It gets exhausting, even though I never actually argue with anyone.

And I'm already exhausted.

As I continue eating, Britney pops one French fry in her mouth at a time while scrolling through her phone.

I watch the shake drain from the bag, trying to not think about anything.

I fail.

Britney is a slow eater.

Like, the slowest eater I've ever met.

Like, we're talking about at least forty-five minutes, if not more, for every meal.

Now, I have absolutely no right to judge the speed someone eats. In fact, I hate that this is going through my mind right now, because I do a lot of things differently, so who the hell am I to say what's right and wrong? But Britney chose to eat her dinner at the predictably busiest time of the night.

What would anyone expect me to do?

She hasn't even touched her sandwich yet. She's just eating one fry at a time.

I can't help it. *How is this going to go?*

Is she going to eat her sandwich now?

Is she going to take it home?

Is she going to explain herself?

Should I ask her about it?

I should probably say something about it, but my inner child is stomping her feet, saying, "This is not fair! I didn't do anything wrong! I kept to myself! I stuck to the schedule! There should not be any drama tonight!"

Maybe it won't be as bad as I'm thinking.

Maybe she'll eat while she's helping me?

She sees I'm done with my shake. She unhooks my bag, throws it away, gives me my meds, flushes me, takes the tube off, and she proceeds to sit back down and pick her phone back up.

Ummmm.

Okay?

I know at the beginning of the book, I said I don't like my assistants to make assumptions about what I'm going to do, but the truth of the matter is I do have a schedule, and the schedule is to give my assistants an idea of what I need help with and when.

Tonight, apparently, it didn't help.

I type, again hating that I'm in this situation. "I'm sorry. I have to go to the bathroom."

Again, using the "I'm sorry" more to buffer the awkwardness.

Nobody should ever feel sorry if they have to pee!

"Do you have to go right now, or can you wait until I'm done eating?"

I feel my eyes wanting to pop open as big as saucers. I fight so hard to keep a normal face.

For one, nobody should ever ask *anyone* to wait if they say they have to pee, especially if they're "working" for them. I could maybe see if she had been cleaning up the kitchen and had told me to head to my bedroom and she'd be there in a minute, but she *knows* when I usually do things and she has a meal in front of her now—during my usual and predictable dinner and bathroom time—that could've been ordered and eaten during her two hours of down-time.

This is not okay!

Second, let's say I could magically hold my bladder for forty-five minutes while I wait for her to finish eating. That would put us behind schedule forty-five minutes. I know for a fact she would not like that. Along with telling me she doesn't like to be rushed in the morning, she has told me she doesn't like to be rushed at night, and that's what my showers do to her.

Because of this, I always make sure to start my shower a good hour and a half before she's supposed to leave and am always finished and in bed forty-five minutes to a half an hour before her shift ends.

How is that being "rushed"?

Before I say something I regret, I quickly spell out, "If you put me on the toilet now, you can finish eating."

I'm really negotiating just so I can be able to pee?

Yep. This is happening.

No wonder I really can't stand needing help with everything.

She agrees, and we head to the bedroom.

Once I'm on the toilet, I asked Britney if she could make it a fast dinner.

I know that is considered "rushing" her, and I actually feel bad about that, but to accommodate *her*, I have agreed to just chill on the pot while she finishes her food.

She simply nods and shuts the door behind her.

I have a clock in my bathroom, and I time a lot of things, like my showers, down to the minute.

So, I decide to time how long this takes her.

Is this a jerk move?

Probably.

But I'm not going to use it against her. I'm just curious to see how long she thinks is acceptable to let someone sit on a toilet for her convenience.

Two minutes now . . .

How would Inside Sara deal with confrontation, I wonder.

I feel like I don't have an argumentative cell in my body. Yes, I like to be playfully sarcastic, and true, a lot of the time I get mad in my head, but I very rarely call out people. One time, my friend wanted to debate with me just for the sake of debating, and I couldn't do it. What's the point? They had their opinions, and I had my opinions, and that was that.

I still feel like that would be the case if I were able-bodied, because that just feels like it's natural for me. However, I feel like Inside Sara would speak up a little more if I didn't like what someone was doing, because I wouldn't have this feeling like I couldn't offend anyone. I believe I would still be very polite when correcting someone, but the worry that somebody might completely walk out of my life simply because I expressed my feelings wouldn't be there.

Six minutes.

Unfortunately, at this point in my life, all the people I'm around most often work for me or assist me. Because of this, my house is not really a safe space where I can say whatever I want and do whatever I want. For now, my house is a workplace for a lot of people. Yes, it's technically still my house, and I technically don't have to follow any rules, but I just find it easier and healthier to go by the social guidelines of any other work environment.

No one has walked out in the middle of a shift because of something I've said to them yet, but here are some of the things I have experienced:

Counterarguments flying at me that are harsher compared to my original statements.

So many cold shoulders that occasionally last throughout the entire day.

A lot of misunderstandings, because I don't get my words exactly right between what I'm trying to say combined with my monotone voice.

Some people are physically rougher when they're helping me—no abuse, no hitting, etc., but I can feel the tension whenever they touch me.

These past experiences make me want to be extremely careful of what I say and how I say it.

Ten minutes.

I often wonder why people are like this. Why do people get so bent out of shape when speaking with me sometimes?

I have two theories about this.

Fourteen minutes.

It's important to note that these are Sara Pyszka Theories. They are solely based on my experiences, and I don't have any scientific evidence to back them up.

My first theory: But I'm Helping You Theory.

Some people think the mere fact of doing anything they consider *help* should be enough. They're thinking about me, and they want to help me. They think they're doing something awesome.

I will never take this away from anyone. Helping people *is* awesome.

However, helping someone when they don't need help isn't something to collect praise for.

Newly hired assistants are perfect examples of this. I have been at my TV, working, minding my own business, and they have approached me with a cup and a towel in hand. It takes me a minute, but I realize they want to give me a drink.

Oh.

I didn't want a drink.

Now, I know they've meant well, but I usually decline and politely explain that if I'm thirsty, I will say so.

Some assistants understand, and some assistants will get this mild/moderate sad look and say something along the lines of, "But I was just being nice."

Of course you were being nice, dude! I appreciate it! But if I don't want a drink, I'm not going to take a drink.

I'd have the same reaction if someone were to rearrange my closet without asking me. They might show me what they've done when I come into the room, and they may be smiling. When I thank them but politely say they should've asked me beforehand, because I had a method to my previous organization, their smile may fade. "But I was just trying to help you."

My "But I'm Helping You Theory" Summary: To the helper, all help is good, and all corrections are bad.

Eighteen minutes.

My second theory: The Pedestal Theory.

I have no idea what anyone actually thinks or feels when they first meet me, but here's my best guess.

They see someone in a wheelchair who has a computer in front of her. They may or may not see my arms are tied down.

They may or may not see my other straps, but they probably don't know those straps are keeping me from flying out of my wheelchair. If they do see them, they might think they're for behavioral issues.

I might be smiling at them, or, depending on my wonderful lack of muscle control, I might be trying to smile at them but actually grimacing.

They greet me.

I meet their eyes for a quick second, and then I look down.

They probably don't know why I'm looking down at the computer in front of me for more than a few seconds, so they probably question how much I'm "with it" or if I'm even with it, at all.

I keep looking down at my screen, and with every second I'm not looking at them or saying anything, it probably makes them lean toward the "she's not with it" side of the spectrum.

If they don't walk away from me, they will finally hear my device say, "Nice to meet you. How's it going?"

Wait. What? They probably think. *She made that computer say that!*

"I'm doing pretty good. How about you?" they scramble to say.

They see me typing.

Holy crap! She really is making that computer do that!

How incredible!

We start to have a conversation.

Holy crap! She's with it!

She's talking to me!

"Sara! That computer is so cool! You are amazing!"

And, bam!

Just like that, they put me on a pedestal.

Because I can work my communication device, because I can drive my wheelchair, because I can have a conversation with them, I'm on a pedestal.

More importantly, I'm on a pedestal because I blew their expectations of me out of the water.

And the more people get to know me, the higher that pedestal raises.

Holy crap!

Not only is she with it, she has a personality!

She's funny.

She's creative.

She's nice.

She's amazing!

And so, whenever I say something they don't necessarily agree with, or worse, whenever I make a mistake, I sometimes feel like I'm falling fifty feet in their eyes.

What? I thought she was so perfect. Why would she think something like that?

What? I thought she was smart. Why would she do something like that?

Of course, they don't say anything like that to me. This is just me pretending to be a psychologist here, but I feel like they get really disappointed in me in the moment and it comes out as anger/frustration.

So, yeah. Those are my theories. Again, not science-based, but Sara Pyszka–based. Every once in a blue moon, I will lose my temper and say a jackass thing, but most of the time, I feel like this is what happens.

Twenty-three minutes.

Okay, this is not a "fast dinner."

I understand she likes to eat how she likes to eat, but . . .

Yeah.

Grrrr.

I think about calling for her, which, if you are unfamiliar with the disability world, basically consists of me making an "ahhhhhhhhh" noise.

Should I call her?

I already asked her to make it a fast dinner. Shouldn't that mean to come in as soon as she's done?

Another one of my downfalls. I tend to go for nice/as nice as I can be instead of specific.

I seriously need to work on that, especially if I'm going to be the boss of so many people.

I need to be specific and direct.

I decide to do the exact opposite of what I need to work on, and I decide to give Britney a few more minutes.

Yep. That would so be me!

Twenty-five.

I wonder. What would Inside Sara do if she had a bad day with people?

Like I mentioned before, my dream job would be working at a camp. Obviously, a lot of things could go wrong.

Grants not being approved.

Having to find extra money.

Co-directors not putting in their fair share of work.

Something breaking down on campus.

If camp was in session, I could have:

Problems with campers.

Problems with counselors.

Problems with programming.

A kitchen disaster.

Weather problems.

If I had a day of drama at camp, I could see myself coming home and not wanting to talk to anyone. I would want to be by myself and decompress.

Maybe I would take a shower right when I got home and wash the day off me. Maybe I would wait until bed.

I could make myself one of my comfort foods for dinner, either mac 'n' cheese or grilled cheese. I can't see Inside Sara craving buttered noodles, but hey! Ya never know!

After dinner, I would probably climb into my big, comfy recliner and either quietly read a book or watch a couple episodes of a comfort show like *Grey's Anatomy*.

If I had a boyfriend, I would want him to sit with me. We wouldn't need to talk that much. Just laying my head on his shoulder would be enough.

Yes, I'm aware most long-term couples are rolling their eyes and/or gagging at me right now.

Oh well.

I probably would still have a bedtime routine, but I wouldn't be as worried about what time I fell asleep. If I went to bed early and woke up early, it wouldn't be as big of a deal. I would just get up and start my day.

But I'm not Inside Sara.

Instead, I'm sitting on a toilet, exhausted, staring at a clock, timing how long it takes someone to come get me.

Thirty-two minutes.

Seriously?

In her defense, I'm timing it, and I haven't called for her.

But . . .

Seriously?

Should I even *have* to call for her?

Thirty-three minutes.

And I'm lucky, because I *can* call for her.

Thirty-four minutes.

What if she were helping someone who couldn't call for her? Someone with a cognitive disability or totally nonverbal?

Thirty-five.

That would be taking advantage of someone!

I know she's taking advantage of me. I know for a fact many people have taken advantage of my calm, go-with-the-flow, yeah-sure-whatever personality. But I think it's so much worse to take advantage of someone who can't stand up for themselves.

Thirty-six.

I think the difference is I know when to say enough is enough.

They are *unable* to say enough is enough.

Thirty-seven.

Okay, this is getting ridiculous!

Thirty-eight.

If she doesn't come in five minutes, I'm calling her!

Thirty-nine minutes.

The door opens.

Oh, my God!

For thirty-nine fricking minutes, she thought it was okay to just do her thing while I sat here on the toilet!

Seriously?

I'm not going to say anything, because, for some reason, I don't feel like I have the right to. However, I will figure out how to handle situations like this in the future.

Story of my life. Figuring out how to address the obvious.

"Ready?" she asks.

I want to say something sarcastic like, "Nope. I need another thirty-nine minutes," but that would be mean. Plus, I know that wouldn't be the right way to handle this.

Just then, a flash of light outside my tiny shower window catches my attention.

Oh, geez.

I saw it again.

Lightning.

Nooooo.

"Is it storming?" I spell out.

"Yeah. Just starting. I hate driving in the rain."

"No shower."

She looks at me, confused, once again. "You don't want to take a shower?"

An assistant once told me that not only could I be electrocuted in the shower when it was lightning, but whomever was showering me could also be electrocuted. Even though I was annoyed at the time, because Inside Sara would definitely not follow the no-shower-in-lightning rule, I thought about it and decided this assistant had been right.

My assistants are, in a lot of ways, responsible for me, but I am, in ways a lot of people don't see, responsible for my assistants.

"I know the chances are very small, but we could both get electrocuted if it's lightning. I don't want to put you in danger."

She's still confused. "Why do you care about your assistants so much?"

I blink.

She didn't just ask me that!

Oh, but she did.

It's like she just punched me in the stomach.

I know I should rise above.

I know I should answer with something else.

But I can't. I'm done.

This day—over it.

My filter—gone.

Why do I care about my assistants so much? Why do I want to avoid situations in which they might be possibly hurt or killed?

"Because I'm fricking human!" I angrily spell out.

Day Three

8:10 a.m.

MY EYES SLOWLY OPEN. I blink a few times just to make sure. My eyelids won't stay shut, and there's light peeking through the blinds. Yep, I'm definitely awake. Suddenly, I'm taken back to the previous night's conversation with Britney.

My brain always does this. If something bad happened the day before, my mind, out of nowhere, will take me back.

Why do you care so much about your assistants?

Because I'm fricking human!

Britney met my answer with an unenthusiastic, unapologetic, "Oh," like she has people telling her that they're humans all the time.

Ummm.

Alright.

Should I *not* care about my assistants, and, as someone once told me to do, treat them like assistive technology, just like my communication device?

Should I make them do anything I want them to do, even though I know they don't like it or are uncomfortable with it?

No! Because I will get pushback! I already get pushback from some of them if I put on a song they don't like or if I ask for something so little as an extra drink during the day!

And if I keep making people do what they don't particularly like to do, I will go through assistants just as often as I change my clothes. Nobody is making anyone work for me. If they don't particularly like what they're doing, they're going to get another job without a second thought, and I really can't afford that.

Not to mention, she totally discredited what I believe is my strongest strength: caring about other people.

Whatever.

It's over.

Britney isn't on the schedule today.

Chloe's coming, though, which just might be another interesting day in itself.

I start turning my neck and realize it hurts.

Oh, hi, cramp.

Even though it hurts, this is good.

This means I slept. This means I was so tired, I passed out and didn't wake up the entire night.

I'll take a cramp that will fade away over no sleep any day.

I finish my turn and look at the clock.

I don't need any coffee right now, because I'm suddenly wide awake, and I'm panicking.

Damn!

Chloe!

You're killing me here!

It's 8:11.

Eleven minutes after she was supposed to be here.

I know eleven minutes might not sound like much to some people, but whenever somebody I rely on for pretty much everything I need is that late, I can't help but panic.

I give each new hire a guidebook filled with what I expect and need from my assistants with one guideline being: "Please try to be on time. You are my lifeline. If you don't show up on time, or don't show up at all, I could be left lying in bed all day and unable to tell anyone that you did not come. If you are going to be late, please call my house, leave a message, and tell me what's going on. I can hear the message."

When Chloe first started working for me, she was just as awesome as Amber. She was always up for anything I wanted to do, on the same level as me with communication, and actually came a little early every day she was scheduled. Whenever she was going to be late, which was extremely rare, she would respect my request and call to tell me what was up.

In the past year, it's like she's become a different person.

If I want to stray from my daily routine a bit, she'll not only tell me another way I should do it—usually a way I can do it completely myself, where she doesn't need to do anything—but she'll tell me all the reasons I should do it her way. For example, if I tell her I want to go to Target to get something, she'll tell me to order it from Amazon and then proceed to argue with me until I finally say, "Nope, Chloe. We're going to Target."

One time, she was getting me up, chattering, chattering, chattering, happy, happy, happy. I mentioned I had to go to the wheelchair shop that day to get my chair fixed. Abruptly, she stopped talking, covered her mouth, said, "I think I'm going to get sick," and ran to the bathroom.

What the hell is with people not wanting to take me anywhere? It's not like they have to do anything special! Just drive me wherever and help me communicate!

And now, if she's late, she doesn't even call anymore. I'm lucky if I even get an apology when she does show up.

I've seen this before with multiple assistants, where they go from awesome to awful in a matter of months. This is called *burnout*, and I just recently found this is a real psychological thing that can happen to anyone.

Before I realized it wasn't just my assistants going through this, I had two theories about why this might happen to personal assistants in general. Even though I now know this can happen to anyone in any field of work, I still think it probably happens frequently to people with personal care jobs.

Is this bad to do? To publish my theories that have absolutely no scientific evidence to back it up?

If open to corrections and suggestions, which I definitely am, I don't think so.

Besides, this is my memoir, which doesn't include any science, anyway. Only my experiences.

Okay, on to my theories.

Theory One. People are being told what to do and how to do it their entire shift. Unlike most jobs where people find a routine they prefer for completing tasks, personal care assistants typically have to follow specific instructions from whomever they are working for. We don't do this to be bossy. We just know what we need, what we don't need, and the best way to do it. I always say my assistants are my hands. I know everything that I need to do; I just need hands to physically do it for me. People with laid-back personalities usually don't have a problem with this, but people with dominant personalities, who like to be in charge, seem to burn out a little faster.

Theory Two. This is very much a static job that doesn't offer much. It doesn't have health insurance. It doesn't have raises. People can ask me for time off, but the state doesn't give them paid vacations. I don't need a head assistant, because I'm the head, so they don't have any room to move up. In today's world, this is the exact opposite of what people want. Even though I require assistants to live, I don't agree with this system. Personal assistants should get health care, and benefits, and raises. They're helping others live their lives!

Along with not getting any benefits, the actual job doesn't change much. If I'm staying at home, writing all day, I basically only need help with eating and going to the bathroom, plus typical house chores and possible emergencies if anything happens to my body. If I'm going somewhere, it's usually to the same places to do the same things. My life isn't that exciting, and to be honest, I like it that way. Again, people who have calm, go-with-the-flow personalities have less of a problem with this. It's the people who have stronger personalities and like to be in charge who seem to get bored and want more for themselves.

I don't blame them for this, and I actually understand where they're coming from. Everything isn't for everyone. If it was, everyone could do everything, and the world would be perfect.

Although it would be pretty awesome, I don't see this as either a good or a bad thing.

Everyone has strengths. Everyone has weaknesses.

It's just how the world works.

Unfortunately, when someone isn't aware of their weaknesses and they start working for me, it could drastically impact the quality of my life.

8:14.

I feel my chest start to tighten with panic.

Inside Sara would just hop right up and start her day.

I wonder if I should start inching myself higher on the bed. When I sleep, I like to be a good foot away from the emergency button, so I don't accidentally hit it in the middle of the night. That's all I need—police and paramedics busting into my house at three o'clock in the morning. I figure, with how often I need it, I'd rather do a little work to be able to hit it than have it easily accessible for an accidental chaotic situation.

I may have to crawl up my bed to reach it, but at least I don't have to crawl out of bed.

That's right. You read that right.

When I first moved into my house, I didn't have someone attach the button to the wall right away.

First idiot move.

I figured, if I really needed it, I could crawl out of bed, and it wouldn't be that bad, because the button would be right there.

Second idiot move.

I also figured that since I trusted that group of assistants so much, I didn't need to worry about someone not showing up.

Third and biggest idiot move!

Let's not even touch on the fact that some other emergency could've happened like a break in, or me puking, or . . . I don't know . . . a *fire!* If you're relying on other humans to keep you alive, you never, ever, ever, ever want to assume that everything will always go smoothly! Even if you have the most awesome group of assistants, they're still humans who have emergencies of their own.

One morning, I was waiting for an assistant to come. My mom had to switch days with her, so it wasn't her original day to work. Because of this, my mom confirmed it with her three times.

8:00 came. No assistant.

8:10. No assistant.

8:15. Something in me knew she wasn't coming.

8:20. I had to admit to myself that she wasn't coming.

8:25. I kicked my covers off, still hoping she would show up.

8:30. I positioned myself to gracefully fall out of my bed.

8:35. My legs were dangling off the bed, ready to do this, still hoping she'd walk into my house, even though I knew it wasn't going to happen.

8:40. Against all logic in my brain, my optimism won't give up. Or, more accurately, I really don't want to throw myself on the floor unless I absolutely have to.

8:45. I told myself she really wasn't coming, and I had to do this. I took a deep breath, sent up a little prayer to the sky, and not so gracefully slid off my bed.

I ended up conking my head on the hardwood floor. I laid there for a second to see if I had a concussion. I'm not entirely sure why I waited to see if I had a head injury when I was already planning to call the emergency service, but it just seemed like the right thing to do at the moment. After determining my head was fine—just a dull headache—I hit the emergency button, and they called my mom, who called the assistant. Not only did this assistant totally not acknowledge she had forgotten she had switched days, but she told me not to worry, that she would be there because she wasn't doing anything anyway.

The people I have to deal with sometimes, I swear!

Later that afternoon, my uncle nailed the button to a wall above my bed.

Okay, let's be real. The person I sometimes have to deal with is myself and my idiot moves.

8:14. Present day.

Damnit, Chloe! You have been late three times this month! Every time, I specifically ask you to call and give me a heads-up. Why can't you just respect me on this?

Any other job, someone would be fired if they were consistently late. For me, it's not that easy. I can't let someone go if I don't have someone else to fill their spot, and I can't always look for someone else if I feel things are going south, because there's a possibility the person I'll be replacing can find out, get mad, and quit on the spot.

This has happened to me once, so I'm not just being paranoid.

This is mostly why I feel like I have to walk on eggshells with everyone. I have had one too many people quit without notice, because of something I did or did not unintentionally set in motion, and it's a hellish situation. I don't give my assistants everything they want out of fear they will leave, but the fact that they could peace out on me anytime is forever and always in the back of my mind.

And if I do fire someone without having a replacement, my mom would have to come up from Florida every week to cover the shift. I have made the horrible mistake of doing this, purely out of annoyance with the assistant, and I thought my mom was going to blow a gasket on me.

I will never, ever, ever do that again unless the assistant puts me in danger.

In my defense, I did make sure her shifts were covered. I didn't fire her until I had a replacement, and after I made sure I would have coverage, all I felt was sweet relief I was going to have a new assistant instead. The world just wanted to play a dirty, evil trick on me—that assistant called seriously five minutes after I let the other go and said she was going to the hospital and couldn't work.

Needless to say, my heart dropped.

So, now you know why I'm extremely careful with everyone. I know it's not right, but in my experience, in this specific situation I'm in, it's literally better to be safe than sorry.

8:16 a.m.

Okay, this is ridiculous!

The only reason I'm more angry right now than concerned is that I've seen a pattern of being late, and I've noticed it became worse, despite talking to her. If there weren't a pattern, I'd be freaking out right now, thinking something happened to her or thinking she wasn't coming.

I feel like I've been trained to learn people's patterns more than the average person, so I know if something is normal or off.

If she isn't here at 8:20, I'm hitting the button!

Britney may say stupid crap, and I may have to push her to do some things, but at least she shows up on time and eventually does what I ask of her. Of course, I would love to have all awesome assistants. That's the dream here. However, given the choice right now, I would rather work with Britney than Chloe.

Okay, I need to think of something else for at least a minute or so. I'm not in denial of what's happening right now and what it probably means.

I need to think of something fun, like what I'm doing today.

I'm going to a camp reunion, and despite hating being in a group setting, I've been looking forward to it for weeks now.

I've gone to so many camps throughout my life, my friend once deemed me The Camp Tramp.

For the record, I only dated one guy from one of the camps I went to, and I wouldn't even classify it as dating, since we never kissed, held hands, or even freaking communicated outside of camp, so that name is purely a reference to all the camps I have *attended* and not the boys I dated there.

The very first camp I went to was a day camp for people with disabilities. It was basically like summer school, only we just hung out all day and had fun events like Carnival Day and Olympic Day. The first year, I didn't really like it, but the second year, I became good friends with my counselor for a period of time and continued to go for the next two years, even recruiting a few of my school friends to work there.

The first sleepaway camp I attended will forever and always have a place in my heart. I know words in a book won't do it justice, but it's very much a part of my life, so I have to try. This camp changed the course of my life, in every way possible. When someone asks, "If you could live anywhere in the world, where would it be?" my answer is always this camp.

When I was thirteen years old, I signed up for a website to get an ePal—basically a pen pal but over email. I've always found it easier to talk to my friends online rather than in person. Even before instant messaging became a thing, my friends and I would sit at our family's desktop computer, emailing each other, one after the other, like how two people have a conversation over texts today. I just found it more comfortable not to have my friends wait in awkward silence while I typed my answers.

I still find talking online is more comfortable.

I thought it would be cool to start a friendship completely over email.

I sometimes joke that I was meeting people online before it was the thing to do. In my head, I'm like, "You met your significant other online? Ha! I was meeting people online twenty years ago."

After posting a short bio about myself, including my likes and that I had a disability, I received about a dozen responses.

This is so cool, I thought. *I'm going to make a lot of new friends!*

There was one email that stood out to me. It was from a girl named Jenn, and she also had cerebral palsy.

I immediately emailed her back, telling her more about my CP, and that I drive my chair with my head because I didn't have any control of my hands.

It turned out that she had the same kind of CP, and she also drove her chair with her head because she didn't have any control of her hands.

How cool!

I then told her I was nonverbal and used a communication device.

You guessed it! She was nonverbal and used the same communication device, although was trying a new one.

No way!

If I hadn't been so young, I would've thought someone was pulling the ultimate prank on me.

The more we talked, the more we found out how similar we were.

We both liked the same music.

We had similar experiences when it came to our disabilities.

She loved to dance, and I loved to dance.

One day, she asked me if I'd ever heard of this therapy camp for kids who use communication devices.

I told her I hadn't and asked her to tell me more.

She sent me the website and told me to try to go so we could meet each other.

After I showed it to my mom, she called the director. Even though the deadline had passed, she begged her to make an exception. She told her my story about meeting Jenn online, and like everyone else who heard it, the director was amazed. She said if I sent in my application that week, along with a video of me using my device, she would see what she could do.

I had a feeling I was going to get in, but when I received the letter confirming it, I screamed.

I was going to camp!

I was going to meet Jenn!

When I arrived at camp, I went into the cabin my mom and I would be sharing with Jenn and her grandma. Parents and family members attended this week with us. My mom is *so* not a camp person, so props to her for agreeing to go!

Jenn and I didn't have the typical response for two friends meeting for the first time.

We didn't run and hug each other, because we couldn't.

We didn't even say anything to each other.

I simply smiled at her, and she smiled back, and that was everything.

Along with becoming better friends with Jenn, I also discovered my current communication device that week.

To be honest, I wanted to try it because everyone else had one, and even Jenn was trying one out.

Yes, for that one week, I was *that* kind of a teenager, and it ended up working out for me.

One afternoon, they let me skip my therapy group. They were having a session on how this device could work a computer, and they thought it would be appropriate for me and my mom to go. I sat by an employee for the company, PJ, and she held up her company device so I could see. As the session went on, my mom remembers my head becoming like a turtle's, stretching further and further out of my shell as I grew closer and closer to PJ's device. Finally, seeing how interested I was in it, PJ ripped off my device, put her device in front of me, stuck a switch to my headrest, and told me to have at it.

One of the most frequently asked questions I get is about how long it took me to learn how to use my communication device. My answer is always "Less than five minutes." People never believe it, but it's true.

I always say this device just came naturally to me. I don't know how else to put it.

I didn't have to use five switches anymore; I could just use one.

I didn't have to match nonsense pictures to make words anymore; I just had a keyboard with word prediction.

I don't know what else to say. This device just felt natural to me.

Needless to say, I started talking right away.

My mom was shocked.

PJ was shocked.

I think everyone at this camp was shocked.

PJ let me use it for the rest of the day and then the rest of the week.

When it was time to give it back to her, she slowly walked up to my mom and whispered, "I can't take this away from her."

My mom hugged her, and because the company was in driving distance of my house, she promised we would be there Monday morning to return it.

PJ didn't tell us at the time, but she was absolutely, positively, completely terrified. She was new to the company, only six weeks in, and she had just let us take her device eight hours away from her. She didn't know us from John down the street. She didn't know if we were going to bring it back. So, when we actually showed up on that Monday morning, she wanted to scream, "I'm not going to lose my job! I'm not going to lose my job!"

I returned it like a good little girl, stopped PJ from having a heart attack about looking for a new job, and started the process of getting my own device.

PJ is now one of my dear friends. Actually, she was the one who named me The Camp Tramp.

She did let me steal her device, so I guess I'm okay with the name.

I went to the camp as a camper for another year and then started volunteering and helping out for several years off and on.

If it were up to me, I would still be helping out each and every year.

When I was at this camp, everyone knew how I talked. Nobody looked at my mom or whatever assistant was with me to answer for me. When anyone asked me a question, they looked directly at me. It didn't matter if it took me two minutes or five minutes to type. Patience came first and foremost at this camp.

The first rest stop after camp was always a culture shock. Nobody looked me in the eye. If someone waited on me, they would speak to whomever was with me instead of asking me. Nobody knew what my device was, so they didn't even think to have the patience with me. Granted, I knew it was just ignorance, and nobody meant anything by it, but still, every time I had my first interaction following a week at camp, it was like, "Hello, Real World."

Unfortunately, my freshman year of college, Jenn passed away. I found out through an email from the director of the camp. I took a moment to remember her and everything she did for me. If I hadn't met her, I don't think I would've been sitting at a desk in a college dorm room a whole state away from my parents.

Thank you, Jenn, for changing my life.

The first sleepaway camp I went to without my parents was with a nondenominational religious group all my friends and I belonged to in middle school. Back then, I was more religious and had more friends than I have today, so I thought this was going to be paradise. Since it wasn't specifically designed for people with disabilities, my parents hired my friend's sister to go with me and be my assistant. Weeks earlier, my mom even drove up to the camp, which was a few hours away, to make sure it was accessible.

It was accessible.

I was going to go away for the weekend without my parents.

All my friends were going to be there!

What more could I want?

Ummm.

Maybe everything I needed to talk to others?

It would not be a true Sara Pyszka adventure without some P Luck.

Let me say it again: My mom drove two or three hours just to make sure there were no steps, because calling wasn't enough, apparently.

My parents had been teaching my friend's sister how to help me for weeks.

My friend was also going, and she also knew how to help me, because she was my friend.

I was so prepared for this not even forty-eight-hour trip.

When we arrived at the camp, my friend's sister put my communication device on my wheelchair. She went to grab the switch that I work the device with. Since I had brought my manual wheelchair that could collapse so I could ride the bus with everyone else, it wasn't automatically on my headrest. It wasn't in the bag that my device was in, either.

We checked my purse and suitcase.

Nada!

We called my mom.

Sure enough, my switch was just chilling on the kitchen table.

My mom offered to drive it up, since, ya know, talking was a vital part of a social gathering with friends, but it was already late Friday night and we would be leaving Sunday afternoon. We decided to just wing it and have everyone ask me yes/no questions, and if all else failed, go through the alphabet.

There you have it. My first weekend away from my parents. Had my communication device but didn't have the thing to operate said communication device.

That should be the very definition of P Luck.

That summer, I went away with the same middle-school group, this time, for a week-long camp.

Here are some highlights of that camp:

I had my communication device, and I had the switch to operate it. Score!

This camp was five hours away. Therefore, my mom did not drive to see if it was accessible.

It was not accessible. Every time I had to go in or out of the cabin, a group of guys would carry me up and down a flight of stairs. I also needed two people to push me up and down this massive hill of gravel.

All my friends were in the same cabin as me. Every night, we had a discussion about a certain topic, and all of us would eventually end up bawling our eyes out. It became the running joke—how many boxes of tissues would our cabin go through each night?

I still wonder what happened to the Christian band full of cute boys that was there the same time we were.

Finally, at this camp, I first heard the "Cha Cha Slide." We must have done it twice a day, if not more.

I didn't go to camps just as a teenager. A year or two ago, I was out to eat with my parents and some of their friends in Florida. The restaurant was right on the beach, and everyone wanted to go to the ocean to watch the sunset. Like most beaches, it wasn't accessible. As you can imagine, sand

and wheelchairs aren't really friends. Immediately and without hesitation, my dad volunteered to stay with me on the sidewalk while everyone else went down to the ocean to snap pictures on their phones.

Oddly enough, I didn't feel sad for myself. I never really had a thing for beaches, probably because I could never move around on them, and I couldn't really care less about the sun setting. But I felt sad for my dad. He didn't deserve to not go down to the water just because it wasn't accessible. He loves beaches. He loves sunsets. I told him multiple times he could go and that I was perfectly okay by myself. He waved his hand and told me he was good. Eventually, his friend came back up and offered to sit with me. Even though my dad came right back, he had taken up this offer right away.

My dad didn't *not* want to go down to the water.

He just didn't want me to be alone.

This made me extremely grateful and sad all at once.

The sadness carried through the next morning. It was more of an "I don't feel like I belong in this world; what can I do to fix this?" feeling. Like anyone who wants an answer, I turned to the trusted Google. I figured there had to be a more wheelchair-friendly vacation spot, even though my parents lived in Florida. I was looking for somewhere that had more than wheelchair ramps, basically.

I didn't have any luck, but I'm the world's worst Googler. Seriously, with all the time it takes me to type, scroll, click, and read, most five-year-olds could probably search the web better than I can. I'm sure there are a lot of more accessible vacation spots.

I then tried searching camps for adults with physical disabilities. I didn't necessarily want to go to a camp. I just wanted the atmosphere of a camp with my family, if that makes sense.

In my Googling, I came across a camp for adults with disabilities who graduated high school. Unlike the other camps I had gone to, they didn't take anyone with a cognitive disability. A traditional high school diploma was a requirement. Even though I couldn't take my family with me, I was intrigued. I didn't know how I felt about going to camp at thirty-two, but I had to admit I was digging the activities I could potentially do. After showing the pictures to my mom and my assistant, they convinced me to go.

The camp wasn't my jam, but I enjoyed the experiences I had—

Rode an adapted bike. Really cool.

Went up a fifty-foot wall in an adapted seat. Awesome.

Took a wheelchair ballroom dance class. Totally freaking amazing.

Tried canoeing, which I will never do again, because I discovered I'm completely and utterly terrified of huge bodies of water to the point we had to turn back around. Who knew?

Overall, I was happy with the experience, though.

I'm generally happy with my camp experiences, which makes this reunion something I've been looking forward to.

And it's now 8:19.

Grrrr!

Chloe! Seriously?

I debate to start the process of hitting the button, but I decide to give her a few more minutes.

I always do that—give people more time than they deserve. But again, I really don't like to hit the button unless I absolutely have to.

I make myself think about camp some more since that seemed to calm me down.

Pretty sure I wrote that previous sentence in my first novel, so for the moment, just call me Brynn Evason.

The camp I'm going to today, I would say, was my main camp.

My main camp? Gah. Now I really sound like a camp tramp.

When I was fifteen, my mom's friend told her about this music camp her daughter with a disability attended. It was forty-five minutes away from my house, and members of the Pittsburgh Symphony helped run it. My mom asked me if I wanted to go, even though she probably knew the answer.

A camp?

Involving music?

Hell yeah, I wanted to go!

Before she got my hopes up, or maybe it was after she got my hopes up, who the hell knows at this point, she called the camp, and explained that I was nonverbal, so she wanted to make sure I would be able to participate, since there was a massive concert at the end of the week.

"Of course," they told my mom. "This is a camp for all abilities. It's our job to find something she can do!"

After my first camp chorus class, I approached the teacher and introduced myself. A few weeks before this camp, I had discovered that my device had the ability to sing. I thought this was really cool. I told him this and asked him if I could do anything for the concert. I don't remember who came up with the idea, but we decided I was going to open the concert by singing the National Anthem.

Me?

The girl who didn't like to drive in front of crowds?

Was going to sing a song?

I wasn't just going to sing—I was going to open up a fricking concert by singing a song.

Who the hell was this chick?

Obviously, I wasn't always an introvert. I think I saw an awesome opportunity, and I went for it. I also think I was still young enough not to know how much other people's thoughts and opinions could affect me.

Andy, my chorus teacher, didn't know anything about my device, and I didn't know anything about reading or programming sheet music, but together, we figured it out. Because of this concert, we developed a forever bond between us.

Every day after class, Andy and I would work together. At first, Andy would have to point to a picture of what music note to choose, I would select it and assign a syllable to it (Yes, I typed out the entire National Anthem syllable-by-syllable and not word-by-word), Andy would show me what line the music note was supposed to go on, and I would raise it one pitch at a time.

He would also give me homework to do, because, ya know, the National Anthem has a thousand notes and a thousand syllables, and we only had four days. One night, I stayed up until one o'clock working. Since I was younger, I felt, ya know, like, really cool the counselors let me do that.

By the time I was done working with Andy, he could say, "Quarter note, B flat," or "Eighth note, C sharp," and I knew what he was talking about.

I'm just going to take a moment to gloat—I was really proud of that. I learned to read sheet music in fewer than four days.

I know that's small compared to other things that I could be proud about, but I don't know. Learning all the music notes, what they mean, and what each pitch is, for me personally, was one of my coolest accomplishments.

It really is little victories, huh?

The night of the concert came. I'm going to say I was so nervous, I blocked the entire performance from my brain. Seriously, I don't remember how I felt before the performance. I don't remember getting up on stage. I don't remember being introduced. I don't remember hitting the button to make my device sing. I don't remember everyone clapping for me. And I don't remember the rest of the show.

It's all good if you're thinking, "She really wrote a memoir when she doesn't remember half of the crap she did?" Because that's basically what I'm thinking right now, too.

Meh. Too late to go back now!

Here's what I do remember:

I was so proud of what Andy and I accomplished together, especially as two strangers.

Everyone that night was getting dressed up: the girls in cute sundresses and makeup, and the guys in nice khakis and button downs. Me? Are you ready for this? My outfit consisted of jean shorts and a white tank top with bright pink lips on it.

Oh, yeah.

Extremely. Classy.

I didn't know how fancy this concert was going to be! I didn't know I was going to have such a big part in it!

The final thing I remember is really wanting to surprise my parents. That was extremely important to me. I think I mentioned to my mom that I thought my device could sing, and I think she brushed it off, so my parents had absolutely no idea what was coming. I asked the director not to give my parents a program.

That job was accomplished, but here's what I don't know, and nobody seems to remember:

My entire family was there. Aunts, uncles, cousins, grandma, grandpa, brother, mom, dad. I just remember my mom and dad not getting a program. If this is true, my question is: how did none of my other family members spill the beans? I tried asking a few of my relatives, and our poor memories must run in the family, because they couldn't remember.

I guess this mystery will never be solved.

I think that same night, everyone asked me if I would go back the following year.

My answer was a big, fat absolutely!

The first time I attended music camp, I remember a girl wrote her own song. I thought that was really freaking cool of her. I think the moment I left camp, or soon thereafter, I knew that was what I wanted to do the next year. Between sessions, I made sure I wrote a poem, figuring that was how songs were written.

After I checked in and got settled at camp the second year, I found Andy. I told him my idea to write a song and showed him my poem. Kneeling beside me, he told me it was really good, but he said he couldn't help me. He then introduced me to someone who could.

Lucas.

At the time, Lucas was a conductor at the Pittsburgh Symphony. He took a look at my poem and agreed to help me. I was expecting him to put my poem to music. I imagined he would write out the music notes like Andy did the previous year, I would program the notes into my device, and I would sing it by myself.

Instead, I got so much more.

Our very first session, he said that my poem was good, but it needed some work before it could be a song. Mind you, at the time, I was listening to Avril Lavigne and Britney Spears. Although they will always be my comfort music, they aren't exactly the greatest songwriters.

That was pretty much the level of my poem.

For some reason, this stranger knew I could do better.

I will always be forever grateful of that.

He went through each line with me, asking me how I really felt and who the song was about. Because he wrote in a musical-theater style and not in a pop style, he also taught me some rules of the genre. For example, in pop music, it's okay to rhyme words like *try* with *life*. In musical theater, that's a massive no-no. In the musical theater world, *try* has to be rhymed with *why*, or *fly*, or *shy*, or *pie*.

I went to music camp two more times after this, and we wrote three songs together between them. These sessions became my golden therapy. I looked forward to these writing sessions all year. He would ask me how I was feeling, I could tell him anything without judgment, and he would help me put it into a song.

I'm telling ya.

Writing. Is. My. Therapy.

Personally, whenever I'm feeling so misunderstood or so alone that my chest is so heavy, it's the greatest feeling in the world to put my thoughts and feelings into words, whether it be a song, a poem, or a book—just let it go out into the world, and have people say, "Okay, I understand now."

And if someone says I wrote about what they're going through and they don't feel as alone anymore, the elephant on my chest disappears entirely and I feel like I have a purpose in this world.

People often ask me what I like more, writing books or writing songs.

This is a hard question for me to answer.

There's nothing like a song that nails right into the core of its emotion and setting my feelings free to an audience. It's like flushing the toxins out of my body. However, I can't do it by myself. Even if I were able-bodied and could play an instrument, I can't come up with a melody for the life of me. I would do the lyrics, for the most part, and Lucas would do the music. Maybe it would be different if I could mess around on a guitar or a piano, but it's hard to picture me doing what Lucas does.

There's also nothing like writing a book. Books I write 100 percent myself. Even though I make an income from it, it gives me a break from needing help all day—something that I so need. When I write, I'm in the driver's seat with both of my hands on the steering wheel, navigating the reader through a part of my life and making them feel all these different emotions. The fact that I can do that, again, gives me a purpose in life.

So, I guess my answer is that I like writing books and songs the same amount, just for different reasons.

When Lucas and I hammered out the lyrics to the first song, he moved to the piano. I figured it was just to come up with the music. When he said he would accompany me on the piano for the concert, I did a double take.

What?

He's going to play with me?

On the piano?

For the concert?

When I finally registered what he said, I screamed.

For the concert that year, I made sure I had a fancy dress.

And cute shoes.

This time, my parents received a program. When they saw I was singing a song called "Please Stay with Me," everyone started whispering, "Who sings this? What's this from? Is this from *RENT*?"

When they found out my song was not from a musical, but rather an original, my entire family cried, including my dad, who never cries.

When I aged out of the camp, Lucas and I continued to work together. It took us twelve years, but we finally had enough songs to make a one-act musical that we performed at the camp where we met.

To be honest, I don't know what we're going to do with the piece, but I'll keep ya posted.

Unfortunately, today I'm not going to see Andy or Lucas. It's not a music camp reunion.

The actual venue where the camp was held also hosted other camps each summer. Music camp and sports camp, which I also attended but didn't really like as much, were for people with all types of disabilities. A different, two-week camp the venue also hosted was for teens with just spina bifida. I became really good friends with a lot of people who went to the spina bifida camp, and I desperately wanted to go, even though I had cerebral palsy.

I mentioned this to a friend I'd made, she straight up asked the director, and they were like, "Sure! We'll see what we can do!"

I believe I went to this teen camp for two years. There were so many amazing memories, but here are some highlights:

Just hanging out in my unit with the girls. Instead of cabins, this camp had a lodge with six units and eight beds. Between activities, we would go to the lodge to take a break. Frankly, this was so everyone could go to the bathroom. However, this was one of my favorite parts of camp. I enjoyed just hanging out and talking. Even if I wasn't part of the conversation, I just enjoyed being there.

I was a weird child.

Scratch that.

I am a weird human being.

Talking to the counselors. Most of the time, because of my communication device, I can't keep up with a conversation. The bigger the group, the quicker I will get lost. When this would happen, a counselor would be at my side in a matter of seconds. Thinking about it now, it sounds like it would be demeaning to some degree, but I didn't take it that way at all. In fact, I found this extremely comforting. They would either let me say my thoughts about whatever topic that had already come and gone, or they'd strike up an entirely different conversation with me. My communication situation can be extremely frustrating sometimes, but it has also led me into some pretty intimate situations.

Feeling like I fit in when I didn't. As someone who is extremely unique, I generally feel as though I'm a jigsaw puzzle. Throughout my entire life, I felt like I fit in with a lot of different types of people, but with each group, something was always a little off. For example, I would have the same interests as a group of friends, but my disability would somehow get in the way. Or someone would be okay with people with disabilities, but our personalities majorly clashed.

At this camp, everyone could physically do more than me. (*Well, no shit, Sara! You did crash their camp! What did you expect?*) A lot of people used wheelchairs, but everyone could talk and use their hands. When they would do an activity, I would need a lot more help than everyone else. Or during a conversation between eight teenage girls, I would be just hanging out. However, despite being different, every single one of my fellow campers respected me and tried to include me as much as they could, and that was enough for me.

They had dances. Need I say more?

Finally, my favorite memory would have to be on the last night of camp. My ex-boyfriend, if I can even call him that, wanted to get back together. When I politely declined, he was an ass to me, making digs at me, not talking to me, not getting out of my way on the sidewalk. In general, he was just being a jackass.

I decided enough was enough.

I looked at my friend after the closing ceremony and typed, "Will you help me?"

"Umm," he hesitated. "Sure."

I then looked at their counselor and repeated, "Will you help me?"

I had them get toilet paper, pink streamers, and shaving cream. We then proceeded to go to town on his bed. If I said, "More toilet paper, streamers, and shaving cream!" they would do it.

I think what made it my favorite memory is that we all were laughing our asses off.

If someone can help me and have fun doing it, that is everything to me.

And my old boyfriend? I don't think he ever talked to me again.

I kind of lost touch with everyone. That's why I'm really looking forward to going today.

With the combination of not having great assistants, writing a lot, and generally not being a fan of social gatherings, I've missed so many get-togethers, I want to cringe. I'm looking at today as a chance to catch up with everyone and to show everyone I actually still care, and I want to stay connected.

8:23 a.m.

I hear my front door open and close.

I scowl at the clock.

For the love of everything holy!

Over twenty minutes late!

And no phone call!

When she gets in here, I'm going to distinctly motion to the clock.

I know that's not the professional way to correct someone. I know I should use my communication device. But I don't care!

This has happened one too many times, and I'm pissed!

I'm going to wait until she looks at me, and I'm going to fling my head toward my alarm clock.

I try my hardest to respect everyone, but when I have so many people disrespecting me on so many different levels, it's very hard not to have disrespectful thoughts enter my head. It's not often that I act on these thoughts, but today, I am!

Chloe opens my bedroom door and slowly walks to my bed.

I wait for her to look me in the eye.

She doesn't.

I then notice she doesn't have washcloths ready.

She runs her hand down her face and sighs.

Oh. No.

No, no, no, no!

No!

Because of my experience with her and other assistants, I already see my entire day playing out.

I push the thought away.

You don't know what she's going to do for sure. Try not to assume anything.

That didn't work.

My past experiences don't escape my mind.

I really try to give everyone the benefit of the doubt, but after I see the same behaviors lead to the same outcomes, it's hard for my brain to assume anything else. I hate that I do this, because it's so not what I stand for. However, I also think it's part of everyone's psychology.

And the fact that she's just standing there with her hand on her face, not saying anything?

Yeah, this is not good.

Immediately, I switch from pissed mode to crisis-management mode.

Even though I'm on my stomach and people have a hard time reading my head movements, I start to spell because . . . what else am I going to do? "Are you okay?"

Chloe's voice is soft. "No, I have a migraine. Third one this week." She rubs her eyes with both of her hands.

She drove here with a migraine?

She lives forty-five minutes away!

How did she do that?

Not to compare anybody, but when I get a migraine, I need to be in a dark room, no windows, no device, with the doors shut. I cannot even tolerate if the hallway light is on, or else I feel like I'm going to get sick.

I also had another assistant who got migraines pretty often. She felt one coming on, didn't feel safe driving, and asked me if I would mind if she slept it off.

Chloe still isn't moving. I still don't know what to do (again, really, what can I do?), so I continue to try to figure something out. "Did you try to get someone to come for you today?"

She paused, seeming as though it's a big effort for her just to talk. "No. I had it when I woke up, and that was six o'clock. I felt bad calling everyone that early."

But that's the point of everyone being a backup. To call them when you don't feel good or don't feel like you can come in.

"Do you feel like you can do all day?"

Still on my stomach. Still in crisis-management mode.

"Yeah. If you take it easy today . . . I should be fine."

I don't know if I'm annoyed or grateful right now.

I guess both.

She came to work when she wasn't feeling good. Not a lot of people would do that. I have to give her credit for that. She didn't leave me hanging, which means she understands my situation and her situation. I can't take that away from her. However, because she didn't want to call anyone for help, I now have to be extremely careful today, which means asking for the bare minimum, which means probably not going to the reunion.

It's a tricky situation, because what am I supposed to do?

How am I supposed to feel?

Some people would call me lucky, because at least she showed up.

At least I have a custom wheelchair.

At least I have a communication device.

At least I have a roof over my head, food in my fridge, and hands to help me.

And I agree. I'm very fortunate.

It's just that sometimes I feel like people think that should be enough for me and that I shouldn't be annoyed when stuff like this happens to me.

Are they right?

Do I want too much?

I'm not sure, but I firmly believe life is murky. I believe a person can be extremely grateful and extremely frustrated at the same time.

"Do you think you can get me up?"

Still on my stomach, but no longer in crisis-management mode, because I guess it's going to be whatever it's going to be.

"Yeah. I think so. Give me a second."

You think so?

Give you a second?

Oh, honey, why didn't you try to get someone else to come?

Again, at least she came.

Ahh! This is so confusing!

Chloe sighs heavily but doesn't move, and that's all it takes for me to start to doubt her condition.

Okay, if she brings up the reunion, I will definitely know. If she doesn't, I can have my guesses.

I swear I can tell if an assistant is actually sick or just wants to get out of something.

Reasons why I'm questioning Chloe at the moment:

She didn't try to get anyone to cover for her. She gets migraines regularly, apparently, and, again apparently, they knock her out for a day or two. Knowing she had to work a sixteen-hour shift, it doesn't make sense she wouldn't at least try to find someone else.

Nine times out of ten, if an assistant is sick, they will explain to me what's going on and ask me what I want them to do. She came in and didn't say anything. I had to ask her if she was okay. I had to ask if she could work today. I had to ask if she could get me out of bed, and only then did she need a moment. Nine times out of ten, this is typical behavior I see from someone who doesn't want to do something but doesn't want to say it.

She's just standing in my brightly lit bedroom, dramatically sighing every few seconds. Again, not to compare anyone, but if I had a migraine and told someone I needed a moment, I would take it somewhere dark and alone.

Finally, every time I want to go somewhere with her, the same thing happens. She seems to come down with something. If anyone else came in and told me they were not feeling well, I would be so much more sympathetic. I would have absolutely no problem canceling my plans and doing everything I could to help them. But with her, it's the same story every time.

Gah! I can't stand that I'm questioning someone's migraine.

It doesn't matter if she's telling the truth. If my assistant tells me they're sick, I have to go with it.

For a few minutes, she just stands in the middle of my bedroom, loudly sighing.

This is making me so uncomfortable.

If she needed a moment, she could go anywhere in my house. I wouldn't mind.

This is like a scene in a movie. I feel like she wants me to see her like this.

But again, I could be very wrong.

Chloe finally starts the process of uncovering me. Immediately, I feel my body tense.

Damn!

I know what's happening.

Son of a . . .

Whenever I get suspicious of something, for example, if someone is grumpy and I think it has something to do with me, or if someone is in a bad mood and not talking, or if I think someone knows what I'm thinking, my CP acts up. Even if I know the best thing to do is to go along with it, to be chill and to push it out of my brain for the moment, sometimes my body doesn't get the message.

I would say this is one of the things I hate the most about my disability. A, it doesn't help anything if I'm spazzing with someone who doesn't feel good, and B, my body is doing the exact opposite of what my brain wants to do, which is to make everything easier for that person. It's very deceiving for the person, even if they know me very well. I've been accused multiple times of doing it on purpose.

But I guess this is part of having neurons that misfire.

When Chloe tries to flip me over, my arm jerks up, almost hitting her in the face. She gasps and jumps back with a disgusted look on her face.

Words cannot describe how I feel when I try to go out of my way for someone, and not only does my body betray my good intentions, but I almost take their eye out, as well.

I seriously don't know what to do right now.

I guess the only thing I can do is go along with whatever my body is going to do.

A long time ago, my mom actually told me it was hard for her to wrap her head around the fact that I don't have any control over my body because I'm so smart. I know she doesn't think this anymore, but this definitely is not or was not the case. Even though I know what I'm doing is wrong, and annoying, and downright embarrassing for me, it's not like I have a switch in my brain I can flip to shut off my body.

Sometimes, my body is going to do what it's going to do, and that just sucks.

I do send up a little prayer to the sky. Even though I know that won't stop my body, I need all the possible help I can get today.

Still making a disgusted look, she manages to flip me over and turns me horizontal on the bed, grabbing me a little harder than she usually would. She takes my diaper off, and without cleaning me, she puts my pullup, socks, pants, and shoes on.

Yeah, today is going to be one hell of a day.

Now, I could've corrected her. When she took my diaper off and didn't immediately wash me, I could've said she was forgetting to. However, I was in a position where all four of my limbs were pressed against the bed. I had tightened my entire body against the bed and was using it to my advantage. If I told her she didn't clean me, I would get nervous, she would try to move me, and there would be a good chance some part of my body would try to take her out again.

I really can't afford that right now.

Some people think that I don't ask for what I need out of fear. I can honestly say that's not true. Sometimes, I know what their reaction is going to be. Sometimes, I don't have the energy to explain exactly what I need. Sometimes, something else is more important at the moment, for example, not having a CP attack.

If I really felt that gross, I would've spoken up, but my only priority is to get to the bathroom and get in my wheelchair without having another CP attack.

Yes, an assistant coming when they don't feel good has to be a major pain in the ass for them. I will never discredit them for that. However, it also puts a strain on me, because I want to do everything I can to help them, and when I can't do that, I always feel guilty.

Chloe manages to get me on the lift, and my body manages to work with me. Once I'm on the toilet, Chloe leans against the door and whips out her phone!

Holy crap!

Seriously?

Oh, my God. Okay. Seriously.

Not only do I have a guideline about not using cell phones while I'm in the bathroom, which she abandoned a few months ago, but how the hell can she scroll through a tiny screen when she has a migraine?

I have a four-inch screen on my wheelchair that shows me what mode I'm in. If I even accidentally turn it on while I have a migraine, I feel like the contents of my stomach are going to see the light of day again.

Again, Sara. Everyone is different. You can't judge her based on your own experiences.

Still, though. I can't help it. I have to ask.

I get her attention and start to spell. "Doesn't your phone bother your migraine?"

Immediately, her chuckling fades away. "Yeah, a little. But I have the blue light turned off. Having it off really helps your eyes."

Still, though. You're reading! And it's still focusing your eyes on light! And tiny print!

I don't understand!

Before I could tell her I was done, she leaned over and looked into the mirror, chuckling to herself some more. "My hair is a mess," she turned to me. "This morning, I stopped at the gas station to get some energy drinks. The lady at the cash register pointed to my hair and said that I must've had a *fun* night last night. Little does she know Mike and I aren't talking."

She stopped to get energy drinks with a migraine?

When she was already going to be late?

What the hell?

"The dog pooped again in the living room, again, you know. Yeah, this is the second time in a week! When I woke up, there was a big pile of dog crap by my shoes! So, I just left it there! I'm sick of cleaning up after him! He wanted a dog, so I'm not cleaning up after it anymore!"

I force down a gag.

Okay, I don't care if this is being judgmental, but if you have animal crap in your house, you should want to get it out right away! Even if you don't want to do it, wake your boyfriend up! The longer it sits on the floor, the longer the stench is going to be in the house!

She lightly chuckles. "Payback! That will teach him to treat me like crap!"

Mind you, I'm still on the toilet. This is weird, but sadly, this isn't the weirdest bathroom situation I've been in.

Once, I was sitting on the pot, doing my own thing, minding my own business, when an assistant ran into my bathroom, exclaimed, "Oh, my God! My boyfriend just took money out of my bank account again!" And she proceeded to hold up the phone to my ear, so I could hear the message from her bank!

Sometimes, I seriously wonder what the hell my life is.

I don't think I will ever forget that.

"He can be such an ass sometimes," Chloe continues. "This will be good for him."

I recently realized assistants absolutely, positively, cannot stand when I try to give them suggestions about their personal lives. I can't blame them. It drives me nuts when they try to tell me what to do, so why should they feel any different? Therefore, I try my hardest to bite my tongue if they happen to vent to me.

Today, though, I don't know if it's the weirdness of the morning or her attitude, but I can't help but spell out, "You seem really unhappy with him over the past few months. You broke up a few times already. Is there a reason why you keep going back to him?"

She peeks in the mirror again, ruffles her hair, looks directly at me, and smirks. "Because it would be punishment for me when we do have a *fun* night."

Oh.

Oh!

Oh! Oh, my God!

Holy crap!

Okay.

As she takes me off of the toilet, I nod to myself. *That's what I get for not minding my own business. Didn't need to know about her sex life!*

Once I'm in my wheelchair, she asks me what I want to wear today. Her voice is soft again, and I realized it had been totally normal in the bathroom.

She hadn't even sounded like anything was bothering her.

In fact, she was even laughing and smiling.

Now, she's quiet and weak again.

Ahhh!

This is probably one of the hardest things I have to do. I hate lying. I mean, I despise lying. I think it's because people have been lying to me my entire life, whether it be because they don't want to do something for me, or they feel uncomfortable with me, or they don't want to hurt my feelings. I remember it starting in elementary school and continuing throughout my life.

Unfortunately, I've accepted it's going to be part of my life forever, and there are going to be times where I can and will do something about it and times where I can't do anything about it.

I push all the thoughts away. I tell myself it doesn't matter if she's lying to my face right now. For right now, I'm the employer, and she's the employee, and all that matters is her answer.

I need to know what I'm doing today before I pick out my shirt

I start spelling, absolutely hating the position I'm in. "I don't know if you remember but—"

"You texted me," she finished my sentence. "You're supposed to go to your camp today. You asked me to get dressed up." She closed her eyes and rubbed her temples. "And apparently, I forgot."

I give her a minute as she sighs.

I don't understand.

How can she be okay one minute and then . . .

Again, doesn't matter if she's lying to you.

Just focus on getting an answer.

I give her another minute.

When she looks up at me, I start to spell again. "Do you think you can go?"

I know the answer. I have to ask anyway. If I don't, I would be assuming that she can't, and I don't want to mess with that.

"I don't know, Sara," she almost whines, which instantly hits a nerve in me. "I can probably drive you, but I will probably just sit in the car while you do your thing. I'm also afraid if we go and if my migraine gets worse . . ."

Yep. Got it. We're not going.

I'm not going.

Even though I saw this outcome as soon as she came in, my heart sinks.

"I mean, it's up to you. I think I'll be fine, but I'm not sure. You decide."

She's seriously putting this on me now?

Ohhh, no!

I'm supposed to decide whether or not I want to drive with her when she already told me she's not sure she could make it?

What am I going to say? "Sure! I will take a chance on my life, your life, and my very expensive vehicle!"

Hell fricking no!

Or . . .

Wait.

Is that what employees are supposed to do? Tell their employers what they think they can and cannot do and have them decide?

I have no idea!

So freaking confusing!

"I could ask my sister to take us. She's not doing anything. I will text her right now."

I appreciate the offer, but I shake my head.

I'm not going to put out someone I don't know just because my assistant can't take me.

And if she really is going to sit in the car the entire time, can you say *awkward*?

And even if she offers to come in, I would never in a million years have her do that.

I made that mistake once, and that was one too many times.

I had to go into work at the company that makes my communication device. Chloe was scheduled that day, and, of course, she claimed she wasn't feeling well. I didn't know what to do. I wanted to respect her, but at the same time, they had said they needed me, and I said I would be there. I don't remember what I said to Chloe, but we ended up going.

I get embarrassed over stuff, but give me a couple minutes, and I will get over it.

This day, I would have to say, was one of the most embarrassing days of my life.

I was assigned to work with someone in their office. These offices aren't that big. I want to say if there are more than three people in it, with one being in a wheelchair, everyone is on top of each other. Chloe took a seat by the door, sprawled out, and closed her eyes.

And when I say sprawled out, I mean it in every sense of the word. She was slouched down in the chair, her legs were spread open, both of her arms were dangling down at her sides, and her head was thrown back.

Honestly, she looked like she was dead.

Holy crap, I thought. *This is happening. Yeah. This is really happening.*

I was working with someone closely that day, so I didn't want to correct her in front of him. Even though she was making me feel a deep shade of red inside, I didn't want to embarrass her or start something at my place of work. Instead, every so often, I would say her name. She would pop her head up, look around, and lay her head back down.

Because I only come in occasionally, all the employees I know always stop in and catch up with me when I'm there. Since it was my first time there in a while, everyone was stopping by. They would see Chloe basically passed out, do a double take, and either lower their voices or say they would come back.

Finally, I couldn't take it anymore. More and more people were starting to see her, and I had to then do some work with the head of the department. I asked Chloe to come stand by me. When she asked why, I think I kinda-sorta shrugged it off and just made her do it. It helped, though. She didn't look like a dead person and even went to get a cup of coffee.

Why hadn't she grabbed a cup of coffee beforehand? I have no idea.

One thing that I really have to start stressing when I interview new assistants is that they're not only helping me with my daily living, but they're also representing me whenever we go out. If they don't talk to me the right way, other people are going to follow their lead. If they're going to act inappropriately, other people are going to think I'm okay with it.

I really need to figure out what to do in situations like this.

"Are you sure you don't want me to ask my sister?" Chloe asks me. "She doesn't work or anything."

I shake my head. Even if someone else drove me, I would really like someone who knows my alphabet code to be with me. Yes, all my friends know I use a communication device. They all know to be patient with me.

However, although every single one of them knows this, sometimes, in a group setting, patience just doesn't exist. I don't feel comfortable going into a group setting without someone to help me communicate faster.

"Do you want to ask Amber or Britney to take you? I'm sure they wouldn't mind."

Now you want to ask someone to cover for you!

No!

Wait!

You want me to ask them, because I want to go somewhere!

Ahhhh!

I don't know what to do!

Again, if I knew she was really sick, I wouldn't be having this internal argument.

I have to ask her a question before I answer hers. "If I don't go to the reunion, do you think you can do all day?"

She sighs yet again. "Yeah. I can do all day. I just don't think I can take you anywhere, Sara."

Here's the thing: I would absolutely love to text Amber and ask if she could come in. Truthfully, I think that's what Chloe should've done first thing this morning. I know Amber would take me to the reunion. I know she would have fun. I know she would make sure I could say whatever I wanted to. However, I really don't like to call a backup just because. There are going to be times when I will really need someone to come in. I don't want to use one of my aces just because someone can't take me to a social gathering.

Am I doing the right thing?

Should I call someone so that Chloe can go home?

I don't know.

I feel so unsympathetic, but I don't want her to think she has an out every time I have to go somewhere.

I tell her I'm not going to go, and not to worry about it, and to grab me any old tunic.

9:52 a.m.

"I'm going to go downstairs and sit in the bathroom," Chloe says after we finish my morning routine. "I need to be in the dark for a while. Are you sure you don't want me to text my sister? I don't want you to miss your thing because of me."

I nod, confused.

If she needs to be in the dark now, which is what I expected in the first place, how would she make it sitting in the car for a few hours, even if her sister drove? It's a sunny day.

"Okay. Text me if you need me. I will have my phone."

Again, I wonder if I'm doing the right thing.

Should I text Amber or Britney to see if they could come in, if she's not going to do much all day?

But she said she could do today. She said it more than once.

Ahh!

I sorely wish there was a class about managing personal assistants in the "real world" just like I had to take my freshman year of college. It would be so helpful for me to have some guidelines right now.

But I suppose every person who uses personal care assistants is in a different situation and has different standards, so I guess it would be impossible to have a class that covers all the possible scenarios that could happen.

I guess it's up to me as an employer to come up with what I can and cannot tolerate.

I make a mental note to take some time to sit down and really think about this.

I also make a mental note to talk to Chloe on a day she's feeling better. This has gone on too long, and I have no idea what I'm going to say, but this has to stop. We need to figure it out.

Right now, I have to do something that's going to break my heart.

In my living room, I turn on my TV and wake my computer. After checking my email, I go to Facebook. I click on the Events page. Forcing away tears, I click the box to type something to the group. In typical Sara Slow Speed, I craft my message.

"Hey everybody. I want to cry right now. I don't think I am going to make it. My assistant has a migraine and can't drive me. I really can't stand depending on somebody. It's hell. My heart is breaking right now. Anyway, I love you and I miss you ALL."

I hit the blue button, making it official.

For a moment, I stare at my post.

This is just not fair.

If I were Inside Sara, I would just get up and go without worrying about anyone, even if I had a boyfriend.

I have to make an effort to show everyone I still care.

Maybe when I have a stable group of assistants, I'll reach out to everyone.

I don't know when that will be, and I don't know what I'll do, but I'll figure out something.

I have a lot of stuff I have to figure out.

Just then, a friend comments on my post. He was the one who helped me trash the jackass's bed all those years ago. "We will miss you, P!"

P became my nickname. I have no idea how or why, but at one point, it was weird for me to hear anyone from that camp call me by my actual name.

I close my eyes. I miss those days. To everyone, I was just P. Somehow, that was enough for me.

His comment tugs on my heart a little. Somehow, I know this is it. Case closed. End of discussion. Nothing else will come of it. I made my decision not to take extraordinary measures to get there, and I have to just go with it.

Still, my reaction confuses me.

What the hell was I expecting? My relationships with everyone in this group had been crumbling for a couple of years now, mostly because I have missed a lot of get-togethers (because of not having the right assistants!). I was hoping to get my foot in the door, I decided that I couldn't, I explained to everyone my situation, and someone from the group politely responded.

It sucks, but I know it is what it is.

But I don't understand why I'm so upset right now.

I didn't expect everyone to change their plans just because I can't be there, nor would I want anyone to do so.

Maybe I wanted to go more than I thought I did.

Probably.

Yeah.

I think that's it.

Alright. Time to get off Facebook!

I've always had trouble with friendships, whether I was in fifth grade or five years out of college. When I started writing this book, I knew I wanted to write about my struggles with friends. I had to. However, I did not or do not want to call out anyone. I kept thinking throughout this process how I would tackle this subject without betraying anyone's trust.

Finally, just a chapter or two before I wrote this one, the perfect solution came to me.

Or so I hope.

In my novels, *Dancing Daisies* and *Switch the Song*, each of the characters represents a certain group of friends in my life. Some people think each character is based on a specific person in my life, and this is not true at all. I've noticed that my friendships have certain patterns to them. The same kind of people almost always have the same kind of behaviors, reactions, etc. I'm going to take some characters from my book and explain what pattern of friendship they represent.

For those of you who read my novels, I think this might be neat for you. Think of it as a behind-the-scenes of the creation of the characters.

For those of you who didn't read them, I hope this piques your interest to do so! I tried to avoid as many spoilers as I could, but one or two may have slipped out. Who's to say?

Okay, first up, we have Meg.

Sara Pyszka

Meg is the best friend to my main character, Brynn. Or, at least, Brynn thought she was her best friend. They would do everything best friends would do: go out, talk about their love lives, watch movies, gossip. Physically, Brynn is a carbon copy of me, so Meg would help her out with anything she needed—eating, drinking, even going to the bathroom. When it was just the two of them, Meg wouldn't make a big deal over anything, but when someone was with them, she would make sure every move she made was seen. When Brynn happen to make a bad move, even if she couldn't help it, Meg would make sure everyone in the room knew about it by calling Brynn out on it.

Eventually, Brynn slowly realizes that Meg was using her and her disability to make herself look good.

Unfortunately, I've had about five Megs in my life. If I had only one or two in my life, I don't think I would put a character like this in the forefront of my book, but since this has happened so many times, I felt like I had a responsibility to show this can and does happen.

I've had people jam out to Taylor Swift with me, and then the next time we were with someone, tell me to my face how much of a dork I am for liking her music.

I've had people help me buy a pair of shoes and then have them criticize me in front of their friends for never wearing those shoes I just *had* to have.

I've had people offer to help me when we're with a group of us and then loudly exclaim at the restaurant that I'm so hard to help.

I've had people come to my house every day just to hang out and then have them loudly exclaim, "It's so hard being your friend!" Their tone still rings in my ear to this day.

I've even had people straight up tell me (about these people), "Sara! They are using you! Get the hell away from them!"

One Meg Moment distinctly stands out in my mind, and if it's still with me after all this time, I don't think it's ever going away.

One afternoon, a Meg and their friend stopped over to say hi. They said they were going to the mall. They asked me if I wanted to come. I wasn't doing anything, and I was bored, so I agreed to go. As they were helping me get ready, they loudly announced, "I feel good! I'm doing my good deed of the day!"

I *distinctly* remember the tone of their voice, but I honestly think I mentally blacked out after that.

I don't remember what I said.

I don't remember what I did.

But I didn't go to the mall with them.

I'm sorry, but even if you feel good about doing something for someone, especially if they call you a friend and you call them a friend, you shouldn't proudly exclaim you're doing your good deed. You're going to sound so insincere, and your friend is going to feel like a box you just want to check off.

Oh, yeah. One more thing a few of my Megs would do: ask me to hang out or go somewhere and then proceed to ask if they could get paid for it.

Gah! I have no idea how I'm not more screwed up!

I mean, I'm definitely screwed up, but here I am, alive and kicking . . . and not going to my reunion because I'm worried about someone who may or may not be lying to me.

Yeah.

I have no idea why the Megs do what they do. I'm not in their heads. But here are my two theories.

Theory One: Insecurity. Every single one of us has flaws. Nobody has ever been perfect, and nobody ever will be. Most of us know this and accept it. The Megs in my life always seem to have flaws they don't want to face. They want everyone to think they're awesome. Therefore, they seem to befriend the weaker man (I despise that term), so no matter what they do, they come off as a good person. And if the weaker man happens to make a mistake, it's even better for their ego.

Theory Two: Jealousy. Despite having a disability and having to deal with uneducated people on a regular basis, I have a pretty good life. I've always had all the equipment I needed. I had a pretty good education. Even though my friendships have always been rocky, I always had someone I could, at least, small talk with. I am financially stable. My parents have always been there for me. I have always had a good place to live. Whenever I saw an opportunity that felt right for me, I jumped on it and usually succeeded. I will never understand why, but some people just cannot stand to see someone like me doing well. And so, when they see me mess up or see one of my flaws, it's like a gold mine to them. They feel the need to call me out on it.

Never in a million years will I understand why this happens—specifically, why people get off on bringing other people down, but luckily, when I meet somebody new, and they seem like they might be a Meg, I quietly get myself out of the situation before it progresses.

Life is too short to be around insecure and jealous people who only want to bring you down.

Sometimes, I feel incredibly sad for my younger self. I would meet a Meg and try so hard to be friends with them until it mentally scarred me. However, I can't change the past. I can only be thankful that I learned from the past and will never make the same mistakes again.

Another thing that I had Meg, the character, do (I'm kinda liking the phrases *Meg, the character*, and *the Megs of my life*) is start dating the guy Brynn was in love with. Brynn would talk about him to Meg every chance she got, so Meg knew what she was doing. She even assured her he felt the same.

This is not a spoiler, because it's revealed in the first chapter of my first novel!

Although this isn't just a Meg thing to do, this happened about four times in my life, if not more. At least four guys I was into (at different times) have went for my friend or my assistant. Even though it's against the girl code, this happens to a lot of people, and again! I felt a responsibility to put it in my memoir.

It probably doesn't happen more than once to the same person, though; I feel like I have a curse on me and I'm going to break some kind of record and win an award, but if it happens again, I don't even think I would be hurt about it. I'd be like, "Alright. Can we go for a sixth time? How about seven? Ooh, let's make it eight?"

I don't know why this is a common trend in my life. I don't know why they think this is okay to do. All these girls knew I had feelings for the guys, so I don't know if they thought my feelings didn't matter or if they felt superior because the guy liked them and not me. I don't know why they always had to keep it a secret from me and not have an honest conversation with me. I don't know if the guys really liked the girls for who they were or if they were attracted to them just because they were helping someone in need. I don't know if people form bonds with each other just by being *my* friends. Most importantly, I don't know why they do it in the first place.

When this happens, I'm always more hurt by the girls than the guys. Sure, it's disappointing when someone doesn't like me or even doesn't even want to try to get to know me better, especially when they have known me and my friend for the same amount of time. I want to be like, "And how do you know, just because she can walk and talk, that she's going to be a good girlfriend?" However, I firmly believe people can't help who they're attracted to. If a guy knows I have a thing for him, doesn't feel the same, and doesn't get my hopes up, I will never hold it against him if he doesn't want anything with me.

How could I?

The girls, however, I really have a hard time with.

Up until a few years ago, I used to talk about the guys I liked to everyone and anyone. It's extremely difficult for me to admit this, because it's so embarrassing, but I think I did it to show people I was just like everyone else. I wanted them to know I like guys. I wanted them to know I was a sexual being. Because maybe if they knew that, they would think of me as their equal.

Now that I'm older, and probably because I have one too many scars, I never talk about my personal life to anyone anymore. Except in this book, which anyone in the world could read, because, apparently, I'm insane. When I do slip up and start telling someone something personal, opinion after criticism after opinion comes rolling in, and I don't have the energy to defend my choices anymore.

Plus, there are so many other ways to be someone's equal that doesn't involve talking about guys.

Okay, Meg is probably the hardest character to talk about, because some of the things she did in the book are very real to my life. I wanted to get the hard stuff out of the way first and then move on to lighter topics.

The next character I'm going to cover is a favorite of mine.

To get away from the madness of Meg, Brynn goes to a sleep-away camp in *Dancing Daisies*. Within twenty minutes of being there, she meets a girl with pink hair and a heart as open as the sky. Randi is a badass, somewhat of a rebel, and she truly doesn't give a crap about what anyone thinks. She is sarcastic as hell, but if someone actually messes with any of her friends, she'll have no problem kicking ass. From their very first conversation, she instantly accepts Brynn into her circle of friends, not even blinking at her disability when others do. Over the course of the two novels, we see Brynn and Randi become best friends outside of camp, from texting about everyday crap to going on a road trip or two.

I've only had about two Randis in my life. Sure, I had a lot of people look past my disability. I had a lot of people stick up for me when I was hurting. I've had friendships where we texted each other every day about nothing in particular. People would joke with me, and I would joke with them. I've watched movies until three o'clock in the morning with people. I've laughed so hard with people that I've peed my pants. I've gone on road trips with people.

I have felt like I could be myself with so many people, and I will always be thankful for that.

Here's the thing: You can get a lot of people in your life who will do a lot of things for you. If you have one person in your life who will do all of that with you and stick with you year after year, decade after decade, that is gold.

That is a Randi.

Do not take your Randi for granted, and do not do anything to screw it up with your Randi!

Unfortunately, another theme in my life is that friends seem to come and go. As of writing this book, I have about two friends who I kinda-sorta maybe almost but not really talk to on a regular basis, and by that, I mean we email once a month, if that. Everyone else that I have these really fantastic memories with? We don't talk anymore. And if we do talk, it's only once or twice a year.

I have theories about why this happens more with me than anyone else.

Gah. I didn't know how many theories I'd come up with until I wrote this book.

Theory One: I didn't know how to be a good friend. I've met most of the people in my life before the age of twenty-two. That blows my mind to think about, but it's true. Like most people under the age of twenty-two, I didn't know who I was. I honestly didn't think my disability stopped me from doing anything. That said, if I didn't know what I was or wasn't capable of, I had absolutely no idea what I should or shouldn't be doing with a friend. For example, when I was little, I would make my friends play school or play house. I would basically make them do whatever I physically wasn't able to do. As little kids do, they would get tired and want to do something else. I wouldn't want to do something else, because I wasn't tired of seeing them doing what I couldn't.

Another example of this: when I was a teenager, I would have my friends put me on my bed, turn music on, and I would move around. I would have them talk to me, but of course, I couldn't talk back. They would be okay with it for a couple minutes, but then they would want to do something else. I, however, was happy just hanging out, so I didn't think we needed to do something else.

As I'm writing this, I'm shuttering to my very core.

And I didn't do it thinking, "My friends should do whatever I want and whatever I say because I have a disability." I truly, legitimately didn't know any better.

I have memories of doing this to so many people in so many different ways, it's disgusting.

If you're one of the people I unintentionally bossed around, I am so sorry.

Like any sane person pushed into doing something they didn't necessarily want to do, all of my friends had drifted away from me.

Frankly, I don't blame them.

I think that's why I really don't like telling assistants what to do, even though my life literally depends on it. I think I was in that situation for so long without knowing it, and felt a lot of people leave my life because of it, that I now fear that everyone is going to have the same reaction, despite this being a totally different situation.

Unfortunately, people typically have only one chance to make a first impression. With how severe my disability is, I feel like my first impression to others is skewed from the get-go, so I have to work twice as hard until people get to know the real me. Likewise, if I even remotely make a mistake, I feel like their impression of me drops a lot faster than anyone else's would. Again, I feel like I have to work twice as hard to bring it back up.

What deeply saddens me about meeting the majority of people I've interacted with before I was twenty-two is that I feel like I learned so much these past few years. I feel like a different person. Over the course of my life, I've met some outstanding people whom I really liked. I felt like they could've been Randis to me. However, because it was years ago when I met them, they have all moved on to the point that I don't feel comfortable reaching out to them now.

To sum up, I feel like I missed out on a lot of really cool friendships because I didn't know myself or what kind of a friend I could be.

Okay. End of Theory One. That was intense, even for me.

Theory Two, which will be a lot shorter.

People in the disability community, whether someone with a disability themselves or someone who knows or loves someone with a disability, see me. They want to get to know me. They think I'm cool. They want to be my friend.

I have no problem with this. I will never discriminate trying to be friends with someone based on disability or their relationship to it. However, just because someone is okay with my disability doesn't mean we're going to be friends.

The most common problem I experience with this is we try to get to know each other, and we find out we have nothing in common.

They might be political. I want nothing to do with politics.

They might be super religious. I send up a little prayer every once in a while, but I'm not a church person.

I love to read. The last book they read might have been in high school.

I could care less about sports while they could never miss a game.

My perfect day off consists of binge-watching a show and getting takeout. They might not be able to sit still and prefer to be out on the town.

I'm not saying I can't be friends with someone who is extremely different. In fact, I'm very open to adopting new hobbies. But, if the only root of our friendship is our disability, things are bound to go south.

I want to say this is a shame, but, really, when I think about it, it's not. Everyone who identifies with a certain group isn't going to be friends with everyone else in said group. Sure, we're going to have a certain respect for one another, but they aren't going to all be friends. Why should disability be any different?

Likewise, if I meet someone with the same interests—reading, writing, music—and they don't have much else to do with the disability community, I don't want to say they aren't okay with my disability, but things get a little tricky because of my disability.

For example, the most important thing I need from anyone is patience. If someone doesn't have patience, I cannot have a relationship with them. Almost everyone I meet who has the same interests or has a really cool personality has their own thing going on. They're busy. Therefore, they don't have patience, especially for someone they don't know. And I truly don't think it has anything to do with me. I just genuinely feel like if I'm not working closely with them or talking to them on a regular basis, they aren't going to have time to befriend a random stranger, if that makes sense.

Theory Three: It's confusing.

Most of my friends now have been assistants who worked for me. Naturally, I like to hire people who have a similar personality to mine so we'll be on the same brainwave. Naturally, we end up bonding over the same interests, talking more, and watching movies and shows together. I even end up going out more when they work just because, naturally, I like to go places with people I like. This seems to be fine when they're working. When they're off the clock, it gets tricky.

Should I text them about something they like?

Should I invite them to an event I'm having?

Do they feel like they have to come?

Will they get paid if they do come?

This isn't much of a problem now, but when I was in college . . . oh boy.

Unlike now, I would have people come for only an hour throughout the day. If I was doing something they were interested in, such as watching something they enjoyed, I would tell them they could stay. In the moment, they genuinely seemed like they wanted to. They would get all comfy in my apartment and we would essentially have a girl's night. A few days later, however, they would tell me they only saw me as their boss, not as their friend.

I don't know why, but this didn't sink in. Maybe because I was twenty and I was hardly, hardly a boss.

I mean, technically, I was their boss, but I sure as hell didn't act like it, and they sure as hell didn't act like employees.

A few days later, they would ask me if I wanted to go out to a bar with some friends. Not thinking about it, I would go, and we would seem to have a great night, even taking some silly pictures. A few days after, the boss/friend thing would come up.

Still, it didn't sink into my thick skull. It embarrasses me to admit this, but I think part of me blocked it out because I enjoyed their company so much and truly thought we were actually friends.

This will never make sense. There they were, telling me I wasn't their friend, and I was just blowing it off like it was nothing.

I don't understand what the hell I was thinking!

I want to say actions speak louder than words, but I can't, because I don't even remember telling that to myself.

We would go to movies.

We would go to the mall.

We would go on road trips.

We would host parties.

I even went to their houses so I could meet their parents.

Still, the You're Not My Friend Thing would keep coming up.

I have no doubt in my mind that situation was just as confusing for them. Maybe they wanted to be my friend but . . . I have no idea. I wasn't in their heads, so I'm not going to put words in their mouths.

It finally hit me one weekend when one of them came to my house in Pittsburgh. She was being my assistant, but we were also having a great time. She was telling me personal stuff, I was telling her personal stuff, and we were genuinely doing what good friends would do. At the end of the weekend, however, she told me she couldn't come see me anymore unless I paid her.

Can you say buzzkill?

I understand where she was coming from. If she thought of me as a job, why would she drive a few hours just to be with me when she wasn't getting paid?

But, damn!

It was like the message they had all been trying to get across to me had finally smacked me in the heart, and when it did, it left a huge scar.

That weekend was the last time I talked to this assistant. I didn't try to reach out to her (why would I?), and she has never tried to contact me again.

Today, whenever someone even mentions her name, either a cold feeling runs through my body or I start to cry.

I know there's nothing I can do about it. I know I can't change the past, but if I could go back in time, I would tell my younger self that sometimes words speak louder than actions. I would make myself get out of these situations.

But then, who's ever in a situation where someone is repeatedly telling you they aren't your friend?

More importantly, who the hell sticks around for that?

Oh, my younger self.

Sometimes, she kills me!

My final thought about why I don't have many friends isn't really a theory but more of a fact. When I finally realized this after almost thirty-four years, I was like, "Oh. Oh! Oh! Holy crap! This makes so much sense!"

Most people my age have a life. They probably have a significant other. They may have children. They are probably starting a family. If they're single, they're doing their own thing. Regardless of their relationship status, people have busy lives, whether it be with family or work. When they do get together with friends, it's usually for a quick activity where they can catch up but also be doing something. Dinner and talking. Drinks and talking. Painting with a Twist and talking.

Gone are the days when a friend would just come over and just talk. When I do see this, it's very rare, because people are so busy.

Then, there's me.

I was down in Florida visiting my parents for a while when I had this epiphany.

My parents were going out to eat and asked me if I wanted to come. I politely declined.

A few nights later, they were going out with their neighbors and asked if I wanted to come. Again, I politely declined.

A few days later, my grandma came down and they were going to get dinner on the beach. I didn't want to go but felt rude not spending time with my grandma.

"You really don't like going out to eat," my mom noted.

I nodded but felt like I wanted to give her more of an answer.

A thought popped into my head. After thinking about it for a minute, I screamed so loud, my mom looked at me like I was crazy.

Oh, my God.

That's it!

That's why I don't like going out to eat! Or anywhere for that matter!

Holy crap!

It makes so much sense!

I don't feel weird anymore!

I don't feel guilty anymore!

I then proceeded to explain it to my mom, who still looked confused as hell.

From what I understand about talking, it comes easily to everyone. I asked my mom if talking is like having work to do. She, again, looked at me like I was nuts. "What do you mean?"

I rephrased the question. "Is talking hard to do?"

"I don't understand what you're asking. No? Because you learn how to do it when you're little, so you just do it?"

I then asked my dad.

"I don't understand. What?"

Again, I rephrased the question.

"I'm sorry, honey. I still don't understand."

Parents! Come on! Not that weird of a question from someone who is nonverbal!

Regardless, I took that as my answer. Talking is such a part of most people's lives, some people have a hard time with the concept that it might be difficult.

Then, you have me.

In that instant of my mom stating that I don't like to go out to eat, a zillion light bulbs went on in my head.

For me, talking is an activity itself. If I'm using my communication device, I'm essentially working a computer like someone would for work. If I'm doing my letter code, I'm moving my head all over the place and not paying attention to anything else. Whenever I go somewhere, I'm basically doing not one but two activities.

Let me go through some scenarios I find myself in:

If I go out to eat, I'm pretty much juggling two things: using a computer to have a conversation and eating, which is also not a mindless activity for me. If I eat beforehand, which I usually do, either the smell of food gets to me or it's just awkward, especially when I'm on a date, because they feel bad.

Same goes with drinks. I don't like alcohol, so there's that. I could meet for coffee, which is a little easier than a meal, but it's the same thing. I'm doing two things at once. Also, meeting someone for coffee is typically a quick thing to do.

Quick and Sara P should never go in the same sentence.

Plus, every time I take a drink of something, I have to let the air out of my stomach, and I sure as hell ain't doing that multiple times in the middle of the restaurant.

Let's say some of my friends decide to have a game night or go bowling. Again, it's two activities, but now I have to decide what's more important to focus on—talking, which mostly leads to mindless conversation, or the game, which, although fun, doesn't really matter in the grand scheme of things.

Some people might think this realization might've made me upset, but it had the exact opposite effect. Whenever I turned down an invitation, something never felt right. I felt like I was pushing everyone away when I didn't mean to. Even when I was a teenager, someone would instant message me, and I would immediately close out of it. It wasn't because I didn't want to talk to them; it was because I was doing something else. Of course, I didn't know this at the time, so I couldn't explain why I was ignoring them.

Now, because I'm aware of what the hell I'm feeling, instead of saying, "Hey. I can't make it to your birthday party. I'm sorry. However, I would love to have you and your significant other over to hang out," I can now say, "Hey. Thanks for inviting me. Get-togethers are a little difficult for me with my communication device. I would love to have you and your significant other over. We can get takeout, but I might not eat until after you leave, because I want to focus on talking to you."

Again, I sincerely wish I knew this when I was younger, but I didn't.

I can only do better from here.

By the way, Randi from my books doesn't represent any of this. She's the friend I would've had if I had known better.

The better you know yourself, the better a friend you can be to others.

After Randi, we have Christine.

When Brynn arrived at camp, she found out her counselor was going to be Christine, a twenty-something-year-old, who volunteered to help a camper with a disability. Although Brynn was a little nervous at first, Christine caught on to everything right away. Because she wasn't much older than Brynn, she understood her need for independence and tried to give her as much space as she could. Because she was also with her all day for two weeks, Christine saw Brynn had low self-esteem and tried to help her with that.

Christine represents how, when I went to camp as a teen, I would become just as close to the counselors as I would to the campers. We would have long conversations. We would laugh until late into the night. We would have random dance parties, even if it was just the two of us. They would help me with activities, and when I wasn't really into it, they would try to make it fun for both of us. When they saw I was upset about something, just like Christine, not only would they try to talk to me about it, but they would give me advice for what to do about it.

This one memory sticks out to me, probably because it's so not something I would even think about doing today. When we would have downtime, we would gather in the hall of the lodge and just hang out. I was sitting in a corner, minding my own business, perfectly content to just be around people. Jackass Boyfriend (dude, he came up in this book more than

I expected he would) came up to me, did something jackass-ish that I don't remember, and wheeled away.

A few minutes later, a counselor approached me, took a seat on the armrest of the chair next to me, and asked me how I was doing.

Without even knowing what I was doing, I began ranting.

I told him about what my ex had just done, and then about what he had been doing all week, and then about our entire relationship.

I must've gone on for an hour while he asked questions and gave me support.

The very best part? I didn't even know his name!

I just kept going on and on and on to this guy I didn't know, and he just kept being patient with me.

That was the beautiful thing about that camp. Whenever someone would be upset about something, someone else would always be there, no matter how well we knew each other.

I'm happy to say not only did I learn his name, but we remained close friends for a few years after that.

Unfortunately, though, all of my relationships with the counselors fizzled out. I will always smile when looking back on the memories we made, though.

Next up. Tommy, another one of my favorites.

Tommy represents a lot of themes in my life, but for the sake of this book, I'm just going to focus on one.

Brynn also meets Tommy at camp. Although for different reasons, they're both outsiders and, almost instantly, they form a bond. Unlike

Brynn, who is sometimes stuck in her own head and thinks she knows why people do what they do, Tommy is always trying to see the big picture. He tries to get Brynn to do the same. For example, the director of the camp stops Tommy from feeding Brynn one night. She automatically assumes the director thinks she can't make her own choices, while Tommy suggests that he just might not understand her and her situation.

There are many, many, many people in my life who have opinions about what I'm doing, how I'm feeling about it, and what I should be doing. They either listen to everything I have to say and A, proceed to tell me not only that I'm wrong, but how I'm wrong, B, make fun of my rant and say that I always complain about everything, or C, tell me to shut up before I even say anything and to just let it go.

I remember, one night in college, I was hanging out with a group of people in my dorm lobby. My friend started telling a story about something annoying that happened to me. I started to type something to add. I don't remember what I was going to say, but I do know it wasn't anything horrible, just an offhand comment I was going to make.

After all, the story was something that happened to me. My friend was telling it for me.

Seconds after I hit my head switch, this guy, who I stupidly had a crush on, made a scene of rolling his eyes and loudly saying, "Here she goes again! Up on her soapbox!"

Everyone at the table laughed.

I didn't say my comment, or anything else for the rest of the night.

I just remember staring into his eyes until he looked away.

My soapbox?

I wasn't even going to complain about anything!

I was just going to add my two cents, because this is my story, after all! The only reason she's telling it is because it would take me forever to type!

You don't even know what I was going to say!

And even if I wanted to complain about it, I have that right!

You can take my soapbox and shove it up your ass!

I have so many examples of people telling me what to do and not do, feel and not feel, say and not say, and think and not think, I could probably collect them all for another book.

That's why when someone takes the time to actually listen to me, truly understands where I'm coming from, and, even if they don't agree with me, they have a respectful conversation with me to try to get me to think about it differently without belittling me, that is, to me, the most attractive trait anyone could have.

I have realized people like the Tommy in my books are extremely hard to come by, especially in today's world. If I do find someone like Tommy, I want them in my life.

If they're a girl, I would want to be best friends with them.

If they're a boy, I would want to date them and possibly marry them.

I said possibly!

I would love to talk about Tommy more, but unfortunately, it would give away a lot. And there's other things that have to be done today.

I open up the web browser to text Chloe. I have to go to the bathroom.

For a good minute or two, I don't hear back or hear anything downstairs.

Again, I wonder if I'm doing the right thing.

Is this even safe? What if she really doesn't feel good and is downstairs? I wouldn't know if something were to happen to her.

A few seconds later, I hear her stomping up the stairs.

"How are you feeling?" I type out.

"Not good," she says in a weak voice as she runs a hand down her cheek. "I was sitting on the floor of the bathroom with the door shut. But I was doing some research on my phone about migraines and what medicines I could take."

I try not to think about how counterproductive that seems as I type. "Are you sure you don't want me to text anyone to see if they can come in?"

"Sara, I'm fine. As long as you're okay with not going anywhere, I told you I'm fine to do all day."

Before I could type anything else, she turns and heads down the hall to my bedroom.

I follow.

Alllllright.

No need to be rude.

Midway down the hall, she turns around and laughs.

"Wait until you hear what the asshole texted me. He really has it coming to him."

Can't wait.

11:01 a.m.

After I go to the bathroom and Chloe finishes telling me what her boyfriend did about the dog crap, she switches back to her weak voice. "I'm going to go back downstairs. I need to sit in the dark bathroom again. Text me if you need me."

I wonder again why she's so against calling someone else in to take over for her.

Not only is she against it, but she seems to snap at me every time I mention it.

I'm just trying to help.

Her own bed has to be more comfortable than my downstairs bathroom floor.

Maybe she really needs the money.

Maybe this is still just an elaborate act to get out of my reunion.

Maybe she doesn't want to go home because of her boyfriend.

If that's the case, why the hell is she still with him?

More importantly, if her romantic relationship is affecting how she treats other people, she should get the hell out!

Then again, I'm not her.

I shouldn't speculate about anyone's relationship.

As a distraction, I decide to reflect on my own relationships.

Definitely not the best distraction for this day, but at least I won't be judging anyone but me.

Let's start with Inside Sara.

I can see myself still being attracted to quiet and smart guys, so I could see myself meeting my current boyfriend in college, either in a class or at the library. We would go on more than a few dates before we made things official. Even though we wouldn't be married, because I don't believe there's a need to get married, we would still be together to this day.

I think we would both be homebodies, but every once in a while, we would go on a weekend hiking trip.

Unfortunately, none of this has really happened to me.

Let's break down my love life.

Or, more accurately, lack thereof.

My love life has been a series of situationships. If you're like me and just found out about this term, a *situationship* is basically more than a friendship but definitely not a committed relationship.

First up, we have Dan.

Dan was in all my classes the first years I was in public school. Like most elementary school crushes, we never had a full-on conversation. I think the most we said to each other was at my first boy-girl birthday party at a bowling alley. He wished me a happy birthday, and even though I despised my communication device, I made sure I replied with a "Thank you."

Talking didn't matter, though. His tan skin and buzzcut were enough for me. Enough that I liked him for three whole years!

If you learn nothing else from this chapter other than I'm completely, utterly, and totally ridiculous, you'll learn I'm loyal to the point it's unhealthy.

Moving on to middle school.

I don't remember what happened to Dan. My guess is that he slowly faded from my memory since we didn't have any classes together.

However, a new guy slipped into my life, Dylan.

Despite my mom knowing Dylan from church, I wasn't really friends with him until one night in sixth grade when, for some strange reason I will never understand, he followed me around at a dance for two straight hours.

From that moment on, my mind was disgustingly in a heart-shaped Dylan bubble.

Gah!

Bleh!

Never mind that we had never really talked until that night!

He was cute. He smelled fantastic. He seemed to like dancing and music just as much as I did. He talked to me like he would anyone else. He was really cute. He didn't seem to care who saw us together. He gave me compliments the entire night. He joked with me the entire night.

Did I mention he was really cute?

Oh, Sara.

Unlike today, where I would consider him to be a creeper, I fell madly in love with him back then.

Oh, Sara.

I invited him over to my house. That became a regular thing. He became close with my family and friends. I would ask him to come to events. We would sit together at lunch. I joined the drama club because of him, and even though he dropped out, I was still in the play and actually had a great time.

Once we turned sixteen, he had no problem driving my van and we would go on adventures together.

My love infatuation with Dylan lasted five years!

Not one. Not three. Five years!

What thirteen-year-old has a crush on someone for five fricking years?

Apparently, me!

I was in high school, sitting at a lunch table, when my heart shattered for the very first time.

Dylan had been becoming friends with more and more people, as high-schoolers typically do.

He was hot.

He was charming.

He was a catch.

At any given lunch, a handful of people would surround us that I didn't really know.

This particular lunch, a kid loudly exclaimed, "So, Dylan! I heard you have a crush on Mr. J!"

Wait.

What?

"You got a problem with that?" he replied.

Oh, my God.

I immediately turned away, fighting back tears.

Oh, my God!

Everyone had tried to tell me.

My friends. My family. My mom.

They had a feeling he could never like me.

They were right.

Out of the corner of my eye, I saw his eyes dart to me. "Shit. Did she hear?"

"I don't think so," my friend whispered to him. "You're good."

He looked relieved. "Good."

Oh, my God!

He wanted to keep it from me?

They wanted to keep it from me?

Why?

As fast as I could, I told my aide I had to get out of the cafeteria. I was having a hard time breathing.

Now that I'm older, I understand that coming out is different for everyone. It's easier for some people and harder for others, especially fifteen years ago. I would imagine it would be even harder to come out to someone who is basically in love with you. Back then, though, I don't think I was even upset he was gay. I was hurt because he claimed to be my best friend and he hadn't told me directly. Sure, I would've been disappointed he didn't share my feelings, but I would've ultimately accepted him for who he was.

But again, there's so much more to coming out than I could ever probably understand.

It took me a solid few years to get over Dylan, but in the meantime, I met Jake.

I firmly believe the only reason Jake entered my life was to show me random things can and do happen.

One night, my friends wanted to go out to eat. I didn't really want to go, but they insisted.

When I had parked my wheelchair at the table in the restaurant and looked up at our host, his giant brown eyes met mine.

Huh, I remember thinking. *That never happens.*

Even with Dylan, he hadn't looked me in the eye until a few days after we started talking.

He then flashed me a freaking gorgeous smile with all white teeth.

Alright! You're cute!

I returned the smile.

My friends didn't notice, but I kept the smile plastered on my face the rest of the night.

Gah!

So girly!

So ridiculous!

The next week, my friends wanted to go out again. Immediately, I suggested we go to the same restaurant. Not only did they have a cute host, but they had this amazing, ooey, gooey, brownie dessert.

This time when we were seated, he made small talk with me, leaning on my wheelchair while I typed. I briefly wondered if we had crossed paths before without my knowing, because this never happened with strangers.

"Holy crap," my friend said when he walked away. "I think he's into you! Did you see the way he was looking at you?"

I started to shake my head when my other friend pointed at me. "And I think you're into him! You're blushing! And smiling!"

Crap!

I had tried to hide my smile, but I failed.

They were on to me.

The next week, we knew we'd go to the same restaurant.

"You should ask him out!" my one friend suggested.

"Oh, yeah!" The other friend cheered. "Ask him out! Why not?"

Because I don't ask people out! I want to be asked out!

Gah!

So unfeminist of me!

This week, not only did he make small talk with me, but toward the end of his shift (we would get there pretty late), he took a seat at the table next to us to fold silverware for the next day. Even though my friends were doing most of the talking, he was still smiling at me.

What is up with this kid?

Why is he all smiley all the time?

He's making me all smiley all the time!

Knowing that I wouldn't do it, my friend took matters into her own hands. "Hey Jake. Would you ever want to hang out with us when you're not working?"

Still smiling, I turned to her. *What the hell are you doing?*

"Sure! I would love to! What are you guys doing right now?"

I turned back to him. *What the hell are you doing?*

It's almost midnight!

"We're probably just going to Sara's for a little. Wanna come?"

What's happening?

Yes, he was cute. Yes, I wanted to hang out with him. But it was almost midnight! Granted, my friend always put me in bed whenever we would go out so we could stay out as late as we wanted and not bother my parents. But, still!

This was crazy.

"Definitely! Just let me talk to my boss and call my girlfriend."

Girlfriend?

Once he went back into the kitchen, my friends seem to echo my thoughts.

"Girlfriend?"

"Girlfriend! What the hell? He definitely seemed into you!"

After we were in the van with a strange boy following us to my house late at night, my friends assured me that he had been flirting with me.

I thought for sure that he was flirting with me, too, although I didn't say anything.

How could I be so wrong?

Did I read into it too much?

Why is he coming over to my house right now?

More importantly, why was he always smiling at me and not everyone else?

When we got to my house, my parents were in bed, so we decided to pop in a movie while we quietly chatted. About half an hour into it, Jake announced that he had to go to his girlfriend's, but not before he gave me his email and screen name and asked for mine.

After he left, I remember all of us thinking the whole thing was weird. Very cool, but just weird.

The next day, the messages started. We would have conversations, but it was mostly just messages. If it was in the morning, it would be, "Hey! Have a great day at school today." If it was in the afternoon, it would be, "Hey! I hope you had a good day! What are you doing this evening?" If it was at night, it would be, "Goodnight! Sleep well!" I thought these messages were extremely cute, but the fact that he had a girlfriend never escaped my mind. Not only were there messages, but he stopped by after school every once in a while, too. I always invited his girlfriend, but he never brought her. He even invited me to his graduation party, and despite not knowing anyone, my friend and I went.

Before it got out of control, I wanted to tell him how I was starting to feel. Maybe it had something to do with Dylan. Maybe not. Regardless, I opened up an email and composed a message like, "Hey, Jake. I feel like I have to tell you something. I respect you, and I respect your girlfriend. I'm starting to have feelings for you, and I don't know what to do about it. I don't expect you to feel the same. I just thought you should know."

I usually heard back from Jake within a few hours.

This time, there was nothing but silence for a week.

"Hey. Thanks for being honest. I have some news! When my girlfriend and I were on vacation, we decided to get engaged. Hope all is well!"

Wait.

Huh?

They're eighteen!

Who decides to get engaged at eighteen?

When I didn't get a response from my email congratulating them, I realized what had happened.

Alright!

That took care of that!

Even though the Jake thing didn't work out, it was a major part of my life. Regardless of whether he'd had feelings for me and was just confused, or if he was just a really nice guy who didn't mean to flirt with me, I still befriended a random stranger who had made me smile. Every so often, when I feel down and think I'll never find someone, I think of Jake, and it gives me hope that random things can happen to me when I least expect it.

If it happened once, it can happen again, right?

Next up, Evan.

Back when meeting people online started to become A Thing, I made myself a Yahoo! profile and included my hobbies, interests, and a picture. I believe I felt neutral toward it—not really into it, not really against it, just kind of like, *This is what everyone is doing? Sure, why not? I'll try it.*

It was my introduction to online dating and having a disability.

It didn't matter how old we were. Whenever I was on a dating site, most of my conversations went something like this.

Guy: Hey. How's it going?

Me: I'm good. How are you doing?

Him: I'm okay. Can you have sex?

Ummm.

Romantic.

Sometimes, they wouldn't even bother with small talk. They would just literally send me a message with that question.

At first, I was appalled. How can they ask that right away? That shouldn't even matter! They should want to get to know me first! Unfortunately, though, I soon learned that's just a part of online dating that everyone with a disability faces. For some reason, people think this is an okay question to ask us, which I obviously don't agree with. From talking with other people with disabilities, I can say everyone has their own way of handling it.

Me? I have never responded to any of these messages, even though they were probably good opportunities to educate people. I just went straight for the delete button.

One day, my friend and I were sitting at my computer with my Messenger opened. A message from Evangoth333.

"Evan Goth?" My friend scoffed. "That sounds promising."

Immediately, I shook my head. I'd been doing this for a few weeks now, and I kinda got a feel for what screen names led to what kind of a conversation I would have.

Or so I thought.

"Hey, you don't know how he's going to be," my friend urged. "Give him a chance. If you don't like him, you can block him."

With my friend's help, I had a three-hour conversation with him.

"That was so cool," my friend said. "He seemed really into you and wanted to actually get to know you. Do you think you'll talk to him again?"

I shyly nodded. Despite seeing only one picture of him, I thought he was adorable. It was his personality I was attracted to. Cool, calm, subtle.

We spoke every day after that.

I would share some of the conversations we had, but I can't. For once, it's not because I don't remember—I had to block them out of my memory.

About a month into talking to Evan, things started to get weird.

Our conversations became more and more intimate. I asked him if we could talk on the phone. I had developed feelings for him, and for once, the other person felt the same. Talking on the phone seemed like the next step. One, I wanted to hear his voice, and two, I wanted to make sure I was talking to who he said he was. Not only did he say he didn't want to, but every time I brought it up, he would tell me he had to go and sign off.

Naturally, because I liked him so much, I wanted to see another picture of him. This was right before people started posting pictures like it was nothing. He kept putting it off and putting it off until, finally, he updated his senior picture.

That was the only other picture I had of him.

Finally, webcams for personal use became affordable and easy to use. Just like the phone, I would suggest that we video, assuring him I would even have someone there with me, and he would sign off as fast as possible.

Even though I desperately wanted to talk outside of instant messaging, I went along with it, surely making up excuses for him. After all, I didn't want to push him away like I had Jake.

Again, I was eighteen. I didn't know what the hell I was doing.

A few weeks later, I woke up my computer to a message from Evan. It said something like, "Hey. I need to tell you something. I was depressed a few years ago, and I think it's coming back. My mom is making me go to the hospital. I probably won't be online for a while. Please know I will be thinking of you every day. Sara, I love you."

He was offline by the time I got the message, but my heart sank.

Oh, my God!

I knew he had depression, but I didn't know he'd been hospitalized for it.

The fact that he was in the hospital and I couldn't talk to him or know how he was doing pretty much killed me.

And he said he loved me?

What the hell?

We always talked about how much we liked each other and always said how much we thought about each other, but that was the first time he had said he loved me.

Even though he was offline, I wrote back, "I love you."

The next few weeks, I was glued to my computer, waiting for an update.

The day finally came.

Apparently, he was still in the hospital and they had given him fifteen minutes on a computer. He told me he was okay, he still loved me, and his doctor thought he was obsessed with me. They wanted him to limit his communication with me. He told me, again, that he loved me and to take care of myself.

First, I screamed in relief. *He's okay!*

Then I was confused.

Obsessed with me?

What's wrong with that?

We like each other.

I'm pretty sure I'm obsessed with him, too.

Obviously, I didn't know anything about mental health back then.

Here's the summary of the next two years with Evan.

Yes, two years.

If loyalty were a disease, I'd be dead by now.

I would message Evan, or he would message me.

We would talk consistently again.

Things would become intimate again.

I would then not hear from him for about a month.

Repeat until the night I knew it was over.

It was my sophomore year of college, and I was sitting at my desk in my dorm room. I'd been messaging Evan once a week with no reply. One night, I logged onto Messenger, hoping that I received something.

Nothing.

Somehow, I knew.

I just knew I would never hear from him again.

I then proceeded to sob.

My roommate asked me what was wrong, but I couldn't tell her. All I could do was cry.

It took me a few years to get over Evan. I think the hardest part for me was I didn't have any closure. He just disappeared.

However, PSA, people! If someone says—in any way, shape, or form—they shouldn't or don't want to talk to you, that's a pretty big sign, and you should run.

Okay, you don't necessarily have to run. Just be extremely careful and don't get emotionally attached like I did.

I think the weirdest thing about this situationship is the fact that, even today, you can find anyone online within a matter of minutes.

Throughout the years, I tried searching his full name. Nothing.

I tried searching his screen name. Nothing.

I tried searching him on Facebook. Nothing.

This is morbid, but I even tried searching for his obituary. Nothing.

Finally, after years of being detached from the situation, I can now say I have no freaking idea who the hell this dude was. He could have been anyone—a guy, a girl, an old man, an older woman, someone I know, someone who knew someone I know. It could have been literally anyone, especially since "he" didn't want to talk on the phone, video with me, or give me any other pictures.

As I was writing this section, I must have thought to myself a million times, *This is a crazy story! I can't believe I'm putting this in! They're going to think I'm nuts! This is something that would be in a novel.*

However, I felt it needed to go in, because, A, it very much happened to me and it hurt me, and, B, yes, online dating is the norm today, but stuff like this can and still happen. People can never be too careful.

So, yeah. Basically, he was the first guy to say he shared my feelings, and I don't even know if he actually existed.

So freaking P luck!

Before I touch on the situationship of all situationships, some of you might be thinking, *But, Sara. You said a lot of guys would go for your friends. I don't see a story about that.*

It's true some guys would do that, but luckily, I never had a huge thing with them. We would all hang out a few times, I would want to get to know the guy more, my friend or assistant would know this but still hang out with him anyway, they would hang out behind my back, I would eventually find out, and that would be that.

I don't want to beat a dead horse.

Plus, I wanted to focus on these four outrageous situations, which are far more interesting.

Okay, onto the situationship that tore my heart out.

I learned so much from this, so to make it not so bad, I'm going to be highlighting some of the things I realized I did wrong. If one person takes away one thing from this, I will feel so much better.

Okay.

Breathe in.

Breathe out.

Here we go.

I would say about six months after Evan disappeared, another guy messaged me online: Alex. For a period of time, the company that makes my communication device had a website that was all about me and my singing that Alex came across. Alex really liked the video of my song and asked me if I had any music coming out.

That's really cool, I thought. *He doesn't want to know anything about my disability. He's all about my music. That's awesome.*

And he was my age! Twenty.

I wrote him back, telling him that music was on hold and that I was writing a book.

He seemed just as interested in my book as in my music and even asked me what it was about.

Not only did I tell him what it was about, but I asked him if he wanted to chat sometime over instant message.

Apparently, I learned absolutely nothing from my experience with Evan.

Sometimes, I seriously wonder about my younger self.

Seriously.

Sooner or later, we were talking every night. He even made sure to get online an hour or two before my assistants put me to bed so we would have enough time to talk.

He seemed to understand everything I tried to say.

I tried to explain my communication device. He repeated it back better than I explained it.

I told him how my wheelchair worked. He seemed to get it just like that.

I know what some of you are thinking, because it briefly flashed through my mind.

Was this Evan acting like someone else?

I'm 99 percent certain that it wasn't. He talked different. He typed different. He was in a different state. He had a different job. However, I'll never know, because I never asked him.

First lesson I learned: if I have a question, I need to ask it, no matter how stupid or ridiculous I think it is. Even if I think I know the answer, I'll never know until I ask it.

For the record, I never actually thought he was Evan, but I should have, at least, brought it up.

About a month in, we decided to talk on the phone. The first time, I had an assistant with me to buffer the silence while I typed. Any time after that, I had my assistant dial the phone and leave. He was perfectly okay with being patient.

A few months in, he told me he was going to be two states away from Ohio and jokingly suggested that I meet up with him. I jokingly suggested to my assistant that we should go. She not so jokingly said, "Let's do it!"

And just like that, I was going to take a random road trip to a different state to meet this guy from the internet.

Safe.

A few days before the trip, my assistant backed out. She said she didn't feel comfortable going and had too much to do. To be honest, I was really bummed about it. We, of course, had expressed feelings for each other by then, and I really wanted to meet him. I loved the idea of doing something completely and utterly random.

Because I was friends with all my assistants, I told them what happened.

"I'll go with you!" one pronounced. "I'm not doing anything."

"Well, I want to go, too," another one said.

Soon, I had four girls ready and wanting to go with me.

Operation Random Boy Road Trip was back on!

The operation then was off again for just a few short moments. I had gotten into a car accident just a few months earlier, and I had just received a brand-new van. Because I didn't want to get in trouble, I called my mom and asked if I could take it to a city that big. She didn't feel comfortable with it, and even though I protested, she stood her ground.

As soon as I hung up with her, one of my friends/assistants looked at me, grinning. "She just said you couldn't take your van."

I looked at her.

"She didn't say you couldn't go. She just said you couldn't take your van. We can take my car. I'll drive. If you're okay with it, we can take your manual wheelchair and fold it up so it fits in my trunk."

Operation Random Boy Road Trip was back on! Again.

The day finally came. I'd bought a new shirt for this occasion and had my assistant straighten my hair that morning. Unfortunately, the city was absolutely disgusting with rain and wind, so by the time I met Alex, I had to wear a super unattractive fleece and my hair was pulled up into an even messier bun than normal.

We left my apartment around noon and drove for five or six hours. We were not only going to a city, but we were going to the heart of it. We wanted to park the car and not move it again. Because of this, we parked near the café where we were going to meet him.

Alex was at a tournament and couldn't meet up until a few hours later. Because none of us were familiar with this city, we had absolutely no idea what the hell we were doing.

In fact, "I have no idea" quickly became the theme of the trip.

"What are we going to do now? I have no idea."

"Do you know where we are? I have no idea!"

"Where are we going to eat? I have no idea."

I think that's when the trip became my favorite college experience. Five girls in an unfamiliar city (which, when put it like that, I highly don't recommend), trying to figure out what the hell was happening and laughing along the way.

Second lesson I learned: I don't need a guy to have fun. I just need people who have an open mind and a willingness to go with the flow.

Finally, after a few hours of killing time and making great memories, the time came.

All five of us went to the café.

You would think one of us would've thought to break up the group at two separate tables, but no.

No no—all five of us sat down at one table and didn't think twice about it.

At least, not at first.

Ahh, poor Alex.

He texted he was on his way. Hello, shot of adrenaline!

"Do you want to go meet him?" one of the girls asked. "I'll push your chair."

I did want to go.

She and another girl went with me. If nothing else, I had a small army with me everywhere I went that trip.

We were walking down the busy sidewalk when I spotted him. I started to smile, but because I wasn't driving myself and they didn't know what he looked like, we just kept on going. It was only when he awkwardly called my name that they knew to turn around.

Oops!

I remember him saying hi to me, then asking me a question, then asking me another, then asking me another.

Immediately, I became even more nervous. I knew he knew I talked with a communication device, but it was like he'd forgotten I needed a little more time to answer. Luckily, whenever we were at the café, he seemed to pick up on my pace.

After a few minutes, everyone started to realize, *Oh, damn. They probably want to be alone.* Alex was visibly nervous, probably because he was at a table with a group of girls, trying to have a conversation with me.

None of us, including me, thought of the date-ish aspect of this trip, which just went along with the "I have no idea" theme.

What did my girls do?

Instead of moving to another part of the café like normal people probably would, one by one, they slowly migrated two tables down.

Oh, us!

We were able to finish our conversation in semi privacy, but can you say *awkward*?

"Do you want to go for a walk?" he asked me out of nowhere.

I don't know why, but that really stands out in my mind. I thought that was just so adorable.

Isn't that what guys say to you when they like you?

Or when they want to abduct you?

Ya know, same difference.

Luckily, I think it was the first reason, since I'm here now, recalling all this for you.

The girls heard him ask me and immediately stood up. I signaled to them that I really wanted to go, but I wanted them to be close by. After all, I was in my manual in a strange city with a strange guy who was going to be pushing me.

I don't even want to say what might've happened to me.

Thankfully, my friends got my message. They suggested we all head to the car, told Alex where it was, and assured us they would stay back enough to give us some space.

Later, they all admitted they were so nervous about me going with him that none of them wanted to take their eyes off us.

Oh, this trip!

I seriously had a small army with me!

Even though I don't necessarily have friends, I've been well loved by everyone around me. Sometimes, I feel like society puts so much emphasis on friends and relationships that I forget I am loved and cared for in so many other ways.

Maybe that should be a lesson in itself.

Once we got to the car, Alex thanked me for coming and told me to have a good ride home.

Yep.

We drove five or six hours just so I could have coffee with a guy, and then we were going to drive five or six hours that night.

Absolutely insane, but I freaking loved every minute of it.

Once we were on the road, the questions and comments started flying out.

"What did you think of him?"

"Do you like him?"

"Are you going to keep talking to him?"

"Were you nervous?"

I mindlessly nodded, but honestly, my thoughts were going a mile a minute.

They kept talking.

"He was nice."

"Very nice, but extremely nervous!"

"Oh, God, extremely, extremely nervous!"

"Guys! He was extremely nervous probably because he was meeting a girl he liked! Give him a break!"

I have to be honest. That made me smile.

Then, his clothes came up.

"What the hell was he wearing?"

"Oh, my God! Yeah! He was dressed like a nerd!"

"Seriously! Couldn't he have dressed up for you?"

They all started laughing.

Ashamedly, I went along with it, partly because my mind was elsewhere, still playing the night over, and partly because I was just a big, huge idiot.

Unfortunately, this wasn't the end of this. Every time Alex came up in conversation, instead of being the guy who I was talking to, he became the guy who dressed like a dweeb. The worst part of this was I didn't stand up for him. In fact, I would make jokes right along with them when his clothes could not have been farther from my mind.

Third lesson: I do not have to go along with what everyone else is saying just to fit in, especially if they're making fun of someone, and especially if I'm starting to have feelings for that someone. If I don't agree with them, I need to speak up! If I'm not going to speak up, I should, at the very least, not agree with what they're saying. Gossiping can be fun and may join everyone together for a moment, but ultimately, is it really worth it?

After the trip, Alex and I continued talking on a regular basis. He didn't shy away.

A couple months later, he said he would be in the same city and offered to drive to me this time.

I believe I said something along the lines of, "Hell yeah! Get your cute ass down here!"

He then asked if he could be my first kiss.

Even though I was alone in my apartment, I took a minute to hide my smile. "Of course," I finally replied.

That fateful night came.

He showed up at my apartment, and we hung out for a little, talking and teasing each other. I didn't know when he was going to do it, so I was extremely jumpy. He suggested we pop in a movie. He also asked me if he could take me out of my chair so I could sit with him.

This is the moment! I thought.

One movie down. No kissing.

It isn't going to happen.

Why?

Alex suggested we pop in another movie.

Warning! The next scene is completely, utterly, 123 percent cheesy, but to me, it was perfect. I wouldn't have it any other way.

About five minutes into the second movie, the two main characters shared their first kiss.

Always awkward when you're cuddling with a guy who has said he wanted to kiss you!

"That looks like fun," Alex whispered. "Wanna try?"

And just like that, albeit with a little repositioning of my body, he kissed me.

And again.

And again.

And again.

Finally, he asked me if I wanted to move to my bedroom. Grinning, I let him carry me to my bed.

And that is how our visits went for the next seven years.

Seven.

Seven!

I will say it again. Seven!

Loyal until the death of me!

Or maybe it's not loyalty. Maybe I'm just a psychopath.

Who's to say?

Regardless, every few months, he would come to whatever state I was in or I would go to whatever state he was in, we would flirt for an hour or so, and then we would make out.

Early on in our situationship, he said his friend's roommate wanted to ask him out. He wanted to know if I would be okay with him saying yes. He didn't want anything to change with us; he just wanted to make sure that I was okay with him dating other people at the same time.

Now that I think about it, I believe it was either his way of either asking me if I wanted to be exclusive or telling me he didn't want to be exclusive. Of course, at that time, I wasn't picking up what he was putting down, if he was even putting down anything!

Here's what went through my mind.

N-n-n-no! I don't want him going out with another girl.

I really like what we have.

Why is he asking me this? He should do whatever he wants.

He must really want to go out with her.

Who am I to stop him from doing what he wants?

Of course, I didn't say any of this to him. I just said, "Okay. Do whatever makes you happy."

Fourth lesson: if I want something to happen, I need to say it. If I don't want something to happen, I need to say it. If I'm unsure about what someone is saying, I need to ask them about it. If someone really cares about me, they'll understand. If someone doesn't, they aren't worth my time.

Communication. Communication. Communication.

Unfortunately, this happened one or two more times throughout our situationship. In fact, a year or two into this thing we had, he even strongly encouraged me to date other people.

It even got to the point where I couldn't tell him I missed him because that was too relationship-y for him.

What the hell was I doing?

Fifth lesson: freaking listen, dude! Sometimes words really do speak louder than actions!

Even though he'd made it crystal clear we were not in a relationship, we would both drive or fly however many hours to see each other, flirt, and make out.

But it wasn't even the making out that did it for me.

He was my person.

Whenever something good would happen, I would text him right then and there.

Whenever I was upset about something, he would drop whatever he was doing and talk to me.

We would video chat for hours about nothing.

He was like my Tommy (from *Dancing Daisies*) in a way. Whenever he disagreed with me, he would spend (sometimes hours) having a respectful conversation with me.

I think that's why I was attracted to him; he could get me thinking in a different way.

Ultimately, there were two visits that made it go from, "This is just a fun thing that doesn't mean anything" to "Huh, I think maybe this could go in a different direction."

The first of these visits, I started to feel more comfortable with him. Whenever people say they feel comfortable with their partner, I feel like they usually mean they aren't attracted to them anymore, but I could be wrong.

This is not what I mean.

Typically, when he was around, I just wanted to be a cute girl and not the girl with a disability. For me, this meant having my assistants do all my personal care, even though he always wanted to learn how to do everything for me. All I wanted was to have him cuddle me and binge watch movies with me.

This visit was different, though. I felt okay with the idea of him helping me eat, taking me to the bathroom, and helping me change. I actually didn't want any of my assistants around, but it was too late to tell them that I didn't need them. I would've felt more than comfortable if it were just me and him for the entire weekend.

The other thing that happened that weekend was I felt like I could just be myself with him. Like I said, I always felt like I wanted to be the cute girl around guys. Sometimes, that included downplaying my disability and letting him choose what restaurants we ordered from and what activities we did. This visit, however, I didn't feel like I had to work to be cute. If I did or didn't want to do something, I felt like I could just tell him.

I just felt like I could be myself. I don't know how else to put it.

When he was about to leave that weekend, I probably did the most stupid thing I could have ever done—I asked him not to tell me if he was dating anyone.

After a long pause, he just said, "Alright."

Saaaarrraaaaaa!

Whyyyyyyyy?

There were a hundred—a thousand—different things I could have said to him, and I'd chosen *that*?

I am a fricking moron!

Sixth lesson: never, ever, ever put my head in the sand! Especially with someone as intimate as this. The more I know, the better I can be.

Knowledge. Is. Power.

Just a few short months after, he came to my place again. This time, he seemed to have an experience similar to mine during the last visit. I'm not going to put words in his mouth, because (ha) I have absolutely no idea what he was thinking, but something seemed to shift for him, too. It was like we had both let down our walls.

He even wrote me an email as soon as he got home, telling me how much he cared about me and how he realized this on the way home, which was something he had never done before.

We're on the same page, I thought.

I didn't know what the page was, but I thought it had potential.

During that visit, we had both decided to do what comes naturally after years of cuddling and making out. We felt like it was the right time, and he was honored that I wanted to share that moment with him.

Not to go into much detail, but I had some unexpected obstacles.

We couldn't.

Or, more accurately, I couldn't.

Damn movies! They don't prepare you for anything!

Afterward, I was feeling so many different things. Disappointment. Confusion. Loneliness. Resentment that I hadn't realized that that certain thing was going to be a problem. Embarrassed that I didn't know my body.

Alex just laid there, holding me and stroking my hair, assuring me it was okay and that it really didn't matter to him.

He couldn't have been more of a gentleman in that moment.

A few days after he left, we made plans for me to come see him.

I wanted to try again.

He wanted to try again.

Again, I thought we were on the same page.

The month before I was supposed to travel, I emailed him asking for dates.

No reply.

It's important to know that this was a not so great time in my life. My brother was leaving, my parents had decided to move, I had decided to stay, I had to find an apartment, and I do not do well with change. This trip was the only thing keeping me going.

I was also mentally relying on him so much more than I should've.

A week went by, and I emailed him again. "We still on?"

No reply.

He would answer my messages about anything else, just not about the trip.

Finally, I received a text. "Hey, can we video?"

Great, we're finally going to talk about the trip!

Although, if I'm being completely honest with myself, I knew this probably meant something else was up.

Immediately, I logged on. He was casually eating mint chocolate chip ice cream. I remember this, because I playfully opened my mouth, saying, "I want some! Give me some! Feed me through the screen!"

He lightly chuckled, but then became serious. "Hey. I have something to tell you. I've been dating someone. I wanted to wait to tell you until I knew it was serious."

My. World. Froze.

No more jokes about ice cream.

"I just want to tell you before you saw it on social media."

Looking back on everything, this was probably one of the most hurtful things he said to me. Although I totally had it coming when I asked him *not* to tell me if he was dating anyone, but he waited to tell me not because we were such good friends, not because we had become intimate (although, in reality, that's probably it), but because of *Social. Media.*

He then asked me not to come see him the next month, because it would look bad to the new girl if another girl came.

Ummmm.

What?

But you wanted me to come just a few weeks ago.

But we both wanted to try again.

But just a few weeks ago, we came up with a sweet letter code so I could talk to you in bed.

I don't understand.

Now, this makes me absolutely furious, even to this day. If I were truly, legitimately just his friend, it wouldn't have looked bad to this new girl. He would've wanted me to meet her.

He tried to tell me more about her, but I couldn't do it. He was being so casual about it, and it was killing me.

However, if I were truly, legitimately, just his friend, *I* would want to hear everything about her.

It was just a giant mess!

I signed off, went into my kitchen, asked my mom to give me a beer, and then chugged it.

I then proceeded to not eat for eight straight days.

For a good week, my inner dialogue went something like this:

He's seeing someone.

He met her online.

They didn't even meet through his work or anything like that.

He was actively looking.

I knew this day would come, and I knew he'd been dating on and off ever since he'd met me, but I don't understand. Why now?

I started to feel so comfortable with him. Why did he start seeing someone now?

He doesn't want me to come. A month ago, he wanted me to.

We were going to try again. Now he's in a relationship.

I always knew this was going to happen, but I don't understand.

Repeat until I drove myself insane.

Along with this twenty-four-hour inner dialogue, I also wrote some emails telling him how I felt. To respect Alex, I'm just going to say they didn't help anything.

Seventh lesson: If a ship is already under water, let it sink to the bottom of the ocean with grace.

Over the next few years, we tried to keep in touch, but things were never the same. We never tried to see each other again. He's married to her now, and although I'm pretty much over it, every once in a while, a cold feeling of knowing that he didn't want to see what was on the next page for us will smack me out of nowhere and I have to take a minute to let it pass.

12:11 p.m.

I text Chloe to tell her I'm ready to eat. I don't particularly like bothering someone when I know they don't feel well, but she seems dead set on staying, so what choice do I have?

Let me rephrase that: I know I always have a choice. But do I want to argue with her and have her potentially get pissed off to the point of who knows what will happen? Or do I want to keep feeling like I'm bothering her?

Sometimes, I really hate the situations I end up in.

She's not upstairs by the time I'm in my dining room.

I try to think of something else, at least for a minute or two.

I have to say I'm proud I could replay the entire Alex story and only feel a little bit sad. A few years ago, I couldn't even think about him without feeling like throwing up, even though I was still trying my hardest to keep in contact with him.

Now, if someone were to ask me about him out loud, I would probably get a bit shaky.

But I feel like I'm getting there.

One day at a time.

I try to picture myself dating.

Honestly, with how unreliable and unenthusiastic some of my assistants are right now, I can't see it happening, but let's go step by step.

First and foremost, I'd have to be extremely careful. Women with disabilities have the highest rate of sexual abuse. As Inside Sara, I'd be very careful regardless, but as someone with a severe disability, that fact always has to be at the forefront of my mind.

Because I don't go out much, I would probably meet someone online.

I would probably swipe right on a hundred or two hundred guys, which just sounds not romantic, in my opinion, before I meet someone who has the same interests as me, doesn't care about my disability, and doesn't bring up sex in the first conversation.

Definitely not my preferred standards, but we're being realistic here, okay?

We would probably talk for a few days before I decide he was cool.

A few more days, and depending on how everything is going, we would probably want to meet in person.

I would suggest coffee, even though I would probably take one sip of my drink. Dinner, I would need my assistant to feed me, and it could be messy. Anywhere else, I couldn't really talk. Coffee, at least, I could focus on the conversation.

I would have to think about when I could meet him, too.

If it was a day Amber was scheduled, I would take my time getting ready, and I wouldn't have to worry as much about what time we were out.

If Britney was working, I would have to explain a whole hell of a lot, from what I wanted to wear to everything I wanted her to do and prepare myself for a ton of unnecessary comments.

If Chloe was on that day? Fifty-fifty chance I would even make the date.

A similar situation like this once happened to me. I was going to meet a guy downtown at a tea house. Only, after I confirmed the date, my assistant admitted to me that she didn't feel comfortable driving downtown. I will always respect everyone's feelings, but when they start to interfere with my plans, it becomes kind of a problem. She even offered to find us another place, which, although appreciated, that is a huge no-no for me. My dating life is between me and the other person, not my assistants.

The night before the date, I had to text him to see if he would meet up closer to my house. Although he said he didn't mind and we seemingly had a great time, I didn't hear from him again.

In theory, rearranging a date just so another person can feel comfortable shouldn't be a reason not to talk to someone anymore, but I can't help but wonder if it had something to do with it.

Dating in my situation, I feel like so many odds are stacked against me, I have to be extremely careful, despite knowing that I shouldn't have to be. Something so little could make a guy turn away.

But back to the imaginary dating scenario.

Assuming that the first date went well, there would be a second date, which very rarely actually happens, but we're being hypothetical here. I would have to tell him I'm limited to the places I can go or else I wouldn't be able to talk that much.

Same with the next few dates. We would have to get extremely creative.

With every date, I would have to, again, consider which assistant is on the schedule. Chances are I couldn't always go when Amber was working, which, like I said, would open its own can of worms and potentially scare him away.

At any given moment, one (or both) of us could lose interest, and I would be back to square one, swiping through hundreds and hundreds of guys.

I think that's why I was so hurt when, right after he told me he was seeing someone, Alex suggested I should just go on ten to twenty dates. Not only is that *so* not my style, but it's really freaking hard to go on once successful date with one decent guy. To go on several different dates with several different guys would be nearly impossible for me unless I made it my full-time job.

Let's say this guy and I, by some miracle, made it through our first few dates. It would be time to see a lot more of each other. Most couples take turns spending time at each other's places. Unless, by a very slim chance, his place is wheelchair accessible, he would always have to come to my place. I wouldn't mind this, but would he?

Would he mind that we would probably eat a lot of takeout?

Would it get old for him that I would eat a lot of shakes while he ate by mouth?

What if he likes to drink? I don't particularly like to drink. I don't mind if someone drinks around me, but would it be boring for him if he's the only one doing it?

Would he mind that I don't cook?

Would it be awkward for him if I had my assistants help me make him dinner every once in a while?

How would my assistants feel about helping me do stuff for him?

Oh, my assistants.

The time would come where we would probably want to be alone. Would they be okay going somewhere for a few hours without getting paid?

How would I handle that?

Finally, sooner or later, intimacy would come up.

To be honest here, I'm not the best at making out, and it took Alex and I a good while to figure out the best way to cuddle. We were still figuring stuff out when he entered into a new relationship. I think that's the other thing that hurt me so much. I had just figured out how to be intimate with him; *we* had just figured it out together. I am absolutely not saying we should have dated just because of this, but I just felt like he brushed it off like snow on his jacket and didn't respect we had this thing that, although not perfect, was unique and rare.

Would this imaginary dude be patient enough to figure out cuddling?

Would he put up with my bad kisses?

How long would it be before cuddling wouldn't be enough for him?

Would he be patient while we figure out the more intense stuff?

What if it turns out I can't do anything more than cuddling? I would be okay with it, but would he?

Gah!

Yeah, definitely not interested in dating.

At least, not right now.

I finally hear Chloe coming up the stairs. Almost like a reflex, I glance at the clock.

Five minutes after I texted her.

This is ridiculous.

I really need some more rules.

She opens up the refrigerator, grabs a shake, and heats it in the microwave.

Oh. Okay.

I kind of foresaw me not eating by mouth today, but really? She couldn't have asked to make sure?

As she looks at the microwave, I see my entire day flashed before my eyes.

She's not going to come upstairs other than to feed me and to take me to the bathroom.

I'm going to try to write today, but I'll probably end up watching *Switched at Birth* to make myself feel better.

I'm not going to get to shower.

And I'm going to go to bed as early as I can to get myself out of this awkward day.

I type out, "How are you doing?"

"Not good," she says in a weak voice as she keeps staring at the microwave.

I wait for her to say something else. She doesn't.

Oh, God. This is going to be even more awkward than I thought.

I would, again, offer to do something for her, but I don't want to hear another snarky comment.

After she gives me a drink and hooks me up, she leans with one hand on the counter. "Sara." Her voice is normal again. "I'm going to ask you a question, and I want you to be honest with me. I won't be offended. Do you want me to quit?"

First thought. *For the love of everything holy! Someone else is quitting while I eat! This is the second time!* When someone quits, it's never an easy conversation. I get nervous. They get nervous. I sometimes panic. Why do people think this is okay? Granted, I'm not eating by mouth, but still! Stuff is going into my stomach! I'm having my lunch!

I cannot see someone doing this to Inside Sara. If they needed to talk to me, they would make an appointment with me.

Second thought. *Wait a minute.*

She didn't actually quit.

She just asked me if I wanted her to quit.

Oh, my God!

This is a trick question!

If I say yes, she can say I fired her, and she can get unemployment!

Oh, my God.

This little . . .

Immediately, all my walls go up, and I am conscious of every word I'm about to say.

Using my communication device for this conversation, I type, "I definitely think this is stuff we need to talk about, but I don't necessarily want you to quit. Can I ask why you would ask me that?"

She sighs. "Because you seem really worried about me."

Oh, dear Lord! First Britney, now her! Who the hell knew worrying about other people would give me so much backlash? Did I somehow not get the memo? Did caring for fellow humans go out of style?

"You asked me again and again why I don't go to the doctor for migraines. I don't have health insurance. This job doesn't offer it, Sara."

Hey, now! I tell everyone I interview I can't offer health insurance! What the hell?

"I mean, my stepdad kicked me off his insurance. I'm not even twenty-six! My mom won't stand up for me! I keep waiting for my boyfriend to put me on his, but he's taking his sweet old time. I don't know what to do! I don't know when I'll be able to go to the doctor!"

I think about suggesting she get her own insurance like many of my assistants do, but I don't think I should talk right now.

"And I know you worry about me driving. It's a lot, if I'm being honest. An hour to get here and an hour to get home. It's a lot, but I'm okay with it. I just know you don't like me doing it."

Okay, this is too much. She's putting all of her issues on me to make it sound like I'm the one who has these issues with her.

Talk about a total mind twist!

I have to say something.

"If you are okay with it, I am okay with it."

"Yeah, but, Sara, I know you don't like it."

Seriously?

I want to look at her like, *Dude! Didn't you hear what I just said?*

"Also." She runs her hand down her cheek. "With the migraines, they don't seem to be going away anytime soon. I'm going to have days like this. I don't know how often, and like I told you, I can't go to the doctor. I feel bad that you can't go to your thing, and I know you must be really mad at me."

What the hell is happening?

"It's all good," I type out. "You have to do what you have to do."

"You still didn't answer my question, Sara. Do you want me to quit?"

Oh, my God!

She really is doing this!

She really is putting this on me!

I'm done eating, but I feel like it's going to come full circle and go up my throat.

Shaking and trying not to upchuck, I type, "Again, I don't want you to quit, but it sounds like you want to be done. I really don't have a problem with any of the things you mentioned, other than I need to be able to leave the house. However, I am willing to work with you. If you want to start looking for another job, I will take it easy on days you're here. I will also start looking for another assistant, and if I find someone before you find a job, I will tell them they can't start right away."

Side note: If someone gave me their notice with time to figure out what I'm going to do, I wouldn't be like this. If they do it in a professional way, I'm okay with it, even though I might be having a panic attack inside. I'm only being like this now, because I feel like she's pushing me to fire her.

"Sara, I really don't want you to do that. I know how hard it is for you to find an assistant. I don't want you to pass up on the perfect assistant just because I don't have a job. And I'm probably going to find a job way before you're going to find another assistant. Let's just be honest. I would rather wait around until you get someone and just do my own thing."

So, you do want to quit!

And you tried to frame it like I want you to quit!

Screw. You.

I don't want to call her out on it, though, because who knows what she would do, and who knows what I would do!

I hate to admit it, but she's right about one thing.

More than likely, it will take me longer to find an assistant than it will take her to find a job.

If I hate anything more than having assistants, it's hiring new assistants.

First, this isn't a typical job. My assistants are considered independent contractors, which means I'm limited to which websites I can post on since they don't work for a company . . . which means I get some downright weird responses.

I'll post the days I need, and they ask me if they could work different days.

I'll post the hours I need, and they say they could work half of that.

I'll ask them to tell me a little about themselves, and they send me their name and number and that's it.

And my personal favorite: "You are always on here. You must be extremely hard to work for. You'll never find anyone!"

Thank you.

As Taylor Swift sings, "Why ya gotta be so mean?"

I'd say for every eight of these emails, I will get one good person.

Most of these people have experience with either nursing or people with disabilities, which I prefer.

I will email them back, telling them more about the job and asking them if they would like to do a phone interview.

Fifty percent will agree. The other half, I never hear back from.

Once on the phone, I will ask basic questions. Where are they from? What is their job history? Do they have any experience with people with disabilities? Are they okay with all my personal care, including taking me to the bathroom and doing my feeding tube? What is their personality like? Do they prefer following directions or giving directions?

If I like the answers and if they sound enthusiastic and personable, I will have them over for a face-to-face interview. There's another 50 percent chance they will show.

I think that's why I hate hiring so much. They could bail at any given moment, and I never know when that could be. In an instant, I could be back to square one.

At the face-to-face interview, I explain the job in detail, show them some general stuff like how I take a drink and get in and out of bed. If they're still interested, I have them come back for three or four days to get hands-on experience to see if we're a match.

I stress to them that if either of us in that time isn't feeling it, they don't have to stay. I don't want them to feel any pressure.

Even after I offer them the job and they start, there's no guarantee it'll work out. After all, I'm trusting a complete stranger with my life. It takes a month or two for me to relax and be like, "Okay. This is going to work."

So, yes, hiring can be extremely stressful, and, honestly, it would be actually nice to have Chloe stick around, but I don't want her to do it just so she can use me, and I especially don't want it if she's going to be "sick" half the time.

Still, I don't want to bring it up. This has the potential to get very ugly, and I still don't know if she's doing it to manipulate me.

"Do you know what you're going to do for another job?" I ask. "Aren't your migraines going to be a problem anywhere you go?"

"I'm not exactly sure. I've been talking to my old boss. He said that I could work a day or two if I need it. But I really want to start my own business selling old clothes. I want to go to thrift stores, buy what I think people would want, and post pictures online. There's a huge market for it. So, once you find someone and until I get my feet on the ground, I'm thinking about going on unemployment."

As she flushes my tube and unhooks it, I want to scream.

But I can't.

I have to be professional.

There were a handful of times where I lost my temper on an assistant. When I say "lost my temper," I mean I just said what I was thinking without my filter on, not full-on yelled at them. Each and every time I did this, they ended up quitting within a week, leaving my other assistants to pick up their shifts until my mom could come up from Florida.

And I can't afford that right now.

So, I scream inside my head.

You!

Thought!

About!

This!

You wanted to quit, and instead of being professional and having a mature conversation, you're using my sympathetic personality to try to make it sound like I wanted you to quit!

Unbelievable!

Immediately, I start typing. "I do not agree with what you're doing. I believe unemployment is for people who lost their jobs. I do not believe unemployment is for people who want to leave their jobs. I need you. I will need you until the day you leave. You are not losing your job. As I stated, I am willing to work with you until you find another job. However, it sounds like you made up your mind. You want to do your plan, and I can't stop you."

Did I just give her the green light to quit?

I don't care anymore!

I did everything I could, said that she wasn't fired, told her I didn't support her, and she's going to do whatever she's going to do.

I'm done with this conversation!

Out of everything she could do, she laughs like I'm the biggest idiot in the world. "Oh, Sara. Unemployment isn't forever. It's just until I start my business."

Why can't you start your business now? You only work for me two days a week!

And what the hell are you going to do about health insurance? Isn't that your first reason for quitting in the first place? It's going to be the same thing if you work for yourself!

Oh, I'm so unbelievably mad right now, but I'm not going to say another word!

"Do you want to go to the bathroom?" she asks.

I nod, fuming.

I go back to my bedroom, and as we do the bathroom thing, Chloe starts telling me all the ways unemployment can help people.

I don't want to hear it. Not only do I have strong opinions on the subject, but she just tried to freaking use me. Now is so freaking not the time to try to change my beliefs!

Once we're done, I drive to the living room. I expect Chloe to head downstairs.

She doesn't.

She heads to the front door. "Hey, I was kind of nervous to have that conversation with you. I'm going to go to the gas station and get cigarettes. I'll be back in ten minutes. You good?"

I freeze.

Oh.

My.

God.

She doesn't have a migraine!

Granted, I don't know for sure, but I'm fairly certain if someone has a migraine, they aren't going to want to drive to a gas station to get cigarettes to smoke!

She probably just wanted to get me to feel bad for her while she quit!

And I didn't go to the reunion because of her "migraine"!

I probably shut the final door on some relationships because of her!

I manage to nod, and just like that, she's out in the daylight.

Once alone, I let out an ear-piercing scream, and then, I proceed to cry.

My Perfect Day

A Few Years Down the Road

M Y EYES WILL FLUTTER OPEN. I'll blink a few times to make sure I'm awake. I am. I'll give myself a few minutes to stretch and look at the clock.

7:16.

Perfect.

This is the first time I'll wake up since I fell asleep last night.

Even more perfect.

Once I'm awake enough, I'll hit the button to make my voice-activated speakers announce I'm ready to get up. Since I'll have twenty-four-hour care, I'll have people do twenty-four to forty-eight-hour shifts now.

I'll take my time hiring, and now I'll have all A people. Ashley, Alison, Anna, and, of course, Amber.

If something were to come up, I'll know the right way to have a conversation about it.

As far as I can see, there will be no need for a Britney or a Chloe, because along with hiring regular assistants, I will have also hired backup assistants, where if something unexpected happens, they can just jump in.

"Good morning!" Ashley will greet me. "How are you doing? How did you sleep?"

I'll nod and smile as my answer.

"That's cool. Me, too! Do you want to take a shower?"

I'll think for a second. In training, I'll tell everyone I might want a shower in the morning, at night, both times, or none at all. It will be whatever the hell I feel like that day.

I'll shake my head. I have a lot of work to do, and I'll want to get started.

"Okay. I shall go get your shake."

I'll recently discover that eating in bed saves me a lot of time. Ashley will flip me on my back, raise my bed to an upright position, tell my voice-activated speaker to tell me the weather and play my favorite playlist.

As she's getting my shake ready, I'll think about how lucky I am.

I'll have all good assistants now.

I'll eat and drink whatever I want without getting backlash.

I'm not hesitant to ask for another drink.

I'll go wherever I want without judgment.

I won't feel like I'll have to defend my decisions.

If I want to do something, I'll just do it.

Everyone has their own version of luck. Good health, wealth, success, love. Luck, for me, is feeling at home in my home and doing whatever the hell I want.

Ashley will roll the IV poll into my bedroom with the bag filled with coffee and my shake. She will hook my tube up to my stomach, vent me, give me my medicine, and connect the bag to my tube.

"What do you want to wear today?" She will ask before she grabs a few choices for tops.

I'll mentally go through what I'm doing today.

First, I'll be writing. I should be able to be at my computer by 8:30, so I should get two or three hours in, which means six hundred words or more.

Always makes me feel good!

After that, I'll eat and get ready to go to one of my other jobs.

I might be going to the company that makes my communication device. I have a new-found love for my job.

I know the device like the back of my hand.

I know everything I want it to do.

I know other people like me probably would like similar features.

Why not be honored that they not only want my feedback, but actually use it and implement it into their mass products to help other people?

Or, I might be going to a meeting about the camp I always wanted to start but I never thought I'd be able to do.

Or, it might not be a camp. It could be just a retreat that brings people with and without disabilities together for a weekend.

Or, it might be a totally different project altogether.

Whatever project I decide to take on, it's going to have something to do with inclusion.

I'll end up at the meeting, where I'm treated as an equal. They patiently listen to every idea I have. If they like it, they run with it. If they think something could be better, they respectfully suggest something else.

When I get home, I'll freshen up. I'll even debate showering, but I don't have time.

A guy will be coming over, and we're having Olive Garden takeout for the second night in a row. The plan is to binge watch a show he got me addicted to.

No, I didn't meet him online like I tried to do for so many years.

Maybe I met him at my job, or one of the events I'm planning, or a random event I attended. We chatted for a week or two, he asked me to go for coffee a few times, and well, this happened.

I'll talk to my assistant about it, and she's going to help me eat and then go downstairs until I need her again.

The other night, he asked to sit with me in the cuddle chair. Even though I really wanted to, I said no. I had flashbacks to my previous situationship, and it just freaked me out.

Maybe tonight I'll say yes. After all, the past will be in the past.

Plus, a perfectly good cuddle chair should not go to waste!

Or . . . maybe when I get home from my meeting, a guy won't be coming over.

Maybe an old friend will be.

Or, maybe I will just be by myself.

I will still get takeout Olive Garden, and I will binge watch one of my shows or listen to a book or listen to music as loud as I want.

I know that all of my work, including my books, will be affecting a lot of people on so many levels, and that's everything to me.

On my perfect day, no matter what I'm doing, I'll be happy.

I'll want to wear something cute, so I'll smile and spell to Ashley.

"You got it! Do you want to wear leggings or jeans?"

At the mention of leggings, I'll smile to myself.

Many, many moons ago, I was very unhappy with how things were going in my life. I created a version of myself without a disability. She lived inside my mind, could do everything I couldn't do, and wore a lot of leggings. I constantly compared myself to her. Once I'm happy with my life, I'll very rarely think of her.

I'll decide to wear the jeans and not think twice about what Inside Sara would do.

About the Author

Sara Pyszka launched her writing career with the 2013 release of *Dancing Daisies*, her debut young adult novel. She published its sequel, *Switch the Song*, in 2017. *Inside My Outside* is her first nonfiction work. It chronicles her experiences as an individual with cerebral palsy who gets around using a wheelchair, cannot use her hands, and relies on an electronic device for communication.

Through her writing, Sara hopes to change perceptions about people with disabilities in a positive way.

An accomplished public speaker and lyricist, Sara lives in Pittsburgh, Pennsylvania.

Thank you so much for reading!

CPSIA information can be obtained
at www.ICGtesting.com
Printed in the USA
FSHW010335220721
83429FS